THE MOUNTAIN SPIRIT

Jacket and book design by Rick Brightfield

Jacket photo: Sunset from Camp II in the Western Cwm International Everest
Expedition, 1971. Photo by John Cleare/Mountain Camera

THE MOUNTAIN SPIRIT

edited by

Michael Charles Tobias
and
Harold Drasdo

THE OVERLOOK PRESS

WOODSTOCK, NEW YORK

The publishers want to thank Ken Bromberg for his editing, but more than that, for his friendly advice.

First published in 1979 by
The Overlook Press
Lewis Hollow Road
Woodstock, New York 12498
Copyright © 1979 by Michael Charles Tobias
and Harold Drasdo

LIBRARY OF CONGRESS CATALOGING IN PUBLICATION DATA

The Mountain Spirit.

1. Mountaineering–Philosophy–Addresses, essays, lectures.
2. Mountaineering–Psychological aspects–Addresses, essays, lectures.   I. Tobias, Michael.   II.   Drasdo, Harold.
GV200.M685   796.5'22   77-020740
ISBN 0-87951-073-0

Contents

Introduction

OF ALL SPORTS, mountaineering may have the richest, most copious literature; first, a wide body of reflection rooted in the legacy of metaphors—scientific, physical, literary, and religious—applicable to exploration, and second, a broader literary perspective concerned with the idea and ethos of the mountain itself. This century, particularly the past decade, has witnessed a marked tendency among writers working in either sphere to pay increased attention to the other. Recent histories and anthologies produced by mountaineers have drawn upon writings of mountain travelers whose activities date from long before the dawn of mountaineering, and a number of works of great general interest or impressive scholarship—one thinks of writers like Marjorie Hope Nicolson, Sir Gavin de Beer, Morris Marples, and Roderick Nash—have paid attention to the history and sociology of adventure as it touches upon the wilderness calling.

In the present volume, by presenting a diversity of perspectives, some separated in time and place, we hope to reveal a unanimous passion stemming from the mountain: a passion which not only affect ancient and medieval sensibility but which continues to exert an unusual influence upon art, introspection, and culture even today. This work is intended to display to those committed to serious mountaineering how universally and variously the mountain experience has been perceived and to persuade the scholar and the passive admirer of mountains that valuable avenues of thought are made accessible through physical activity in the hills. In the history of ideas the mountain has been the agent of an alluring, occasionally seminal catharsis. Its immense popularity within the larger contemporary wilderness boom suggests the need for a forum such as that fashioned here.

We have tried to indicate boundaries and landmarks by our selection of material. However, to pursue our aims too systematically would have been unwise, since it would have defeated our intended purpose. For we are anxious, above all, not to lose sight of the *qualities* of the mountain experience, and the most certain means of keeping a sense of those qualities is through the pens of a wide variety of writers, each dealing with his own interest. In order to match our desire to break new ground while keeping abreast of rapidly developing fields, we present original work, rather than anthologizing material already published. The only contributions not produced for this book are the previously unpublished Dōgen translation and the short piece by Samuel Beckett.

Considering the scope of this declaration of intent, it will be obvious that the selection of a title presented a problem. Originally conceived of as *A Mountain Aesthetic,* it became apparent that *The Mountain Spirit* more completely covered the book's variety and content.

Many readers may feel that the contents, set against the reported aims, show bias or idiosyncrasy: the proportion of space devoted to the East may cause some comment but this emphasis can be defended. Eastern writers had produced a massive literature before the peoples of the West showed much interest in the hills, and while nearly all prehistories of Western mountaineering repeat the same short list of names and ascents, early Eastern literature reveals a disproportionate interest in the mountain spirit.

Essentially, it is the unfamiliarity of the Eastern approach that deters most Western readers. We look at these writings as a traveler in a foreign country who encounters men of another color and observes differences from his own people but registers no important distinctions among the strangers. We tend to class Indian, Chinese, and Japanese writings of whatever period as a single group. Our attitudes are reinforced, on the one hand by the superficial difficulties of belief and nomenclature that shape or cloak the content, and on the other, especially in the more accessible writings such as Chinese nature poetry, by a seeming homogeneity and absence of essential individuality.

We hope that the material presented will go some way toward dispelling these impressions, and it gives us special pleasure in this context to include in full the two extraordinary texts from Kūkai and Dōgen. It will be seen that these two present a striking contrast: Kūkai, elaborately courteous and transparently humane, looks at the hills and is inspired to rapturous lyricism; Dōgen bends his sternly metaphysical eye upon the mountains and upon those who would know them, and he reasons to the edge of his intelligence on the mysteries of the natural world. It would hardly be possible to find a greater distinction in temperament and in the way the mind works than in the words of these two Japanese.

In the matter of selection we suspect that few would see eye to eye in representing the same field of interest in so limited a space. To take a single example, the most tractable type of aesthetic response must surely be that relating to human movement. If we were to treat the matter at book length we would know exactly what to include: writings from a dozen rock climbers and mountaineers who have expressed themselves on the subject; works-in-progress on field studies of skill, such as that of W. T. Singleton; a discussion of the general field of movement aesthetics, as in the writings of June Layson; ideas on topophilia, touch, and space, following Gaston Bachelard; material from a number of contemporary climber-photographers and a sucession of filmmakers from Leni Riefenstahl to Robert Carmichael; an exploration of the interesting relationships in programming and expression between rock climbing and some forms of dance. The two short pieces actually offered must seem eccentric choices at a glance. John Gill deals with movement in a severely determined form in his discussion of extreme boulder problems. In Al Chung-liang Huang's piece on T'ai Chi, the movement is free, related purely to the mountain sensation. Yet, together, the two give some indication of the range of kinaesthetic possibilities.

In series, the contributions as a whole offered innumerable possibilities—innumerable whether juxtapositions were to stand on contrast or on affinity since each juxtaposition rejects a dozen intriguing relationships. The arrangement provided simply reflects the editors' readings of ancient and modern, action and introspection, East and West. But having allowed ourselves space elsewhere within the book to follow our own patterns of thought, we will say no more about these matters. Our contributors are best left to speak for themselves.

—Harold Drasdo, Llanrwst, Gwynedd, U. K.
—Michael Charles Tobias, Big Sur, California, U. S. A.

CONTEMPORARY MEDITATIONS

Arne Naess
Modesty and the Conquest of Mountains

THERE ARE MANY WAYS of *experiencing* mountains. I would rather assert, however, that mountains have innumerable aspects, or, even better, the term "mountain" may be used to designate vastly different entities. What I describe in what follows are *mountains.* They are connected with what others call mountains through some sort of interpersonal, social structure, a marvelous common frame of reference. Thus I may *locate* the mountains I speak about, I may give details about minerals they are said to consist of, I may even discuss their age—all this without getting into trouble with identification. But the common frame of reference is *not* the mountains themselves—not the mountains *I know.* The motive here for trying to describe mountains as I know them is not the rather indifferent detail that *I* know them, but that many others know them the same way, but do not always, or not consistently, act upon their knowledge.

Now what *are* they?

The words I use must come as an anticlimax, perhaps. They are very common words, they are crude, and only an intense willingness to go along with me can help me to convey what I know.

Mountains are big. Very big. But they are also great. Very great. They have dignity and other aspects of greatness.

They are solid, stable, unmoving. A Sanskrit word for them is *a-ga,* that which does not go. But curiously enough there are lots of movements in them. Thus a ridge is sometimes ascending, there is a strong upward movement, perhaps broken with spires, towers, but resuming the upward trend, toward the sky or even toward heaven. The ridge or contour does not only have movement up and up, but may point upward, may invite elevation.

When we are climbing a mountain, it may witness our behavior with a somewhat remote or mild benevolence. The mountain never fights against us and it will hold back avalanches as long as it can, but sometimes human stupidity and hubris and a lack of intimate feeling for the environment result in human catastrophes. That is, catastrophes for mothers, fathers, wives, children, and friends. (The climbers themselves die in a way I cannot class as catastrophic.)

So much about mountain appreciation and worship, or the cult of mountains. Many may feel the same way, but will perhaps not feel the same way about mountain people. On the other hand there are many who basically feel the same way about mountain people, but have no tendency toward mountain worship. This may perhaps be most simply explained through a short account of my own first encounter with mountain people.

When fifteen years old I managed through sheer persistency of appeals to travel alone in early June to the highest mountain region of Norway—Jotunheimen. At the foot of the mountain I was stopped by deep rotten snow and I could find nowhere to sleep. Eventually I came across a very old man who was engaged in digging away the snow surrounding and in part covering a closed cottage belonging to an association for mountaineering and tourism. We stayed together for a week in a tiny nearby hut. So far as I can remember, we ate only one dish: oatmeal porridge with dry bread. The porridge had been stored in the snow from the previous autumn —that is what I thought the old man said. Later I came to doubt it. A misunderstanding on my part. The porridge was served cold, and if any tiny piece was left over on my plate he would eat it. In the evenings he would talk incidentally about mountains, about reindeer, hunting, and other occupations in the highest regions. But mostly he would play the violin. It was part of the local culture to mark the rhythm with the feet, and he would not give up trying to make me capable of joining him in this. But how difficult! The old man's rhythms seemed more complex than anything I had ever heard.

Enough details! The effect of this week, along with similar experiences later, established my conviction of an inner relation between mountains and mountain people: a certain greatness, cleanness, a concentration upon what is essential, a self-sufficiency; and consequently a disregard of luxury, of complicated means of all kinds. From the outside the mountain way of life would seem Spartan, rough, and rigid, but the playing of the violin and the obvious fondness for all things above the timberline, living or "dead," certainly witnessed a rich, sensual attachment to life, a deep pleasure in what can be experienced with wide-open eyes and mind.

Unnecessary to add: local mountain cultures are incompatible with those that are cosmopolitan and urban. The intrusion of new values and lifestyles rapidly undermines the alpine culture. Individual Sherpas and their families have enhanced their wealth and status through expeditions, but their communities and culture have suffered unduly. Their great festivals and religious life are fading. But there is some cult of mountains still remaining! Thus, Tserigma (Gauri Sankar) is still worshiped. When we suggested to the Sherpas of Beding, beneath Tserigma, that they perhaps might like to have its fabulous peaks protected from "conquests" and big expeditions, they responded with enthusiasm. A special meeting was announced, and the families voted unanimously to ask the central authorities in Katmandu to refuse permission for climbing expeditions to Tserigma. Gönden, the leader of Beding, walked all the way to Katmandu to contact the administration.

But in Nepal, as in so many other countries far away, local communi-

Sikkimese mountain girl. Photo by Michael Tobias

ties have little chance of being heard. The Sherpas would not mind "losing" the money they could earn from expeditions to Tserigma, but central administrations do not think the same way. As is to be expected, the great alpine clubs the world over have largely ignored the initiative of Gönden. Perhaps the organizers of expeditions tend to think that mountains, being great stone heaps, need no "protection," and that the "enlightened" Sherpas certainly would *tolerate* their climbing friends going anywhere. They are in part right. But I do not think we should in this case make use of their tolerance.

These reflections are supposed to serve the idea of modesty—modesty in man's relationships with mountains and with mountain people. As I see it, modesty is of little value if it is not a natural consequence of much deeper feelings, and even more important in our special context, a consequence of a way of understanding ourselves as part of nature in a wide sense of the term. This way is such that the smaller we come to feel ourselves compared to the mountain, the nearer we come to participating in its greatness. I do not know why this is so.

George Steiner
Cairns

Walking

W FORGET THAT the preponderance of Western thought, motions
of spirit (Dante's phrase), acts of feeling and inward recognition
arose *walking*. That reflection and imagination and the current of silent
speech that generates, cradles, transmutes the impulses of the subconscious, were organized by the pulse and pace of walking. And that the
quality of such thought and sensibility is immediately shot through by
the particular economy of bodily forces which walking entails. That the
relations of perception between muscle and distance, between eye and
terrain, between skin and weather, experienced by a walker are enveloping
and distinctive. We forget what space and time signified, felt, "tasted" like
to one who reckoned the map and the hour in terms of walking from
point to point, from town to town, across borders. (Kant was, reputedly,
a metronomically exact walker; how does this constancy relate to his
categorical determinants of space and time?) A walked world is radically
different from one traveled over in a train, automobile, or airplane. In
what ways is the present dialectic of political-ethnic ecumenism and the
equally strong counterforce of parochialism a direct reflection of the
compressions of climate and landmass, of time and physical setting that
come of flying? Only the eccentric or archeologist of feeling now knows
what it is to walk the bounds of reality, to restore to native logic the
capacities of the body and the dimensions of the environment.

This logic was inherent in the romantic movement. Wordsworth
walks from Calais to the St. Gothard and back. Coleridge regards twenty
miles over mountainous and boggy terrain as average. Hölderlin, not a
strong man, walks from the Rhineland to Bordeaux and back via Paris.
Hebbel walks the length of Germany. (Byron's clubfoot does not prevent
him from forays into the Alps, but he is essentially a rider, and his longer
poems are instinct with a rider's motion and modulations of cadence.)
The revolutionary and Napoleonic wars transform men of a perfectly
ordinary physique into prodigious walkers. Thus Stendhal *walks* to Moscow and back in 1812, and we cannot begin to gauge the aesthetics of
energy in *The Charterhouse of Parma* or *The Red and the Black* without
reflecting on what this means. To put it abruptly: the two great poles of
ego and nature, of personal consciousness and felt world, which define
romanticism and of which modernism is the direct heir, were determined
by, sprang from, walking. Rousseau knew this. He articulated the new
subjectivism around a gamut of walks—the whole way from the enormous
cross-country marches of the young man to the "promenades" of the old.
We have forgotten.

Associations

WHEN A SUNDAY skirter of hills and funicular tiger like myself tries to image, to put into words, his sense of the mountains, clichés and spurious profundities cascade. The slow movement of Mahler's Fifth Symphony and the ascendant arcs in Bruckner's Eighth. The total but hammering stillness of the air in a high dingle or cwm. The stone smell, like metal, just above the tree line. The archetypal rummage of symbols—paternalistic, sexual, death-laden—which legend, psychoanalysis, Jungian animism, and nineteenth-century painting have attached to high peaks, to tenebrous valleys, to crevasses, and to what Hölderlin called the *helle Nacht*, the "luminous, lambent night" of spindrift and vapor in an alpine cirque. Even the very great artists and poets overstate or become formulaic. Coleridge's, Shelley's, Byron's versions of the Mont Blanc group or Jungfrau massif are finally pompous and indistinct. Nietzsche's Engadin can overdramatize and bully (it is in the strenuous yet marvelously elastic *gait* of his later philosophic writings, writings composed during walks around Sils, that the mountain experience is best translated). Hills are more manageable: Wordworth's "Prelude" is matchless on Skiddaw and Helvellyn, as are Keats's letters. Cézanne's successive versions of the Mont St. Victoire are "of the hills hilly," internalizing to the touch and, with uncanny exactitude, the feel of rock and scree and light. Auden's *Ascent of F6* is almost embarrassing, but he is confident on the Northumberland fells and amid the dark, humped lava hills of Iceland. The thing is terribly difficult to do well. D. H. Lawrence is frenetic and banal on the Bavarian alps but superb when he evokes the Rockies and the brooding weight of the Mexican *cordillera*. Ramuz is fine when he treats the mountains as the furnishings of work for those who live among them. Broch's *Bergroman* is not free of vaporous solemnities, but no one has come closer to pinning down in words the play of light and weather, of sound and scent around the snow crests and rock walls of the Tyrolian alps (the *Nordkette* above the luminous cut of the Inn valley). And there is a perfect poem by I. A. Richards about leaping a crevasse in the dark—which is, to that great Platonist-mountaineer, "the only way to live."

But for the armchair-scrambler, his muscles burning, his breath steamy with doubt over the whole mousey venture—"can I reach that lowest, almost hotel-like refuge," "can I puff to the top of the ski-lift?"—the problem is the opposite. To keep lofty overtones at bay, to keep the great dark chords from sounding around his wobbly knees. To *see* what is *there* (through the sweat on his glasses). To know ridicule, and not mind too much.

Sea and Mountain

WANTED: A contrastive political theory of both. Already the ancient Greeks felt the issue to be a vital and confusing one. The empirical-symbolical readings of the sea are those of "openness," "freedom," "sophistication." The man who dwells near and travels across open water is, almost by definition, a free man, a tolerant perceiver of the world's diversities, a spirit whose relationship to nature is at once wary and intellectually inventive. By contrast, the mountaineer is enclosed, prone to xenophobia and archaic imaginings. His comportment has in it strong traces of a primal, almost animal state of solitude and territoriality. Of necessity, he spends a good part of his existence in shadow or raw cold. The inhuman dimensions of the mountains both exalt and dwarf his individuality. The avalanche and the rock fall lie in ambush. He speaks in dialect. He stands, often in precarious verticality, at the cleft or narrows, not in the open agora. His horizon is a wall, where the sea is a gate flung open by the light. Yet, note the antique observers, it is frequently the mountaineer who is most jealous of his freedom, and the harbor man who is servile. It is the Thracian, it is the aboriginal of the Caucasus who will not be subdued, where the Minoan or the Syracusan bends to the despot.

The paradox persists in later "geopolitical" speculations. To Milton, to the romantics, to the political exiles of the nineteenth and twentieth centuries, Switzerland incarnates liberty and the Rousseauist dream of plebiscitary government. At the very same time, the poetics and metaphysics of elitist thought, from de Maistre to Nietzsche and Heidegger, are closely knit to the actual or allegoric presence of high mountains. The Bavarian and Tyrolean alps, the Eiger, the needles of the Dolomites play a notorious role in the fantasy lives, in the *rites de passage*, of the National Socialist and Fascist movements (Riefenstahl's allegorization of the assaults on the Eiger remains a formidable witness).

This equivocation is considered, most deeply, in *The Magic Mountain.* Starting with its famous first sentence, the whole novel turns on the pendulum motion between the North Sea coast and the ice cones above Davos. Twice, the structure of narrative and of meaning is that of ascent, from the *Flachland* to the summits, twice it is that of descent into the world of humane commitment which is also that of death. In the heart of the pattern stands the snowstorm, the literal white-out in which Hans Castorp's soul is driven to the roots of its being and solicited by the inhuman order of elemental agencies. In the political dialectic which is the axis of the book, the mobile sea argues against the mountain. Thomas Mann does not choose explicitly. He is as ambiguously at home in the Hanseatic ports and marine Venice as in the Berner Oberland. But he knows that the polarity is fundamental, that it classifies the sensibilities and the utopias of Western culture since the pre-Socratics. Norway is the puzzler: the one landscape where great towers of rock and snow anchor directly in a racing sea. Ibsen's *Brand* is driven by this crazy conjunction.

I N THOSE SMALL autobiographical notices one is asked for, I list music, chess, and mountain walking as "recreations." The word should be: "obsessions," "compulsions," uttermost desiderata. Not that I have anything to contribute, actively. The only musical instruments I play are, as the undergraduate jibe has it, high fidelity and low fidelity. In chess

Marginal

I am a desperate wood pusher, a Knight-to-Rook-4 fugitive because opening theory leaves me hamstrung. And my mountain walking is, increasingly, that of a mildly obese turtle, breathing loudly, triggering derisive miniature avalanches from underpebbles, and straining to keep my balance on the most domestic of slopes. Nevertheless, the three things are indispensable to me. And somehow, I know that there are relations between them. Not by vague, archetypal association. But somewhere in an intensely crucial, deep-buried synapse where the fields of force, of energized space in the musical sequence and on the chessboard meet with the play of sinew and distance that is climbing. Where the charged silences between bars congrue, somehow, with those that give to a chess game its stifled violence, and can, in turn, be matched with the mountain whorls of quiet (the words get it wrong, unavoidably). And there are precise spots, one in a valley upward from Aosta and under the Monte Rosa glacier, where the immaterial concreteness of music, the alternate rush and repose of chess, and the fact of the mountains come together, in a fusion that is, to me, more compact with meaning than any other experience. I *know* this to be so, in the skin of my being. I cannot articulate or prove it.

Having written (inadequately) about music and chess, I construe these cairns. In the margin. To thank.

John Martin, *Manfred on the Jungfrau* (1826). Courtesy of Birmingham Museums and Art Gallery

You, ye Mountains,
Why are ye beautiful? I cannot love ye . . .
I feel the impulse — yet I do not plunge;
I see the peril — yet do not recede;
And my brain reels — and yet my foot is firm.
There is a power upon me which withholds,
And makes it my fatality to live.

— Byron
Manfred

Tom Lyon
A Mountain Mind

I HAVE THE uneasy sense that talking about mind, in a book devoted to something as solid as mountains, may seem to be an abstraction about an abstraction. In the concrete health and naturalness of mountain travel, with wild beauty all around, just *there,* what need for analysis, especially analysis of consciousness? Well, I will try not to be too finespun about it, but I think there is a "mountain mind"—a mind which is more complex and more whole than the ordinary, nonmountain, or, as it might be called, tame mind. I certainly wouldn't argue that this mind is necessarily to be found in mountaineers, or that it couldn't exist in a lowland city, but I do think there is an interesting level or quality of consciousness which is associated with the experience of wilderness and which seems particularly associated with mountains.

There are two major capabilities to the human brain, according to the psychological research of Dr. Robert Ornstein and others.[1] One capability or style of consciousness is to process information in sequential and hierarchical patterns, to see objects one at a time in separateness, and to categorize and make distinctions. This type of consciousness is associated strongly with verbal skill. It is, as Ornstein points out, the major mode of consciousness in modern, industrial cultures. With its built-in "set" for entity, this kind of consciousness is able reflexively to consider itself as self-subsistent—an ego in other words— and to consider the rest of the objects of the world as likewise independent and "egoistic." This style of mind is what we call "rational consciousness." Its tendency to be dominant, reflected in the cultural situation, is probably a logical result of this ability to focus on itself as a separate entity, and thus to be prey to a progressive security need arising from the sense of alienation. It is as if, having separated itself from the stream of things, the detached and rational pattern of consciousness must continually assert and protect itself. In time, a mechanism or logic of exaggeration can develop, and what is originally only a particular pattern in human consciousness, a neutral capability to process information in terms of entity and sequence, can become a desperate caricature of fear and grasping, running aggressively over the other "separate entities" of the world. It assumes that these other entities must likewise be engaged in self-serving ("survival of the fittest"), and thus comes to see life as a grand battleground. The historical result is that from the position of separateness, with modern technological power at our command, we seem now to be succeeding in forcing the world into a certain pattern. We are breaking up natural mutualisms, simplifying complex wild communities, cutting ties—in short, we are making the world answer to our own peculiar, separatist mythology.

The horrors of the Christian-capitalist-communist-industrial world have been so amply documented that it would be silly for me to continue beating this dead horse. The point I think relevant here is that the sequential or entity orientation, when overemphasized, tends to cut us off from our roots in mutualistic nature. We are one of the systems being isolated. Then, to protect the hypothetical psychic "center," we take apart the rest of the world's knit, or interdependence, so as to arrange it around ourselves as a kind of wall against our always threatened dissolution. The project is endless, I think, because having in effect lost the whole world, nothing less than the whole world could suffice for security. We program ourselves for a state of endless psychic scarcity.

However, we have a second major capability of consciousness, as proven scientifically in the research of Ornstein (and demonstrated for centuries in literature and mythology) and this mode or style tends to balance the entity orientation. On this side of the mind (the right half of the cortex, according to Ornstein, the left half has the proclivity for entity), information is processed according to its general configuration. This mode tends to give a holistic aspect to sense data, to emphasize the relational or mutualistic flow and interdependence among seeming objects. Instead of linear reason, the right side of the brain deals in intuition; its findings and insights are rather more difficult to verbally communicate. In this relational capability of consciousness, the sense of specialness or "ego" on the part of the perceiver is not so pronounced. In romantic terminology the right side is "heart," the other side is "head." ("I stand with the heart," said Herman Melville. "To the dogs with the head!")

The opposition is familiar. We have lived with this apparent dualism for a very long time, calling it various names. "Conscious" versus "unconscious," "fact" versus "feeling," "spirit" versus "flesh," if the speaker is a Puritan; in the Buddhist tradition, it is *svabhava* thinking versus *nihsvabhava* thinking;[2] according to Carlos Castaneda's don Juan, it is the "tonal" versus the "nagual"; in cultural terms, especially in Western civilization, it is "civilization" versus "wilderness." On the one side is all that is rational, open, familiar, aboveboard, and godly; on the other is all that is dark, mysterious, all that upwells from strange and unknown sources in nature—all that should be (as our own cultural project has it) repressed in the individual and rearranged or subdued in external nature. So, under the exaggeration of the entity orientation, we have a culture which is resolutely egoistic, disrespectful of nature, devoted to administration—which is to say, control of spontaneous activity—and at the same time obsessively fearful of even the slightest opposition.

Now I am being very quick with this, superficial, but I believe that this fundamental duality is essentially the map of human consciousness as found in the currently predominant culture. And I think that as long as this dualism prevails, the project of industrial culture will be to repress wilderness, either through obvious physical exploitation or through a more subtle process of administration in which the wilderness "area" becomes hedged around with a specific boundary and an elaborate set of administrative rules—ghettoized, so to speak.

For most of us, wilderness areas or mountains function to help us reimmerse temporarily into the holistic type of consciousness. We reassert half-forgotten physical and emotional knowledge, we are placed in a matrix rather than existing as alien manipulators, and we have an opportunity to experience, among other things, the spontaneity of weather, the cycle of daylight and nightfall, and the surrounding, enormously complex patterns of vegetation, water flow, and animal life. Robert Marshall, the great American exponent of the recreational theory of wilderness, believed such experiences to be psychologically necessary as a respite from the pressures of civilized (that is, repressed) life.[3] Marshall particularly recommended strenuous physical activity in wilderness. In terms of Dr. Ornstein's research, Marshall is proposing wilderness as an avenue into the neglected right side of the brain. In wilderness, we may actually experience the so-called "primitive" mythopoeic consciousness of being in the world.

For most of us, however, time in wilderness is vacation time, clearly set apart from the "real" world. This fragmentation of time corresponds to the geographical and political fragmentation of the wilderness area. We are conscious of going into a special, segregated situation; the essential dualism of the tame mind may not only remain unaltered, it may be reinforced. Eventually, we come back to the city, as we knew we would.

This seems to be a typical pattern. But it may happen that wilderness experience, and mountain experience in particular, with its awareness-heightening element of danger, can provide a setting for consciousness that quite transcends both sides of the duality I have been describing. A recognition may begin to dawn that is neither totally alien and rationalistic nor totally "oceanic" and mystically negated as a self, but includes both and goes beyond. To take almost at random merely one suggestive example from the rich possibilities in mountain literature, Reinhold Messner says, "Being in the mountains encourages one to meditate and to find and retain an internal balance. . . ."[4]

How does such a balance arise? Perhaps it is as simple as Kenneth E. F. Watt's speculation that there may be an "optimum rate" of stimuli for the human perceptual system, and wilderness is the natural source for that rate.[5] Perhaps in wilderness we find little external encouragement for an overweening sense of egoistic importance and little evidence for rectilinear interpretations of life. Everything we see is calmly going about its business of existence; we do not (rationally) understand the totality of the patterns before us, around us, in us. We cannot understand them in linear and verbal fashion, because they do not operate in that simple way. So, little by little, the surface consciousness may recede from its domineering position, somewhat nonplussed; and, little by little, in balance, the other mode of consciousness opens. The "unconscious," the "wisdom of the body," "the wisdom of the heart," whatever this aspect of the psyche may be called, begins to feel its natural, evolutionary correspondence with the coevolved world of nature. And yet the rational sense is not lost. What awakens now is akin to a new sense, a paradoxical but undeniable sense which combines both modes of consciousness in their rightful proportions, letting them both operate, and thus (mysteriously) goes beyond them into the realm of paradox, which is to say, the real world. We are, we now see, both particle and stream, ego and connection, and so is everything else. C.G. Jung said that the contents of the unconscious "are without exception paradoxical or antinomial by nature, not excluding the category of being."[6] Perhaps in wilderness we are simply getting the chance to affirm our natural paradoxicalness, our likeness through and through to the rest of paradoxical nature. The traditional opposites, alienation and merging, are now held in suspension, each free to express its own pattern, but known now from a deeper standpoint. Are we here somehow keyed into the "quick" of life? We stand suddenly respectful, not knowing with rational precision what it is that fulfills us, but not really caring to have that kind of grasp. D.H. Lawrence said in his poem, "The Third Thing,"

Water is H_2O, hydrogen two parts, oxygen one,
but there is also a third thing, that makes it water
and nobody knows what that is.

The atom locks up two energies
but it is a third thing present which makes it an atom.

THE EXPERIENCE of John Muir is an interesting practical example of the development of this higher insight. Muir's early training was firmly (even fanatically, it seems) Christian; he received, in short, the heavily dualized, special-creation mythology that characterizes Western culture.[7] Then, at the University of Wisconsin, he took scientific training, which probably would have further emphasized his entity orientation. He was proceeding in a fairly typical direction, a skillful industrial inventor on the rise, when an accident gave him four weeks of enforced quiet. Having punctured the cornea of one eye, he was kept in a darkened room on doctor's orders. During his confinement, Muir decided against continuing in the cultural mainstream. After the accident, he says in his autobiography, he decided to devote the rest of his life to wilderness travel. Upon recovery, he wandered from Kentucky to Florida, then took ship for California and eventually found his way to Yosemite. But the impetus for Muir's first extended mountain-wilderness experience came not from a desire for it, per se, but from a disagreement. The state geologist of California had declared that the dramatic Yosemite Valley was the result of a cataclysm; Muir believed it to be the result of glaciation. (One of his professors at Wisconsin had been influenced by the great glacial theorist, Louis Agassiz.) To prove his thesis, Muir traveled deep into the Sierra Nevada looking for evidence of glaciers. He developed an amazingly light backpacking style, going without a sleeping bag and carrying small amounts of simple food.

John Ruskin, *Mer de Glaçe, Chamonix* (1860). Courtesy the Whitworth
Art Gallery, University of Manchester, Manchester, England

He spent weeks at a time living alone in the wilderness, patiently taking notes and imbibing the general scene. After long, "loving study," as he called it, Muir found enough evidence for a convincing account of the Sierra's glacial past, and his theory was accepted. However, his notebooks and journals of the period are probably more significant as a record of a radiant and comprehensive consciousness. Muir had both a scientific faculty and an intuitive, physical-emotional sense of place, and then something else. His writing glows with the fusion of perceptual capabilities and the mysterious apperception of the paradoxical life quality, the "inner." He had lain on the rocks, sensing their grain and guessing how they might crack under tons of flowing ice, and he had experienced day after strenuous day and through reflective, quiet nights, going inside the wilderness, devoting himself to it, and accepting its conditions.

Traveling light in the mountains, with his attention focused primarily on the data he was gathering rather than on the self and its delights and trials, Muir became open to the wilderness around him. "These beautiful days," he wrote ". . . saturate themselves into every part of the body and live always."[8] His study of the Sierra and its glacial history enlarged in his mind until he realized he was describing only one microcosmic example of the universal pattern of flow and interpenetration. He became capable of gnomic, comprehensive statements like "The clearest way into the Universe is through a forest wilderness."[9] In short, without straining for it, as if absorbing it unknowingly through his body or out of the side of his eye, Muir came to sense all life as wilderness.

Some of Muir's inheritors, I suppose, have idealized wilderness and thus distanced themselves from it. But Muir's experience with wilderness was spontaneous, implicitly trusting. Again and again in his writings he recommends that we trust nature, inner and outer wilderness that is, to reestablish the basic connection. It is a matter of relaxation, or "going home," as Muir put it. "Going to the mountains is going home."

Our problem is that from the ordinary or tame mind's standpoint, wilderness is the Other, so that even when we favor the wild and put down the tame, we are not quite wild. We are not yet seeing the "third thing." We might realize that the civilized mind is, in the end, just another spontaneous, natural pattern which is quite as wild and valid as anything else the fecund universe has grown. But to see the archadministrator, ego, as a wild and authentic being, part of a pattern, requires a leap into paradox. Once achieved, we can look at ourselves with a certain irony and calmness, as a natural being looking at a natural being. Nothing special. Somehow, we become less urgent and demanding. What is all around, the wilderness that includes civilization, can be seen in something like its full nature because, finally, we don't want anything from it and we don't want it to be anything else. We are enjoying a bit of free space. Now we may, perhaps, get to know what the poets mean, and what any ordinary day tries to tell us. And if we slip back, as we often annoyingly do, we can later see ourselves as merely having made a trip into one of those valley regions that make mountains so interesting.

Mount Edith Cavell, Canadian Rockies. Photo by Ed Cooper

On one side, the longing to be plunged into the undifferentiation of the heart and hearth; on the other, to keep absorbing space in an unslaked desire. And since extent offers no limits, and since with it grows the penchant for new wanderings, the goal retreats according to the progress made. Whence the exotic taste, the passion for journeys, the delectation in landscape as landscape, the lack of inner form, the tortuous depth at once seductive and disheartening.

— Emile Cioran
A Short History of Decay

Rawdon Goodier

"In a Hard Intellectual Light…"

AFTER THE MEETING I caught the plane north from Birmingham. It was a fine autumn evening and I could see the blue outline of Welsh hills away to the west. Pressing my head against the window, I craned to see the ground. The sun was already low and the ground detail, every tree and hedgerow, each hummock and hollow of the old cultivation ridges in the pastures, was picked out sharply by the lengthening shadows. The lowlands of Cheshire and Lancashire soon gave way to the foothills of the Lake District, and my eye was drawn in immediate recognition to the lake at Coniston with Ruskin's house near its head and, beyond, the quarry-scarred slopes of the "Old Man" where I first climbed twenty-five years ago. Then swiftly over the green hollow of the Langdales beneath the Pikes, Helvellyn out of sight below, then Ullswater, and northward over the border and into cloud.

I've always liked to fly over mountains and, in flying over them, to relive occasions among them. I've even experienced something of the same feeling when studying aerial photographs of mountain country under a stereoscope, trying to understand the patterns revealed, the mosaic of vegetation, the strange regularities produced by frost and wind, the signs of past ice ages or ancient settlements: walking in the mind's eye through unknown valleys and ascending unknown peaks. Wordsworth caught the essence of this experience when he described, in the introduction to his guide to the English Lake District, a model of the Alps he had seen in Lucerne:

> The spectator ascends a little platform and sees mountains, lakes, glaciers, rivers, woods, waterfalls and valleys with their cottages and every other object contained in them, lying at his feet—all things being represented in their appropriate colours. It may easily be conceived that this exhibition affords an exquisite delight to the imagination, tempting it to wander at will from valley to valley, from mountain to mountain, through the deepest recesses of the Alps. But it supplies also a more substantial pleasure for the sublime and beautiful region with all its hidden treasures, and their bearings and relations to each other, is thereby comprehended and understood at once.

His words returned to me as I looked down on the Lakeland landscape

—"exquisite delight to the imagination . . . their bearings and relations to each other . . . comprehended and understood at once." Yes, as usual he'd got it right. But "bearings and relations" stimulated another train of thought, and I remembered what Mummery had said about mountain geography in the introduction to his book *My Climbs in the Alps and Caucasus:*

> I fear no contribution to science, or topography, or learning of any sort is to be found sandwiched in between the story of crags and seracs, of driving storm and perfect weather. To tell the truth I have only the vaguest idea about theodolites, and as for plane tables, their very name is an abomination!

Mummery's words have continued to strike a sympathetic chord with climbers, most of whom share his distaste for the pedantry and reductionism of the commonplace scientific approach which seems to make it such an uncomfortable companion in the hills. Yet what was it that Wordsworth had said? . . . that the comprehension of their bearings and relations to each other affords a "more substantial pleasure" than the "exquisite delight" gained in wandering in the imagination. So perhaps understanding does not preclude pleasure after all and may even complement imaginative delight.

And so, stimulated by that aerial view of the Lakeland hills, I found myself once again reflecting upon these personal dichotomies, of which the duality between the objective and subjective experience of mountains seems deeply and confusingly embedded in the mountaineer's psyche.

I think the mountaineer is unusually prone to be torn by such dualities. Even if he avoids carrying city thoughts with him up into the hills, he looks down from their summits onto the flatlands and regrets the necessity of return. Or, from the cities of the plain, he yearns for the hills. With increasing age he may no longer visit them and they become mountains of memory, the mountains of then as against the lowlands of now, mountains of youth as against the marshlands of age.

How separate I kept my early climbing activities from my development as a biologist—as if subconsciously fearing that the objective vision of science would somehow contaminate the purity of the mountain experience—so that I was able to climb for several seasons in the Alps but add nothing to my knowledge of their natural history. Yet a casual discussion with William Pearsall, one of my professors, surprised me when he mentioned how much he enjoyed reading that rather esoteric mountaineering work, *Brenva* by Graham Brown. Pearsall wasn't a noted alpinist, and it intrigued me to speculate on what he could find in such a work. So I turned to his book, *Mountains and Moorlands*, which had been published the previous year, to discover a text which is still the best overall account of the ecology of British mountains, a classic of its kind, and a book in which Pearsall's real affection for the hills shines through.

But my interests in mountain ecology were to develop slowly, for the following years brought unexpected opportunity to spend much of my time climbing on the sea cliffs of Cornwall. There, on the granite slabs of Bosigran, I came to experience for the first time that sort of "high" associated with physical movement on rock that must be akin to the essence of dance—remembered still with unusual clarity: the bite of crystal-line rock under the fingers, the sounds and smell of seabirds, gannets diving, glimpses of basking sharks and the brooding megalithic hinterland of West Penwith. Intensive climbing had led to new routes, self-conscious entries in the Bosigran logbook and preparatory work on a new guide.

At the same time I felt an unease, a shadow of doubt amidst all the joy . . . what was it that had changed? Nothing, it seemed, except perhaps some crystallization within the mind. The thought grew that the desire to make a mark on posterity by attaching names to routes led nowhere that I wanted to go. That sort of indulgence was coming to an end even though it had contained within it the experiences which had been the seeds of change, experiences that were to make me want to absorb everything that the mountains had to offer rather than to impose myself upon them; to begin, perhaps, to approach mountaineering more as an art to be cultivated than a sport to be pursued.

Yes, that was it, pursuit, the word is important. One *pursues* sports and knowledge. Though mountaineering became aligned with the subjective, romantic, antiscientific attitude, a paradox is revealed when its vocabulary is examined—first ascents, last problems, conquests—for surely the relation here is with exploration and science, the first ascent being the equivalent of the scientific discovery to which the author's name is attached, the guidebook description equating to the scientific paper. Perhaps it is no cause for surprise that mountaineering, essentially a post-Newtonian enterprise, shares a language with science. But that it does seems to indicate that it has, after all, moved some way from the outlook championed by Mummery. The reason for this convergence with the ethos of science has been the intrusion into mountaineering of the fallacy that the achievement of harder routes, the conquest of higher peaks, marks some sort of progress which is equivalent to progress in science. But there is nothing in mountaineering corresponding to science's body of testable knowledge, and the fallacy has been compounded by the adoption of the confusion, implicit in much thinking about science until recently, that the increase in scientific knowledge may be equated with some sort of moral progress, a doctrine which found its roots in the Protestant ethic of salvation through individual striving. Thus, in spite of its early protestations of innocence and its refusal to justify itself by science, mountaineering has indirectly come to pay tribute to the prevailing scientific ethos by demonstrating its allegiance to the Western, Judeo-Christian, dualistic tradition. And this is revealed by the language it uses.

If, however, mountaineering is regarded as an art rather than a sport, the implications are altered. If there is such a thing as progress in art, it is different from that in science. The works of Beethoven cannot be said to be "better" than Bach's, or those of Goethe better than Shakespeare's, in the same way that it can be said that the explanations of Einstein are better than those of Newton.

But if mountaineering is cultivated as an art, what kind of art is it . . . or should it be? What is being created by the activity?

Matisse considered the perception of the external environment as being the condition for creative work, "the process whereby the artist incorporates the external world within himself, until the object becomes like part of his own being, until he has it within him. . . . It is the forms of the outer world which enrich the inner life. The inner life is not welter, but a shaped and active seeing." Van Gogh, in a letter to his brother, claimed to "devour nature ceaselessly" and later found himself "in surroundings which entirely engross me, which so order, fix, regulate, renew and enlarge my thoughts that I am quite wrapped up in them. And I can write you full of what those silent moors tell me."

For these as for many other creative artists it is the description of the human response to the environment that is the product of their artistic endeavors, a re-creation of the state of consciousness that the act of perceiving the external environment produces in the artist, the transmutation of feeling into form. This would seem to suggest that the artist's is a purely subjective and usually romantic response. But that response, though perhaps characteristic, is not universal. In a letter, Goethe refers to a young poet who

> does very well anything confined to the inner experience, feeling, disposition and reflection on these, and he will deal successfully with any theme where they are treated. But he has not yet developed his powers in connection with anything really objective. Like all young men nowadays, he fights shy of reality, just as every ideal must come back to it. . . .This is just what our young contemporaries find difficult, indeed impossible, this change of heart and mind from the limitations of what lies within us to the boundlessness of what lies without, from what is simple and born with us to what surrounds us in so many forms.

We see in Goethe the perfect expression of the classical, Apollonian attitude of artistic objectivity, which, like scientific objectivity, directs itself primarily to the "out there" rather than to the "in here," to the analysis of the world in terms of underlying form as opposed to the intuitive response to immediate experience. The romantic tends to disparage an objective, classical attitude toward mountains because he sees that it apparently forces him to interpret all experience in terms of preselected models, without realizing that, even for himself, as a romantic, his perception is a type of understanding rather than a result of the direct effect of the mountains on his senses and that his own response is shaped by his cultural paradigms.

But need these dualities be in opposition? Writing about them in

The Birth of Tragedy, Nietzsche suggests that we need to succeed in "apprehending directly rather than merely ascertaining that the arts owe their continuous evolution to the Apollonian and Dionysiac duality." Sometimes the romantic attitude is equated, not so much with an antithesis to intellectual objectivity, but with a sort of instinctive, "preintellectual awareness," a kind of "groovy dimension" which is a precursor to conscious recognition, the stage before we force our perceptions into their molds of objective models or subjective paradigms. But surely everything in our understanding must pass through this stage of preintellectual awareness. It is here that all our intuitions, all our ideas have their source, and it is here, before we impose dichotomies by our selection of the evidence, that we must look for their resolution in unity. After all, a dichotomy is a branching into two. To resolve the duality we must seek the stem before the branching.

The art of mountaineering gives us the opportunity to resolve these dichotomies within ourselves by following them back to their source in preintellectual awareness—which thus, in a sense, becomes also a confluence in postintellectual awareness. And in the art of mountaineering the resolution is through action.

But the question recurs. If mountaineering is an art, what will be the form resulting from the transformation of feeling induced by the experience of mountains? Well, it is clearly not the new route, or the guidebook, or the scientific description of mountain geomorphology, flora, or fauna. While with Van Gogh we find ourselves "devouring nature ceaselessly" in "surroundings that entirely engross us . . . and order, fix and regulate our thoughts," the *making* cannot be transferred, for the subject of the making, whether we succeed or fail, is ourselves. Nothing less can account for mountain madness, for the driving desire to associate and identify ourselves with the hills. We let the mountain experience impose itself upon us, displacing other influences; the eye is subdued by the mountain form, the touch by the rock surface or the moss cushion, the ear by the seashell-like sound of distant waterfalls. Time becomes measured with the footstep, space by the span of one's arms reaching for the next hold. This is the sort of experience within which the dualities converge and meet. But the fact that they meet does not mean that the dualities no longer exist or that they have no meaning. The description of mountain geomorphology and the Wordsworth poem still stand. To deny the validity of either is to preclude perception of their confluence.

On that journey of a year ago the plane starting its descent broke in upon these thoughts. Below, through dark chasms in the clouds, I could see the lights of lowland towns. The mountains seemed as far away as ever. Maybe, for most of us, there is no final resolution, no soothing confluence, no perfect balance between the Yang and Yin, the summit rarely if ever gained. And yet perhaps to have glimpsed it, to be aware of its possibility, is enough.

TWO EARLY
EASTERN TEXTS

Carl Bielefeldt

Dōgen's Shōbōgenzō Sansuikyō

I T IS EASY enough to find mountains in religious literature. Throughout history and in all parts of the world men have looked on the mountain as the abode of the gods and the resort of the holy, and have seen in its form an expression of the hierarchical structure of religious truth and the arduous course of man's spiritual quest. Yet it is rare indeed to come upon a religious text which concerns itself directly with the nature of mountains providing us with an explicit mountain metaphysic. Again, it is easy enough to find nature in the tradition of Zen. For centuries the masters of China, Korea, and Japan have surrounded themselves with nature, have contemplated and been enlightened by nature; and their sayings, their poetry, and their art everywhere celebrate the spiritual significance of the natural world. Yet it is rare indeed to come upon a text which offers a detailed explanation of how a great Zen master actually looks upon nature, of what he sees and does not see in the landscape around him. Such a rare text is the *Sansuikyō* (The mountains and rivers sutra).

The *Sansuikyō* is one book of the *Shōbōgenzō*, a large collection of writings by the famed Japanese master Dōgen (1200-1253), founder of the Sōtō school of Zen. Dōgen's *Shōbōgenzō* is remarkable in several respects. It represents one of the earliest texts of the Zen movement in Japan, composed in an age when the school, long prominent in China, was first beginning to attract the attention of the Japanese. Dōgen himself was one of the pioneering Japanese monks who traveled to the Southern Sung to study and transmit the Chinese Ch'an tradition. In the history of Japanese Buddhist literature the *Shōbōgenzō* represents one of the first, and undoubtedly most interesting, attempts to express the teachings of the religion in the vernacular, rather than in Chinese—the traditional literary language of Far Eastern Buddhism. Dōgen clearly had a deep love for language and an extraordinary sense of its possibilities. His *Shōbōgenzō* remains one of the great masterpieces of Japanese religious literature. Even more importantly perhaps, in terms of Zen intellectual history, the *Shōbōgenzō* stands as one of the few premodern attempts to provide reasoned philosophical interpretation of the enigmatic sayings of the great Chinese Ch'an masters. This is not to say that Dōgen is a systematic philosopher in the style of classical Buddhist dogmatics; he is himself a Zen master, trained in the koan tradition of the Southern Sung. Yet beneath the bold paradox and striking poetic imagery inherited from this tradition can be seen a man of powerful intellect and wide learning engaged in an explication of the premises of his faith. Indeed, in the *Sansuikyō* Dōgen attacks in the strongest terms those in his tradition who would deny the reason and reject the possibility of Buddhist metaphysics.

The ninety-five texts which constitute the modern redaction of the *Shōbōgenzō* span almost the entirety of Dōgen's teaching career. The *Sansuikyō* belongs to the early period, perhaps the most intellectually creative. According to the colophon of a manuscript of the text generally thought to be in Dōgen's own hand, it was composed in the autumn of 1240, some thirteen years after his return from China and seven years after his establishment of Japan's first complete Zen monastic facilities at Kōshōji, near Kyoto. Three years later Dōgen was to abandon these facilities and retire to the mountains and rivers of Echizen, where he founded the monastery of Eiheiji, the subsequent headquarters of his school. Several months before he wrote the *Sansuikyō*, Dōgen composed a work known as the *Keisei sanshoku*, based on a verse by the Sung poet Su Tung-po:

> The sound of the stream is His long, broad tongue,
> The mountain, His immaculate body.
> This evening's eight-four thousand verses—
> How will I tell them tomorrow?

In the *Sansuikyō* Dōgen returned to the theme of this poem to explore the meaning of mountains and rivers as the dharma body of the Buddha.

Like most of the books of the *Shōbōgenzō*, the *Sansuikyō* takes the form of an extended commentary on several thematically related passages drawn primarily from the Ch'an literature. The basic principles of this commentary are set forth in a brief introduction, which may be paraphrased as follows: The mountains and rivers around us right now are a sutra, a revelation of the eternal truth taught by Buddhism. These things around us are occurring as specific conditioned events, and at the same time are perfect in themselves. Both their conditioned occurence and their inherent perfection are made possible by the fact that they are empty of any fixed nature of their own.

From these premises Dōgen proceeds in his commentary to explore the eternal mountain as a stream of events, and the restless river as a perfect reality beyond our notions of stillness and repose. It is noteworthy that these premises are not Dōgen's invention, nor the invention of the Ch'an masters he interprets; they are as old as Mahayana Buddhism, and their presence here reminds us of the profound debt that the Ch'an tradition owes to the *prajñā-pāramitā* literature. Indeed the entire argument—if such it can be called—of the *Sansuikyō* should serve as a warning against the tendency to read too much Taoism into the Ch'an understanding of nature. There are, in fact, numerous allusions to the Taoist tradition in the *Sansuikyō*, but they are there to enhance the flavor, and not the substance, of the work.

One such allusion—the flying of the Taoist wizard—appears in the final sentence of the introduction; it points to the last, and in some ways most interesting, section of the *Sansuikyō*. Here Dōgen draws the conclusion that insofar as mountains and rivers are perfect in themselves, embracing all reality, they are indistinguishable from the practice and verification of the Buddha dharma. Hence, the Buddhist religious life is not an activity taking place within the world but the basic activity of the world itself; mountains and rivers are themselves living the life of the mountain sage. Here again we need not see this teaching as unique to Dōgen, indeed it is probably inherent in the ancient Buddhist use of the term *dharma* to mean both religion and phenomenon. Yet there is perhaps no doctrine more central to Dōgen's style of Zen, a style which seeks at every turn to understand Buddhist practice as enlightened activity and to ground the religious life in the living body of the Buddha.

The following translation of the *Sansuikyō* is based on the text published in Terada Tōru and Mizuno Yaoko, eds., *Dōgen, I, Nihon shisō taikei*, 12 (Tokyo, 1970), pp. 331-41. My translation owes much to the many Japanese commentaries and textual studies, both ancient and modern, which have been made on the text; but I have tried throughout to remain close to the language of the original and to avoid confusing translation with commentary. In keeping with the character of this volume, I have left the text free from all but the most basic annotation. Those who seek more complete information may consult my "Shōbōgen-zō Sansuikyō" (M.A. Thesis, University of California, Berkeley, 1972), of which the present translation is a revised version. I should like to offer this work to the late Suzuki Shunryu Roshi of the San Francisco Zen Center, who introduced me to Dōgen's Zen, and who first encouraged me to undertake the translation of the *Sansuikyō*.

Katsushika Hokusai (1760-1849), *Boy and Mount Fuji* Edo period, Ukiyoe school. Courtesy of the Smithsonian Institution, Freer Gallery of Art

They were special words, set at a height. . . . Once there were such words.
. . . They were not simply beautiful phrases, but a constant summons to superhuman behavior, words that demanded that the individual stake his very life on the attempt to climb to their own lofty heights.

— Yukio Mishima
Sun and Steel

Dōgen

Treasury of the True Dharma Eye: Book XXIX,

The Mountains and Rivers Sutra

Translated from the Japanese by Carl Bielefeldt

THESE MOUNTAINS AND rivers of the present are the actualization of the word of the ancient Buddhas. Each, abiding in [its own] dharma state, completely fulfills its virtues. Because they are the state prior to the *kalpa* of emptiness, they are living in the present. Because they are the self before the germination of any subtle sign, they are liberated in their actualization.

Because the virtues of the mountain are high and broad, the power to ride the clouds is always penetrated from the mountains; and the ability to follow the wind is inevitably liberated from the mountains.

THE MASTER TA-YANG SHAN-K'AI addressed the assembly: "The blue mountains are constantly walking. The stone woman gives birth to a child in the night."[1] The mountains lack none of their proper virtues; hence, they are constantly at rest and constantly walking. We must devote ourselves to a detailed study of this virtue of walking. The walking of the mountains is like that of men: do not doubt that the mountains walk simply because they may not appear to walk like humans. These words of the Patriarch [Ta-yang] point out the fundamental meaning of walking, and we should thoroughly investigate his teaching on "constant walking."

Because [the blue mountains] are walking they are constant. Their walk is swifter than the wind; yet those in the mountains do not sense this, do not know it. To be "in the mountains" is a flower opening "within the world."[2] Those outside the mountains do not sense this, do not know it. Those without eyes to see the mountains do not sense, do not know, do not see, do not hear this truth.

He who doubts that the mountains walk does not yet understand his own walking. It is not that he does not walk, but that he does not yet understand, has not made clear, his walking. He who would understand his own walking must also understand the walking of the blue mountains. The blue mountains are neither sentient nor insentient; the self is neither sentient nor insentient. Therefore, we can have no doubts about these blue mountains walking.

We do not realize that we must clarify the blue mountains on the basis of innumerable dharma realms. We must carefully investigate the walking of the blue mountains, the walking of the self. And this investigation should include walking backward as well as backward walking. We should carefully investigate the fact that since that very time before any subtle sign, since the age of the King of Emptiness, walking both forward and backward has never stopped for a moment. If walking had ever rested, the Buddhas and Patriarchs would never have appeared; if walking were limited, the Buddha dharma would never have reached the present. Walking forward has never ceased; walking backward has never ceased. Walking forward does not oppose walking backward, nor does walking backward oppose walking forward. This virtue is called "the mountain flowing, the flowing mountain."

The blue mountains devote themselves to the investigation of walking; the East Mountain devotes itself to the study of "moving over the water." Hence, this study is the mountains' own study. The mountains, unchanged in body and mind, maintaining their own mountain countenance, have always been traveling about studying themselves. Do not slight mountains by saying that the blue mountains cannot walk, nor the East Mountain move over the water. It is because of the impoverishment of the common man's point of view that he doubts the statement, "the blue mountains walk"; it is because of the shallowness of his limited experience that he is surprised by the words, "flowing mountain." Without having fully understood even the words, "flowing water," he simply remains sunk in his ordinary perception.

Thus, the accumulated virtues [of the mountain] represent its name and form, its very lifeblood. There is a mountain walk and a mountain flow, and there is a time when the mountain gives birth to a mountain child. The mountains become the Buddhas and Patriarchs, and it is for this reason that the Buddhas and Patriarchs have thus appeared.

Even when we have the eyes [to see mountains as] the appearance of grass and trees, earth and stone, fences and walls, this is nothing to doubt, nothing to be moved by: it is not the complete actualization [of the mountains]. Even when there occurs a time in which [the mountains] are perceived as the splendor of the seven treasures, this is still not the real refuge. Even when [the mountains] appear as the realm of the practice of the Buddhas, this is not necessarily something to be desired. Even when we attain the supreme [vision] of [the mountains as] the actualization of the inconceivable virtue of the Buddhas, this is not yet the complete reality.[3] Each of these appearances is the particular objective and subjective reward [of past karma]. They are not the karma of the way of the Buddhas and Patriarchs, but narrow, one-sided views.

Turning the object and turning the mind is criticized by the Great Sage; explaining the mind and explaining the nature is not affirmed by the Buddhas and Patriarchs; seeing the mind and seeing the nature is the business of non-Buddhists:[4] sticking to words and sticking to phrases is not the speech of liberation. There is [speech] which is free from such realms: it is "the blue mountains constantly walking," "the East Mountain moving over the water." We should give this detailed investigation.

"The stone woman gives birth to a child in the night." This means that the time when "the stone woman gives birth to a child" is the "night." Among stones there are male stones, female stones, and stones neither male nor female. These stones give support to heaven and to earth. There are heavenly stones and earthly stones. Although this is said in the secular world, it is rarely understood.[5] We should understand the true nature of this "birth." At the time of birth are both parent and child transformed? We must study and fully understand, not only that birth is actualized in the child becoming the parent, but also that the practice and verification of the phenomenon of birth occurs when the parent becomes the child.

THE GREAT MASTER Yün-men K'uang-chen has said, "The East Mountain moves over the water."[6] The import of this expression is that all mountains are the East Mountain, and all these East Mountains are moving over the water. Therefore, Mount Sumeru and the other nine mountains are all actualizing themselves, are all practicing and verifying [the Buddha dharma]. This is called "the East Mountain." But is Yün-men himself liberated from the skin, flesh, bones, and marrow of the East Mountain and its life of practice and verification?

At the present time in the land of Sung there is a certain crude bunch who have by now formed such a crowd that they cannot be overcome by the few true [students of the way]. They maintain that talk such as this "East Mountain moving over the water" or Nan-ch'üan's "sickle" is incomprehensible.[7] Their idea is that any talk which can be grasped by thought is not the Zen talk of the Buddhas and Patriarchs; indeed, it is precisely incomprehensible talk that is the talk of the Buddhas and Patriarchs. Consequently, they hold that Hunag-po's stick and Lin-chi's roar, because they cannot be comprehended or grasped by thought, represent that great awakening preceding the time before the germination of any subtle sign. The "tangle-cutting words" often used as teaching devices by the great masters of the past are impossible [they say] to comprehend.

Those who talk in this way have never met a true teacher, and lack the eye of study; they are worthless little fools. There have been many such sons of Māra and lawless shavelings in Sung China for the last two or three hundred years. This is truly regrettable, for it represents the decline of the great way of the Buddhas and Patriarchs. Their understanding is inferior to that of the Hinayana *śrāvakas*, more foolish than that of the non-Buddhists. They are not laymen and they are not monks; they are not humans and not *devas*; they are dumber than animals studying the way of the Buddha. What these shavelings call "incomprehensible talk" is incomprehensible only to them, not to the Buddhas and Patriarchs. Simply because they themselves do not comprehend it is no reason for them not to study the way the Buddhas and Patriarchs comprehend. Even granted that it were incomprehensible, it would then follow that this comprehension they now seek to maintain must also be wrong.

Such people are common throughout Sung China, and I have seen them with my own eyes. They are truly to be pitied. They do not know that thought is words; they do not know that words are liberated from thought. When I was in China I made fun of them, but they never had an explanation, never a word to say for themselves. This [idea] of theirs about "incomprehensibility" is in fact nothing but a false notion. Who could have taught it to them? Though they have no natural teacher, they are the natural children of heresy.[8]

We should realize that this [teaching of] "the East Mountain moving over the water" is the very bones and marrow of the Buddhas and Patriarchs. All the waters are appearing at the foot of the East Mountain; and therefore, the mountains mount the clouds and stride through the heavens. The mountains are the peaks of the waters, and in both ascending and descending their walk is "over the water." The tips of the mountains' feet walk across the waters, setting them dancing; therefore, walking extends freely in all directions, and "practice and verification are not nonexistent."[9]

WATER IS NEITHER strong nor weak, neither wet nor dry, neither moving nor still, neither cold nor hot, neither being nor nonbeing, neither delusion nor enlightenment. Solidified, it is harder than diamond: who could break it? Melted, it is softer than milk: who could break it? This being the case, we cannot doubt the many virtues realized [by water]. We should, then, study that occasion when the water of the ten directions is seen in the ten directions. This is not a study only of the time when men or *devas* see water: there is a study of water seeing water. Water practices and verifies water; hence, there is a study of water speaking water. We must bring to realization the path on which the self encounters the self. We must move back and forth along, and spring off from, the vital path on which the other studies and fully comprehends the other.

In general, then, the way of seeing mountains and rivers differs according to the type of being [that sees them]. There are beings who see what we call water as a jeweled necklace. This does not mean, however, that they see a jeweled necklace as water. How, then, do we see what they consider water? Their jeweled necklace is what we see as water. Or, again, they see water as miraculous flowers, though it does not follow that they use flowers as water. Hungry ghosts see water as raging flames or as pus and blood. Dragons and fish see it as a palace or a tower, or as the seven treasures or the *mani* gem. [Others] see [water] as woods and walls, or as the dharma nature of immaculate liberation, or as the true human body, or as the physical form and mental nature. Men see these as water.[10] And these [different ways of seeing] are the conditions under which [water] is killed or given life.

Thus, what different types of beings see is different; and we should reflect on this fact. Is it that there are various ways of seeing one object? Or is it that we have mistaken various images for one object? We should concentrate every effort on understanding this question, and then concentrate still more. Given this [multitude of perspectives], it follows that the training on the way of practice and verification must also not be merely of one or two kinds, and the ultimate realm must also have a thousand types and ten thousand kinds.

If we reflect on the real import of this [problem], although we say there are many types of water, it would seem there is no original water, no water of various types. Nevertheless, the waters which vary in accordance with the different types of beings do not depend on body or mind; they do not arise from karma; they are not dependent on the self or the other: dependent on water, [water] is liberated.

Therefore, water is not earth, water, fire, wind, space, or consciousness; it is not blue, yellow, red, white, or black; it is not form, sound, smell, taste, touch, or idea: nevertheless, the water of earth, water, fire, wind, space, and the rest is spontaneously appearing. This being the case, it becomes difficult to explain by what and of what this present land and palace are made. To say that they rest on the wheel of space and the wheel of wind is true neither for oneself nor for others;[11] it is just speculating on the basis of the suppositions of the small understanding, and is only said out of fear that without such a resting place [things] would not abide.

The Buddha has said, "All dharmas are ultimately liberated; they have no abode."[12] We should realize that although they are liberated, without any bonds, all dharmas are abiding in [their own] state. However, when men look at water they see it only as flowing without rest. This "flow" takes many forms, and our [way of seeing] is just a one-sided human view. [Water] flows over the earth; it flows across the sky; it flows up; it flows down. [Water] flows around bends and into deep abysses. It mounts up to form clouds; it descends to form pools.

The *Wen-tzu* says, "The tao of water, ascending to heaven becomes rain and dew, descending to earth becomes rivers and streams."[13] Such is said even in the secular world. It would be shameful indeed if those who call themselves descendants of the Buddhas and Patriarchs had less understanding than the layman. [This passage] says that, although the way of water is unknown to water, water actually functions [as water]; and although the way of water is not unknown to water, water actually functions [as water].

"Ascending to heaven, it becomes rain and dew." We should realize that water climbs to the very highest heavens, and becomes rain and dew.

And this rain and dew is of various kinds in accordance with the various worlds. To say that there are places to which water does not reach is the doctrine of the Hinayana *śrāvaka*, or the false doctrine of the non-Buddhist. Water extends into flames; it extends into thought, reasoning, and discrimination; it extends into enlightenment and the Buddha nature.

"Descending to earth, it becomes rivers and streams." We should realize that when water descends to earth it becomes rivers and streams. And the essence of rivers and streams becomes sages. The foolish common people think that water is always in rivers, streams, and seas, but this is not so: [water] makes rivers and seas within water. Therefore, water is in places that are not rivers and seas; it is just that when water descends to earth it acts as rivers and seas.

Moreover, we should not think that when water has become rivers and seas there is then no world and no Buddha land [within water]: even within a single drop of water incalculable Buddha realms are actualized. Consequently, it is not that water exists within the Buddha land, nor that the Buddha land exists within water: the existence of water has nothing whatever to do with the three times or the dharma realm. And yet, [water] is the koan of the actualization of water.

Wherever the Buddhas and Patriarchs are, water is always there; wherever water is, there the Buddhas and Patriarchs always appear. Therefore, the Buddhas and Patriarchs have always taken up water as their own body and mind, their own thinking.

In this way, then, [the idea] that water does not climb up is to be found neither in Buddhist nor non-Buddhist writings. The way of water penetrates everywhere, above and below, vertically and horizontally. Still, in the sutras it is said that fire and wind go up, while earth and water go down.[14] But this "up and down" bears some study—the study of the up and down of the way of the Buddha. [In Buddhism] where earth and water go is considered "down"; but "down" does not mean some place to which earth and water go. Where fire and wind go is "up." While the dharma realm has no necessary connection with up and down and the four directions, simply on the basis of the function of the four, five, or six elements we provisionally set up a dharma realm with directions. It is not that the *asaṃjñika* heaven is above and the *avīci* hell below: *avīci* is the entire dharma realm; *asaṃjñika* is the entire dharma realm.

Nevertheless, when dragons and fish see water as a palace, just as when men see palaces, they do not view it as flowing. And if some on-looker were to explain to them that their palace was flowing water they would surely be just as amazed as we are now to hear it said that mountains flow. Still, there would undoubtedly be some [dragons and fish] who would accept such an explanation of the railings, stairs, and columns of palaces and pavilions. We should calmly consider over and over the reason for this. If our study is not liberated from these confines, we have not freed ourselves from the body and mind of the common man; we have not fully comprehended the land of the Buddhas and Patriarchs;

we have not fully comprehended the land of the common man; we have not fully comprehended the palace of the common man.

Although men have understood what is in seas and rivers as water, just what kind of thing dragons, fish, and other beings understand and use as water we do not yet know. Do not foolishly assume that all kinds of beings must use as water what we understand as water. When those who study Buddhism seek to learn about water, they should not stick to [the water of] humans; they should go on to study the water of Buddhism. We should study how we see the water used by the Buddhas and Patriarchs; we should study whether within the rooms of the Buddhas and Patriarchs there is or is not water.

FROM TIME IMMEMORIAL the mountains have been the dwelling place of the great sages; wise men and sages have all made the mountains their own chambers, their own body and mind. And through these wise men and sages the mountains have been actualized. However many great sages and wise men we suppose have assembled in the mountains, ever since they entered the mountains no one has met a single one of them. There is only the actualization of the life of the mountains; not a single trace of their having entered remains.

The countenance [of the mountains] is completely different when we are in the world gazing off at the mountains and when we are in the mountains meeting the mountains. Our consideration and our understanding of nonflowing should not be the same as the dragon's understanding. Men and *devas* reside in their own worlds, and other beings may have doubts about this, or, again, they may not. Therefore, without giving way to our surprise and doubt, we should study the words, "mountains flow," with the Buddhas and Patriarchs. Taking one [view], there is flowing; taking another, there is nonflowing. At one time there is flowing; at another, not-flowing. If our study is not like this, it is not the true dharma wheel of the Tathāgata.

An ancient Buddha has said, "If you wish to avoid the karma of *avīci* hell, do not slander the true dharma wheel of the Tathāgata."[15] These words should be engraved on skin, flesh, bones, and marrow, engraved on interior and exterior of body and mind, engraved on emptiness and on form; they are engraved on trees and rocks, engraved on fields and villages.

Although we say that mountains belong to the country, actually they belong to those who love them. When the mountains love their master, the wise and the virtuous inevitably enter the mountains. And when sages and wise men live in the mountains, because the mountains belong to them, trees and rocks flourish and abound, and the birds and beasts take on a supernatural excellence. This is because the sages and wise men have covered them with virtue. We should realize that the mountains actually take delight in wise men and sages.

Throughout the ages we have excellent examples of emperors who have gone to the mountains to pay homage to wise men and seek instruction from great sages. At such times [the emperors] respected [the sages] as teachers, and honored them without abiding by worldly forms. For the imperial authority has no power over the mountain sage, and [the emperors] knew that the mountains are beyond the mundane world.

In ancient times [we have the examples] of K'ung-t'ung and Hua Feng. When the Yellow Emperor made his visit [to Kuang Ch'eng-tzu], he went on his knees, prostrated himself, and begged instruction.[16] Again, Śākyamuni Buddha left his father's palace and went into the mountains; yet his father felt no resentment toward the mountains, nor distrust of those in the mountains who instructed the prince. His twelve years of cultivating the way were spent largely in the mountains, and it was in the mountains that the Dharma King's auspicious event occurred. Even a veritable *cakravartin* does not wield authority over the mountains.

We should understand that the mountains are not within the human realm, nor within the realm of heaven. They are not to be viewed with the suppositions of human thought. If only we did not compare them with flowing in the human realm, who would have any doubt about such things as the mountains flowing or not flowing?

Again, since ancient times, wise men and sages have also lived by the water. When they live by the water they catch fish, or they catch men, or they catch the way. These are all traditional water styles. And going further, there must be catching the self, catching the hook, being caught by the hook, and being caught by the way.

In ancient times when Te-ch'eng suddenly left Yüeh-shan and went to live on the river, he got the sage of the Hua-t'ing River.[17] Is this not catching fish? Is it not catching men? Catching water? Is it not catching himself? For someone to meet Te-ch'eng he must be Te-ch'eng; Te-ch'eng's teaching someone is his meeting himself.

It is not the case simply that there is water in the world; within the world of water there is a world. And this is true not only within water: within clouds as well there is a world of sentient beings; within wind, within fire, within earth there is a world of sentient beings. Within the dharma realm there is a world of sentient beings; within a single blade of grass, within a single staff there is a world of sentient beings. And wherever there is a world of sentient beings, there, inevitably, is the world of the Buddhas and Patriarchs. This truth we should study very carefully.

Thus, water is the palace of the true dragon; it is not flowing away.[18] If we regard it as only flowing, the word *flowing* is an insult to water; for it is [the same as] imposing *nonflowing*. Water is nothing but the real form of water just as it is. Water is the water virtue; it is not flowing. In the thorough study of the flowing, or the nonflowing, of a single [drop of] water, the entirety of the ten thousand dharmas is instantly realized.

As for mountains, there are mountains hidden in jewels; there are mountains hidden in marshes, mountains hidden in the sky; there are mountains hidden in mountains. There is a study of mountains hidden in hiddenness. An ancient Buddha has said, "Mountains are mountains and rivers are rivers."[19] The meaning of these words is not that mountains are mountains, but that mountains are mountains. Therefore, we should thoroughly study these mountains. When we thoroughly study the mountains, this is the mountain training. Such mountains and rivers themselves spontaneously become wise men and sages.

> *Treasury of the True Dharma Eye.*
> Book XXIX.
> *The Mountains and Rivers Sutra.*
> In the hour of the rat [12-2 A.M.]. eighteenth day, tenth month of the first year of Ninji [November 3, 1240], at Kannon Dōri Kōshō Hōrinji.

Hsu Tao-ning (d. c. 1066-67), *Fisherman* (detail). Courtesy of the Nelson Fund, William Rockhill Nelson Gallery of Art, Atkins Museum of Fine Arts, Kansas City, Mo.

A hundred yards of even ground will never work such an effect as a rock or mountain of that altitude.

— Edmund Burke
Philosophical Enquiry into the Origin
of Our Ideas of the Sublime and the Beautiful

Allan Grapard

On Kūkai's Stone Inscription for Shōdō

THE FOLLOWING IS a translation of one short work written by Japan's greatest religious figure, Kūkai (773-835), who is better known under his posthumous title: Kōbō Daishi (The Great Master of the Expansion of the Law). Founder of the Shingon School of Esoteric Buddhism, Kūkai was at once a remarkable philosopher, an artist of talent, a renowned poet, an important engineer, and a great writer.

Although he is commonly known in his country as the "Mother of Japanese Civilization," only one substantial work about him has been published outside Japan. He left many works of religious philosophy which were to decisively influence later developments in his country's religion and thought, and one of his disciples, Shinzei, collected his poems, letters, and shorter works, to create a voluminous book which has luckily survived to present times. This book is extremely important because it represents the only detailed source of information to which one can refer when trying to inquire into Kūkai's personality and life. It is made up of some one hundred and ten items, all in classical Chinese. Many of these items bear the stamp of Kūkai's religious, political, and literary genius.

The essay here translated was written in 814, when Kūkai was forty-one years old. The landscape he is describing is one of the "sacred spaces" of Japanese religions, having been called, at certain periods in Japan's history, "Pure Land in this World." Originally the term "Pure Land" designated the metaphysical space in which the Buddhas and Bodhisattvas reside; but as a result of the interaction between Japan's indigenous religion (Shintoism) and esoteric Buddhism, it came to mean "a spatial point in our world where Buddhahood in this very existence could be realized because of a significant environment." The syncretism permitting this change forms the basis for a large segment of Japanese religion.

The area described is now called Nikkō and is world-famous for the architecture and somewhat baroque art of its temples and shrines. However, the place name has a complicated history and that complexity is mirrored in the name of the mountain which is the setting for the text. A glance at the elements involved may be of interest.

This mountain, today known as Nantaizan, was originally called Futarayama. The pronunciation of the first two ideograms is the key to the problem: when they are pronounced *Futara* (the Japanese pronunciation), the sound lends itself to a significant analogy with the Sanskrit word *Potalaka* (in Japanese, *Fudaraku*), which designates the "Pure Land" where the Bodhisattva Avalokitesvara (in Japanese, *Kannon*) resides. This divinity, an object of popular devotion in China and Japan, is a manifestation of the Buddha's compassion, and many devotees pray to be reborn in his, or more often her, paradise. The association, then, allowed the Japanese to believe that the Futara Mount was, in this very world, the "Pure Land." The ancient indigenous belief that Japan was, as a whole, a "sacred space" lent support to this interpretation and is at the root of the Shinto-Buddhist syncretism. But now, when the two ideograms are read in the Sino-Japanese system, the pronunciation obtained is: Nikkō. Tradition says that Kūkai changed his pronunciation to allow the sound to be written with two different ideograms meaning "the light of the sun."

Why should he do that? Because, on the one hand, the doctrine of Shingon's esoteric Buddhism is expounded by the Body of Essence of the metaphysical Buddha Māhavairocāna, whose name is translated in Chinese and Japanese as "the Great Sun." On the other hand, the central divinity of Japan's indigenous pantheon is Amaterasu, the Sun. Such an analogy is at the origin of the Japanese syncretism, and Japanese tradition is correct in attributing to Kūkai the first significant expression of a phenomenon which was to have tremendous consequences on the life of the nation.

It was in fact the monk Shōdō (735-805?) who built the mountain's first Buddhist temple. Today this temple is known under the name of Rinnōji and belongs to the Tendai School, but it has not always been so: Kūkai tells us that Shōdō built a Jingūji, a Buddhist temple constructed on the grounds of a Shinto shrine. (This might be compared, in France for instance, with the building of a Catholic church above a Roman temple, itself built over a Gallic shrine on top of the volcanic Puys de Dôme; the striking and tragic difference is that, in France, the appearance of one meant the complete destruction of the other, prohibiting a truly creative syncretism.)

Reverence for the indigenous divinities, allowance for other creeds—such is the tolerant atmosphere surrounding the early interaction particular to this mountain. Shōdō later built a temple belonging to the Kegon School, and Kūkai may have been especially interested, for he held the doctrine of the Kegon School in high esteem: the central Buddha of the two schools is related, and syncretic beliefs that the Japanese divinity of the Sun was but the manifestation of the Buddha at a lower level had already, if we believe the tradition, been expressed by the Kegon School.

The famous monk Ennin (793-864), during his travels to eastern Japan, changed the allegiance of the temple to the Tendai School. From Ennin's time on, the mountain assumed immense significance and was adorned with a large number of temples and became a famous center for practice and learning. It was a center for the mountain ascetics (*yamabushi*) of the Shugendō's Tendai branch, precisely because of the belief that it was the actual Pure Land of Kannon, and it became the second most important center of the Tendai School, after Mount Hiei in Kyoto.

Alas, the Buddhist Schools amassed tremendous wealth and so thoroughly entered the political arena that they were seen as a threat by Toyotomi Hideyoshi (1536-1598), who crushed the temples, especially those belonging to the Tendai School. The whole center of Kyoto was reduced to ashes, and the same fate almost befell Nikkō.

It was only with one of the great religious figures of the Edo period, Tenkai (1535-1643!), that the area entered a new age and its importance revived. Here again, Shinto-Buddhist syncretism was paramount. At the time of the death of a great political figure, Tokugawa Ieyasu, a controversy arose as to whether he should be buried according to Tendai's syncretism (known as Sannō Ichijitsu Shinto) or according to the Shingon form (known as Ryōbu Shinto). Eventually Tendai won the case, and a mausoleum enshrining Ieyasu was built in Nikkō. Ieyasu was looked upon as an Avatāra who had come to save Japan. Hence, he was called Tōshō-daigongen: the Great Avatāra Illumining the East. Today this mausoleum and the temples surrounding it are an international center of attraction. But while the site was formerly one of the best examples of Shinto-Buddhist syncretism in Japan, the official separation of Shintoism and Buddhism in 1871 changed its tenor. Now we see three separate institutions: the Shinto shrine Futara Jinja, the Tokugawa mausoleum Tōshōgu, and the Buddhist temple Rinnōji. There is no indication of their former unity.

THIS IMPORTANT WORK of Kūkai may now reveal him in a novel light as an early proselytizer for the beauty of nature. The mountain has become a favored spot for climbers; the lakes are famous as resorts for Tokyo's rich; and the Kegon Waterfall at the end of the southern lake is seen as the focal point of one of the most celebrated landscapes in the country.

Kūkai

Stone Inscription for the Śramana Shōdō Who Crossed Mountains and Streams in His Search for Awakening

Translated from the classical Chinese by Allan Grapard

"Mount Sumeru and Vulture's Peak are places where uncommon people reside. The lake Anavatapta, abode of the dragon, is where one finds marvelous beings. These uncommon people choose by divination these places of residence, where they transform and manifest themselves.[1]

There must be a reason for that. Pray be kind enough to treat this subject."

THE ENVIRONMENT CHANGES in function with the mind: if the mind is filthy, the environment will be polluted. But also the mind is influenced by the environment: when the surroundings are quiet, the mind becomes calm. Thus mind and environment meet in an invisible manner, like the Tao and the virtuous efficiency which resides in the Obscure.[2] Śākyamuni, who is constantly among us, keeps His eyes on us for our benefit and Mañjuśrī, the firmly established, confronts and leads us to the Path. The manifestation of the Buddha on Mount Kailāsa relates to the saying of Confucius that those who are humane admire mountains; and the bridges [of compassion] built over the sea to Mount Potalaka relate to the saying of Confucius that those who are wise admire water.[3]

I [Kūkai] want to speak here of a person, the Śramana Shōdō, whose mind could be compared to a well-polished mirror, or to calm waters, reflecting objectively all phenomena. He was from Haga, in the province of

Shimotsuke, and belonged to the Wakata family. When he was not yet of the age at which one spares the life of an ant,[4] his mind was advanced enough and his heart pure enough to be able to receive the Complete Ordination. Annoyed by the useless desires of the four classes of people, his only appetite was for the Triple Truth and for the practice leading to Nirvāṇa. Despising the noises of this world, he had appreciation only for the pure sources in the forests.

In this very same province is a mountain called Fudaraku, whose peaks soar into the Milky Way, whose snow-covered summit touches the emerald walls of the sky. Bearing in its bosom the roaring thunder which marks the passing hours, it is the abode of the Phoenix, twisted like the horn of a sheep. Rare is the presence of demons, and none the traces of human steps: I have asked and have been told that no one had ever climbed this mountain before. The Master of the Law [Shōdō], thinking back to Siddhārtha, let the plaint arise in his heart and, seeking courage and strength, urged his will onward. And so, he started the ascent of the mountain in the last part of the fourth moon of the first year of the era Jingo-Keiun [767]. So deep was the snow and steep the huge cliffs, and tremendous the roaring of the thunder through the mists, that he had to rest for some time. After three weeks on the slopes, he decided at length to return home. Then, during the first part of the fourth moon of the first year of the era Tenyō [781], he decided to try once more but failed to reach the summit. Then again, in the middle of the third moon of the following year, he copied sutras in honor of the Shinto divinities, drew iconographic representations of the Buddha, tore his robe to pieces, wrapped his feet in the cloth, and with utter commitment[5] searched for the Way. Bearing on his back the sutras and the representations, he reached the foot of the mountain, where he spent seven days and nights worshiping and reading the sacred scriptures. Thus he formed an unshakeable decision and pronounced the following vow:

> If the Divinities of Heaven and Earth have any knowledge of human affairs, I pray that they look upon my heart-mind. I intend to offer these scriptures and representations at the very top of this mountain and to revere with awe the divine splendor, so that plentiful will be the happiness of all human beings. So, Divinities, increase my strength, and may the poisonous dragons disappear like the sight-barring mists, may the spirits of the mountain show me the way and all help me to fulfill my wish! If I do not reach the top of this mountain, I shall never be able to achieve Awakening!

After having uttered this vow, he moved across the flashing snows and walked over the young leaves shining like jewels; when he had gone half the way up, his body was exhausted, his strength had left him. He rested for two days and finally came to see the summit: his ecstasy was like that in a dream, he felt a vertigo like that of Awakening. He was suddenly able to penetrate the sea of stars without having to resort to a wooden raft, and he succeeded in seeing the cavern dwellings of the Immortals without having to swallow the Marvelous Drugs. Overcome with satisfaction, then overcome with sadness, he found it difficult to control his spirits.

The shape of the mountains, from east to west, was like a sleeping dragon, providing a limitless view from the summit. From north to south, it was like a seated tiger, inspiring one to live there in quietness. It was as if these mountains were taking Mount Sumeru as their companion, or drawing to them the Cakravada Mountains,[6] and using them as a sash. Mount Heng Shan and Mount T'ai Shan seemed absurdly low, and Mount K'un Lun Shan and Mount Hsiang Tsui Shan seemed ridiculously inferior. Those were the first places illumined by the rising sun, and where the moon could be seen until late into the night. Without needing the Divine Insight, he could see as far as ten thousand li.[7] Who could desire to ride the Crane of the Immortals when the white clouds lay well below his feet?

Without the help of a loom, a thousand kinds of flowers wove a well-patterned brocade. Whose was the alchemy responsible for so many magnificent aspects of nature? Looking to the north, he saw a lake which he estimated to be one thousand acres in extent: it was rather narrow from east to west and long from north to south. Then turning to the west, he saw another, but smaller lake, which appeared to be of two hundred acres. Then, turning to the southwest, he could see yet another large lake which, all considered, was well over one thousand ting wide; not too broad from east to west, it was elongated on the north-south axis. The high crests of the mountains of the four horizons rippled on the lake's surface, and the trees and stones were adorned with many a natural splendor. A silvery snow covered the earth, and the flowers which opened on the branches looked like gold. The mirror-like surface of the lake, being selfless, could not but reflect the ten thousand phenomena, and this reflection of the mountains and lakes was enough to leave him [Shōdō] breathless. But winds and snow surprised him while his eyes were not yet tired of admiring the landscape. Thus he built a hut to the southwest and dwelt there; he made offerings and prayers, and so nearly three times seven days passed. Having fulfilled his wish, he returned home.

In the third year of the era Enryaku [784], in the last part of the third moon, he ascended again, and in five days reached the shores of the southern lake. At the beginning of the fourth moon, he managed to build a skiff six yards long and one yard wide. With the help of two or three young followers, he pushed the oars into the waters and they enjoyed the landscape. In whatever direction they looked, there was a display of many a divine splendor. Looking east, looking west, abundant and calm were the waters.... At the end of the day, in great excitement, they reached an island by the southern side, which was about nine hundred yards away from the shore and had a circumference of more than nine thousand yards. On the different islets around, there was a profusion of beautiful flowers. Later they spent some time on the lake located to the west, more than fifteen li away from the eastern one. The northern lake is separated from the southern lake by thirty li. Although all lakes bring beauty to its perfection, none surpassed the southern lake, whose waters were of a deep blue color and as pure as a mirror, and of a depth impossible to measure. One-thousand-year-old pines and oaks faced the lake, bending their dark green foliage over the water; cryptomerias and ground cypresses of several yards' circumference, soaring up above steep rocks, looked like the tops of blue towers. Five-colored flowers mixed their hues on a single branch, and the birds chanting away the hours united their different voices into one single melody. White cranes danced on the shores, blue geese fluttered on the water. The flapping of their wings echoed like chimes in the crisp air, their voices echoed like gems striking one another. The breaths of Heaven used the pine trees as lutes, the rolling waves used the pebbles as drums. Thus the five keynotes played forth the Heavenly Harmony, and the Eight Qualities of the water were secured in its calmness. Time and again the drapes of mist and the veils of clouds were filled with the peals of thunder emanating from the Dragon-King Nanda; the lanterns of the stars and the torches of lightning looked like manifestations of the "All-Pervading Perfume." The reflection of the full moon in the lake allowed one to perceive the Mirror-Wisdom of the Bodhisattva Samantabhadra, and the Sun of Wisdom in the midst of emptiness let one awaken to the Self possessing the Universal Knowledge. In this supreme environment he decided to build a temple, to which he gave the name Jingūji. There he lived and practiced the Way during four years, at the end of which [788] the temple was moved to the northern shore of the lake, which had beautiful sands and from whence the view to the four directions was free of any obstacle. There, the colors of flowers never seen before, difficult to name, astonished the eyes; delicate scents, the nuances of which are hard to describe, gave rise to ecstasy. The Immortals must never have known about this place and must have gone elsewhere. Here, it was difficult to make a distinction between divine and human beings. How regrettable it is that this area is not mentioned by Tung-fang Shou, how disappointing that Wang Sun never visited here! Although one thinks of the hungry tiger, none was to be seen, and so was Wang Tzu-ch'iao, always seeming to escape. Here the Lotus World is to be seen in the ocean of one's mind; here the True Aspect of phenomena could be meditated upon the mountain of the white-haired tuft of the Buddha.[8] Clothes made from the surrounding vines protected one from the cold, and the shade under the trees allowed one to escape the heat. It was a delight to eat the herbs hereabout and to drink the pure water.[9] Whether walking or seated, one was away from the filth, here where the voice of the crane went easily from the deep valleys to Heaven.[10]

Hearing this, the Emperor Kammu gave to Shōdō the title of Master of Lectures of the Province of Kōzuke—we are in a time of benefit to all [through Buddhism], when one forgets all ill feelings. Later, a temple of the Kegon School was built in Shikinoyama, in the district of Tsugana; Shōdō moved there for the benefit of all beings, and expanded the Way. In the second year of the era Daidō [807], there was a drought in that province: the Governor ordered the Master of the Law to perform the rainmaking rituals, and the Master carried them out on top of Mount Fudaraku. Consequently, the space was filled with the sweet nectar of rain, and the crop was abundant and rich. It is impossible to describe in detail all the actions of this Buddha-like monk. Ah, how difficult it is to stop the wheel of time and how easily the world of humans changes! The age of seventy came quickly, and the four elements making up his body lost their vigor. Having done all that he had to do, his life closed on perfect accomplishment.

Doctor I, a former official of the province of Shimotsuke, who knew well the Master of the Law, came to the capital[11] at the time of his own retirement. Expressing regrets that nothing had been written by the Master about this splendid area, he requested some words from my brush. In spite of my repeated protestations, he was able to force me to compose poor verses born from my own ignorance. So I [Kūkai] composed the following inscription:[12]

> From the egg yolk the earth is split,
> To Heaven ascend the Pure Breaths;
> Toad and crow begin their rotation,
> The myriads of beings appear and wriggle about. [13]

> Mountains soar and oceans mix,
> Obscurity and light go their different ways;
> The waves of phenomena appear and disappear,
> While water shows the Essence.[14]

> Out of a single particle of dust, a whole mountain,
> In a single drop of water, the depths of a lake;[15]
> Dust and drops accumulate and mix,
> Designing and decorating the divine residence.[16]

> The high crests, too high to be wrapped in clouds,
> Defy the scaling by the Phoenix itself;
> Ah, snowy and shiny summits,
> Who could see you, who could reside on you?

> The Sramana Shōdō,
> Strong as a bamboo, resistant as a pine tree,
> Revered the Awakened,
> Recited the Law.

> Converting himself to Avalokitesvara,
> He venerated Śākyamuni;
> Searching for the Way he fervently undertook austerities,
> And entered the imposing mountains.

> Like the dragon he scaled the immense peaks,
> Like the Phoenix he crossed the valleys;
> Protected by all the clairvoyant divinities,
> He looked over mountains and rivers.

Dangerous and steep cliffs!
Deep and clear waters!
Splendid and marvelous flowers,
Amongst the birds' voices!

From Heaven and Earth all sounds,
Close to the divine lute's melody;
Chosen abode of the Divine Beings,
Where harmonious sounds mark the passing hours.

One single sight erases all plaints,
And all suffering ceases naturally;
Indeed without comparison in this world,
Rather, of the Heavenly Spaces' Nature!

Even Sun Ch'o would have thrown away his brush,
How could the eloquent Kuo P'u have expressed it?
Ah, who, animated by the same will,
Would not follow the very same Path?

For two human beings, acquaintance does not necessarily rely on face-to-face meetings and long dialogues; if there exists an identity of essence between the two, great indeed can be their intimacy. I have never met in person the Master Shōdō. Luckily enough, I have been able to hear from Doctor I of his honest and pure inclinations, and this same doctor asked me to set down some words on Mount Fudaraku. Although I have no special genius, I have expressed what humanity requires, not being able to refuse this request. Thus I have added words lacking harmony on the white sheets. Words and sentences are weak and I am afraid that they have not succeeded in making the Obscurity even more obscure. . . [17]

Having nothing to offer but broken pebbles, I have nevertheless tried to express myself with sincerity. Never shall I forget, nor allow this ever to escape from my thoughts.

—Śramana Henjōkongō, of the Western Mount.[18] Kōnin fifth year [814], on the thirtieth of the eighth moon.

Moose's Tooth from Sheldon Amphitheater. Photo by Bradford Washburn.
Courtesy of the Museum of Science, Boston

The Mountain, the reality, Theseus seems to argue, must recall us from
the dream, the opiate of non-remembrance.

— H. D.
Helen in Egypt

STYLE AND MEANING
IN MOUNTAINEERING

Southeast Face of Mount McKinley. Photo by Bradford Washburn. Courtesy of the Museum of Science, Boston

Photo, page 69: Don Sheldon beneath Mount Dickey. Photo by Bradford Washburn. Courtesy of the Museum of Science, Boston

David Roberts

Alaska and Personal Style:

Some Notes in Search
of an Aesthetic

L IKE NO OTHER wilderness, mountains demand the eye, beg us to fantasize and speculate in advance of contact. The sea, by contrast, seems all of a piece, like the desert or the jungle: one edges timidly into it, fearing not worse, but too much of the same—the terror of ordinariness, of getting lost. In the mountains the urge is to be ensconced, to find and reach the heart of difficulty; the corresponding fear is being stranded there.

It is in that sense, Mallory's sense, that mountains are "there" as other kinds of wilderness are not. To traverse the Northwest Passage was to see it for the first time. To reach the South Pole was to discover it. But the summit of the Matterhorn had teased men's eyes for centuries, a self-evident locus of the inaccessible—and therefore, whether hideous or desirable, a place men had to reach.

A S MOUNTAINEERS, we may be artists of a certain sort. Visual art-ists, in the first place, whose challenge is to see the route where lay-men see only cliffs and ledges. As mountaineers, we are also devout pil-grims, spending weeks in the rites of adoration that planning an expedition requires, hours in numb worship on the glacier below the mountain, staring through binoculars and cameras. On the climb itself we become athletes—the long-distance kind—summoning up the stoic virtues of patience and self-denial in lieu of the clever and flashy antics of our brethren on local crags. We may, in a quite limited sense—a sense the nineteenth century would have seen as perversely overspecialized—be explorers.

But we are not creators. The object we would give life to was there before we came; we demonstrate it, perhaps, but we do not invent it. There is a less significant difference between two ascents of a given route than between two sonnets. Whatever a Brahms ballade has about it that is unmistakably Brahms, that individuality evaporates from the climbing route. The mountaineer's creative despair—the impossibility of putting a genuinely personal stamp on the climb he gives all but his life to—is also his chief glory. For who among us has stood at the base of a mountain wall, having just forged its first ascent, and not thrilled at the aura of unsolved mystery that still haunts about it?

NOWHERE IS THAT PERSONAL stamp more elusive than in Alaska. Its mountains, isolated from gold-rush outposts of civilization by huge expanses of uninhabited land, threw up enormous logistical obstacles to the first explorers. Isolated as well from the development of mountaineering technique in Europe and the Western U.S., Alaskan climbing matured in its own tardy, idiosyncratic way. The image of "Alaskan snow slogs" has its accuracy: no mountain in Alaska over fifteen thousand feet boasts anything like the uniqueness of Jannu in the Himalayas, of Jirishanca in the Peruvian Andes, and none requires exceptional technical ability. Due to the sheer vastness of the state, some of its most spectacular ranges, like the Cathedral (Kichatna) Spires, were discovered by climbers only in the last fifteen years.

In the period from 1890 to 1930, all the efforts of mountaineers in Alaska were bent toward ascending the highest peaks. The early expeditions had a grandiose boldness about them. Setting out from Fairbanks, Seward, Tyonek, they labored for months simply to approach the mountain, traversing hundreds of miles of muskeg, forest, and river by the most discouraging of increments. The men who conducted those treks were not, most of them, alpinists; but they had mastered a means of wilderness travel that has all but vanished today. Small wonder that so many, when at last at grips with the mountain, turned back appalled by the danger of avalanches and the ferocity of the weather. Their style was that of the best subarctic overland voyages, and cannot on the whole be weighed by climbing standards. Frederick Cook, for all his later infamy, for all the scorn heaped on him by his companion Robert Dunn (in his classic *The Shameless Diary of an Explorer*), accomplished in 1903 what no one has duplicated since—the complete circumnavigation of Mount McKinley.

Nor can the boldness of these voyages be judged by Himalayan or Andean comparisons. On the approach to Everest in the 1920s, a porter strike meant a serious nuisance. In the Alaska Range in 1899, when Joseph Herron's Indian guides deserted overnight, his was a question of survival, which only a lean winter as the uninvited guest of a tiny band of Kuskokwim natives resolved.

In those first forty years, McKinley, Logan, and St. Elias were climbed, as were a few of the slightly lower snow giants like Mount Blackburn. The Duke of the Abruzzi's 1897 success on St. Elias had a personal stamp about it—Abruzzi's nonchalant glacial competence and comfort, brass bedstead and all. The 1925 ascent of Logan was a masterwork of logistical build-up, no matter how tedious the pace—the stamp of its indefatigable fifty-year-old leader, Albert MacCarthy.

But the tour de fource of Alaskan climbing was the 1910 Sourdoughs' ascent of the north peak of McKinley. Mountaineers none of them—Lloyd,

Taylor, McGonagall, Anderson—they found their blithe way through the complex of defenses that had baffled Wickersham, Cook, Browne, and Parker. The summit push from 11,000 feet to 19,400 and back in less than a day by Taylor and Anderson, carrying a fourteen-foot sapling, stands today as one of the most extraordinary feats in mountaineering history. Twenty-seven years later, asked how he had felt on the summit, Billy Taylor said, "Well, of course, the altitude made you feel light-like. You had to watch yourself or your feet would come up quick." Why hadn't they used climbing ropes? "Didn't need 'em."

Then came Bradford Washburn. At first only one of a number of Ivy League climbers attracted to Alaska in the 1930s—others included Adams Carter, Charlie Houston, Bob Bates, Walter Wood, Bill Ladd, and Terris Moore—Washburn gradually became *the* Alaskan mountaineer. No other man has had a comparable impact, or so dominated the scene for as long a time.

It was not technical difficulty that was Washburn's forte. By today's standards the routes he pioneered were easy, involving almost no rock climbing. But for pertinacity, for originality, for sheer logistical perfection, Washburn's first ascents deserve the highest praise. The hybrid of styles he used on Mount Sanford, horse-packing in, skiing 6,000 feet in an hour's glide down from the summit, evinces the sunny smoothness of his plans. The splendid final ridge on Mount Hayes testifies to his snow-climbing nerve. But it was in a desperate situation that Washburn's style emerged at its purest. Stranded with Bates in the gigantic St. Elias Range after pilot Bob Reeve had barely escaped the first glacier landing in Alaskan climbing history, Washburn bagged the unclimbed 17,000-foot Lucania, traversed over 15,000-foot Mount Steele, and bombed down the Donjek River to the Alcan Highway, cutting the floor out of his tent among other economies to save weight. Quintessential Washburn—especially the cocky grab of Lucania in the face of what others would have treated as the grimmest of forced marches. He made of his impatience a marvelous virtue, anticipating the alpinist's linkage of speed to safety by nearly a generation.

I T IS FITTING that Washburn also became the world's foremost aerial mountain photographer, as well as the first to apply flying to base-camp access. For no historical event has so transformed Alaskan climbing as the use of the airplane. Moreover, no climbing area in the world has evolved a comparable dependence on aerial technology. In the Himalayas, Andes, Patagonia, climbing is largely unaffected by air flight. In the Alps and Rockies flight is irrelevant except in rescue efforts. But in Alaska scarcely an expedition ventures forth without vital dependence on a bush pilot.

The plane has its capacity to trivialize. The mountain that took a 1910 explorer months to reach can now be squeezed in during a two-week vacation from a Wall Street office. There have been "expeditions" in the Alaska

Range that lasted less than seven days. If you add a radio, you have an instant-crump capacity that can turn a mountain experience into something like a drive-in movie.

But the airplane creates its own aesthetic. Above all it demarcates, almost shockingly, "in" from "out." One moment you are out, in Talkeetna, sipping a last beer at the Fairview, scribbling postcards to the next of kin. Two hours later you stand alone on a glacier, afraid to walk a hundred feet because of the crevasses, in a wilderness as empty as you will ever behold. The transition is disturbing, sometimes cruel. At the end of a trip, waiting to be picked up, every party goes through the acute stages of "airplane jitters." Sample dialogue: "He'll probably come just when we've got dinner cooked." "Nah, I bet he's backed up for days. I expect him tomorrow." "Hold still, I think I hear something." "I thought I heard it too, but now I don't." "It's clear here, but it could be socked in in Talkeetna." "For all we know he cracked up a week ago in the Chugach." "Where is he, damn it?" "Listen. Do you hear that sound?"

There are all too many expeditions now that fly in without the slightest idea of which way to head should they have to hike out. Minus a radio, the tyranny of the prearranged pick-up date imposes an artificial constraint on the organic mountaineering balance of ambition matched against difficulty. There is no recourse, in the event of an accident, but to wait. In the most remote parts of Alaska there are planes overhead nearly every day. But it is astonishing how hard it is for them to see you. You stamp a message in the snow, to no avail. Your pilot, armed with an X on a map to find you for the airdrop, circles endlessly miles down-glacier while you wave your arms in vain. It is then that the sense of being trapped can come over you. And for all the times that everything works out at last, there is the odd expedition that loses all its food in a botched airdrop, that misses its pick-up date, that has a pilot who forgets to come.

THE LACK OF NIGHT in Alaska has its own peculiar effects. By obviating the forced bivouac, it grants an eerie freedom. More than one summit has been claimed in the course of a continuous push of more than twenty-four hours. But the absence of a natural schedule can seduce a party into overextending itself, and can take its toll as well in tiny irritations. The classic five-day storm seems all the drearier with nothing but gray to the universe, day and night, with no "morning" to cast its spell of hope over previous darkness.

Night's absence also profoundly affects the snow. A slanting, constant sun means only a few degrees difference in temperature between noon and midnight. At the lower altitudes the snow fails to "set up" for days at a time. Perhaps nowhere in the world are the snow conditions worse. One travels the glaciers at "night" to escape its sloppiest moments. Whole faces are out of the question because of constant avalanching. The wind adds its sculpting touch, creating here mushrooms of rime ice, there the hollow, airy, unconsolidated stuff that is the most frightening snow of all. The result is to add to the climber's sense of being an unskilled workman, to make him feel all the more a plodder and a blunderer. The arabesques that enlighten ice climbing in the Alps or the Andes are seldom possible in Alaska. A party may find, as Al Steck's did on Logan in 1965, that a snow shovel is its most effective technical device. The rock climbing learned in Yosemite or Colorado adapts well to Alaskan granite. But where does one practice floundering and flailing, or swimming through spindrift, or tiptoeing across windslabs, or wallowing in glacial slush?

NO SINGLE CLIMB in Alaskan history is more of a landmark than the first ascent of Devil's Thumb in 1946, by Fred Beckey, Bob Craig, and Clifford Schmidtke. Technically far beyond anything else then done in Alaska, the climb had a style that was wholly admirable as well. Making fast pushes from a high glacier camp, taking the inevitable bivouacs in stride, climbing in tennis shoes on the hard rock pitches, the trio validated an alpine-style approach years ahead of its time.

Devil's Thumb stood as a standard of excellence until eight years later when it was matched by Beckey himself. For Beckey and Henry Meybohm, 1954 was as fine a season as climbers can have. They made the first ascent of the northwest ridge of McKinley in May, then with Heinrich Harrer the first ascent of Deborah in June and the first ascent of Hunter in July. On Deborah, especially, the technical boldness displayed by Beckey on the Devil's Thumb saw the party through what all three later described as "the most sensational ice climb any one of us had ever undertaken." It was Beckey's knack to ignore the intimidation of being hundreds of miles from civilization, of the atrocious and dangerous weather: he treated Alaskan peaks almost as he would have the Cascades. It was his vision to foresee that the finest climbing in Alaska was to be had not on the loftiest peaks, but on those of moderate height and size.

The legendary impatience—of a wholly different sort from Washburn's —was there from the start. When Fritz Wiessner's bad knee precluded the first Devil's Thumb attack, Beckey caught the boat for Wrangell, telephoned Schmidtke and Craig, and was back in the Stikine a week later. On Deborah and Hunter, the three men used Don Sheldon's plane like a taxi. Yet they strolled the seventy miles down the Kahiltna and back to civilization after Hunter, just as they had hiked out two months before from McKinley.

Later Beckey forays complemented his vision: the return to the Stikine with Kor, Mather, and Davis in 1964 for the ascents of Mussell, Ratz, and especially, Burkett Needle. Yet other jaunts—like an attempt on Mount Kimball in six days' round trip from Los Angeles—were so impetuous they seemed almost parodies of the earlier successes. But Beckey, with his trunk of secret photos, his half-apocryphal files, doesn't look back.

In the 1960s the Europeans, with Cassin on McKinley and Terray on

Huntington, finally took notice of Alaska. Some of the most difficult of the lower peaks were climbed, and routes of a high technical standard emerged. Two expeditions set stylistic examples that, while not immediately spawning imitators, showed a highly innovative spark. The Hummingbird Ridge, Logan's finest route, involved extreme snow climbing over so long a stretch that fixed-rope support—used to the point of overkill by other expeditions in that decade—had to be partly eschewed. In cutting themselves off from retreat, Steck's party showed a commitment reminiscent of early Arctic voyages. On the Moose's Tooth four climbers from Munich succeeded where Beckey and others had failed, mainly by dint of going all-out for the summit in an incredibly fast time. During the same month, it was taking Terray weeks to work his way up Huntington. Neither the German ascent nor the Hummingbird Ridge assault has received the credit it deserves.

IN THE MIDST of such technical ferment, Vin Hoeman was something of a throwback. He was not a good rock climber, and he knew little about big-wall technique. He was phenomenal on really bad rock and snow, and his drive made it impossible to keep up with him on the trail or kicking steps in a couloir. Though he died on Dhaulagiri at only thirty-two, he remains by a healthy margin the mountaineer who has made the greatest number of first ascents in Alaska.

Unlike most of the climbers who have taken the state to heart, and who have made the significant climbs there, Vin chose to live in Alaska as well. He felt a proprietary zeal about its mountains. In a formidable system of note cards, he kept track of every fact he could dig up about the Alaskan ranges, cataloguing every peak that had what he called "IVR"—independent vertical rise, meaning an altitude of a thousand feet or more above the highest col connecting it to any higher mountain. The system bordered on fetishism. Because Vin's writing was so small, a climber's life could usually be encompassed on one side of a card. A few, like Washburn, rated two sides. Vin himself was the only three-card climber in history.

The system dominated his very perception of mountains. Near Igikpak in the Brooks Range, he turned his back on the second-highest peak, a fine unclimbed tower, because it lacked IVR by a hundred feet or so; instead he clomped off up-valley to nab a nameless talus pile that happened to have no higher neighbors.

Vin was a peak-bagger, but he had a style and vision of his own. He loved the challenge of messy and difficult terrain, of marathon treks to arcane destinations. He bushwhacked fiercely, and climbed slopes with a spiderlike crawl. He was a connoisseur of the obscure. The epitome for him of an ideal expedition was what he called the Grand Traverse: the ascent of the highest peak in a range by traversing it from roadhead to roadhead. The perfect Grand Traverse would make the first ascent of that mountain. In 1968 Vin himself led what may well be the only such Grand

Traverse ever accomplished in Alaska—the first ascent of the highest peak on the Harding Icefield, packing in with horses along the beach from Homer, up the Fox Fiver to the icefield, climbing and naming Truuli Peak, continuing down the Resurrection River, and coming out to an unexpected hero's welcome in Seward. It was his favorite trip. It crystallized his love for Alaska, and was probably his most elegant accomplishment.

THE LAST FIFTEEN YEARS have seen an explosion of interest in big-wall climbing on relatively low-altitude peaks, those under 13,000 feet, particularly in the granite labyrinth of the Cathedral Spires and along the awesome corridor of the Great Gorge of the Ruth Glacier. It is in ranges like these that the real singularity, as well as the future, of Alaskan mountaineering lies. Still in progress is a shift from the fixed-rope expeditionary method to the purest alpine style.

For the first time ever there is beginning to be something like a "scene" in Alaskan climbing. In the Cathedral Spires, competition is approaching the kind of intensity that made the Bugaboos the place to be in the 1960s, the Tetons in the middle 1950s. So many good climbers have appeared, with such ambitious sights, that one wonders how far the limits can be pushed. A temporary answer looms in the form of routes that are coming to be known as great prizes through repeated failure—most notably the east face of the Moose's Tooth. Yet it seems all the more difficult in today's scene for the personal mark, the innovative stamp, to be printed on the face of Alaskan climbing.

If there has been a harbinger of a new style in the last few years it must be the remarkable Californian, Charlie Porter, who shuns any publicizing of his feats, even slide shows or journal notes. In the summer of 1976 Porter had the kind of season scarcely seen since 1954. His ascent of the west face of Middle Triple Peak in the Cathedral Spires with Russ McLean—an eleven-day epic on the sheerest face in the range, as well as the mountain's first ascent—may be technically the hardest climb yet accomplished in Alaska. (Porter broke a finger when hit by falling ice early on the climb, but continued.) Bolder still was his solo ascent of the Cassin route on McKinley. It may be that soloing the great mountains is the next dizzy step in upping the Alaskan ante: witness Jon Krakauer's climb of Devil's Thumb in 1977, after walking in from the seacoast.

FOR ME THE EXCITEMENT at first was simply that of the unknown. On the north face of McKinley in 1963, my first expedition, each time I led there was a pleasure I could taste at the thought that no one, ever, had stood where I stood then. In the next two years, on Deborah and Huntington, that shallow thrill modulated into the deeper but gloomier charm of all-out commitment. My best friend and partner, Don Jensen, was a guru of dogged and obsessive dedication, and on Deborah he taught me through his own grim example how a mountain could become the only thing that mattered. At the time his intensity frightened me. Now I see it as the germ of his own odd kind of self-transcendence. Yes, it could get you killed; it could also, and did, get us up the west face of Huntington, a route otherwise beyond our abilities or nerve.

After Huntington I took a special interest in the more remote ranges, the ones Washburn hadn't photographed and scarcely knew about. The challenge in the Cathedral Spires, the Revelation Range, Igikpak, and the Arrigetch, sprang from an embarrassment of riches. Every peak we turned to was unclimbed. We didn't need to look for routes; the mere ascents were usually difficult enough. In those years, the late 1960s, there was still among us a clannish pride: no one else, we thought, cared about a place like the Revelations, or was soon likely to. It was a greedy happiness, the kind that revels in obscurity.

Now Alaska has been discovered. In a given summer there are still significantly fewer visitors to the Ruth Gorge than loiter about a single cirque in the Wind Rivers, but the view up Arrigetch Creek toward Xanadu is fast becoming a postcard cliché, and a photo of Middle Triple Peak from the air has been made into a jigsaw puzzle.

But by far the most striking change the years of my climbing in Alaska have spanned is the adaptation of alpine ethics to the big climbs. The shift is wholly and irreversibly to the good; not only is fixing a route tedious and stodgy, but few expeditions in the fifties and sixties cleaned their routes afterward, so that more than one great line, like the Cassin, is festooned today with rotting handrails. Still, the old style had its own aesthetic, its peculiar rewards and terrors. Simply because of the lengths of time it required climbers to be exposed to danger, it was, I think, at least as hazardous as the alpine approach.

On Huntington in 1965 we spent twenty-six days pushing our route before we reached the summit; we had four nightmarish days of descent. That month of moving supplies, eating, and sleeping built up a gradual but oppressive identification with the mountain. Don called this slow seeping of the mountain into our very pores a "communion." We knew all its moods, from the stormiest to the windless perfect summit day we seized before it could change its mind. We were like cripples, unable to climb a single pitch, we thought, without securing it for future passage; the movement of our gear was as important as the movement of ourselves. But when the summit we had despaired of for weeks finally burst upon us, it had the power of grace. And now, years afterward, the whole experience still sings.

On the southeast face of Mount Dickey in the Ruth Gorge in 1974, we climbed a route technically harder than Huntington, and more than half again as long, in only three days. The intensity was of a different sort. In place of the wormlike burrowing-in during a storm on Huntington, on Dickey I felt an extreme vulnerability to the weather. We reached the final slopes just as the storm that could have done us in broke in full

Terray Ridge, Mount Huntington. Photo by Bradford Washburn. Courtesy of the Museum of Science, Boston

Keep your eye fixed on the path to the top, but don't forget to look in front of you. The last step depends on the first. Don't think you're there just because you see the summit. Watch your footing, be sure of the step, but don't let that distract you from the highest goal. The first step depends on the last.

— René Daumal
Mount Analogue

fury. In memory, there is a kind of looking backward, downward, over the last slick cliff we climbed in the drizzle that prefigured the blizzard, a half-glimpsed "what-if?" hanging in the past like an old guilt. The joy was more of efficiency than of movement. No three days of my life have been more intense; and I had bad dreams about Dickey during every one of the fifteen nights following. But three days are not a month, the climb of calculated maturity not the ultimate adventure of a youthful plunge into something entirely beyond one's previous notion of the possible.

I HAVE RECURRING DREAMS about Alaska, dreams that refer to earlier dreams more clearly than they do to my life. I have a dream McKinley, much smaller than the real one, which I can never quite circumnavigate. I could draw a map of my dream Cathedral Spires, to which I have undertaken some forty or sixty expeditions, failing again and again to find the way to that high shelf glacier above which all the finest peaks extend, still unclimbed. On my dream Huntington, Sheldon amazingly lands his Super Cub at the 10,000-foot level on a snow patch a little bigger than a dining-room table. But nothing he brings or tells us can get us through the overhangs above.

Climbs end, but the deep-stirred psyche never rests. In it our terrors reenact the struggle between our puny need to move upward and the inorganic world's dogmatic downward insistence. There the tamed scale of the child's playground wars with the unassimilable hugeness of the wilderness. Always there, human hopefulness resounds, the dreaming faith that, in an eventless world of rock and ice, something is about to happen.

Over: Eroica, XS. Photo by Ken Wilson

Harold Drasdo
Reading the Big Wall Image

Mount Analogue:

> ... the symbolic mountain—the way that unites Heaven and Earth, a way which must exist in material and human form, otherwise our situation would be without hope.
>
> —René Daumal

North American Wall, El Capitan:

> ... the finest single climbing experience I have had so far. Staying on the route was like trying to track a deer across the Grand Canyon. Inch up and peer, ease up and peer. The route meanders back and forth, abruptly turning and changing direction. Feeling joy at being alive, feeling energy, feeling adrenalin, laughing. Every day one or all of us would have to perform some maneuver so extreme that whoever was safe and sound on the belay station would laugh till he almost fell out of his slings. We didn't want to top out till all the water was gone.
>
> —Ellie Hawkins

THERE IS A MYTH of the Tsimshian Indians, from the Canadian Pacific Coast, in which the protagonist—an "outcast hero" type—faces a series of trials of strength. In turn he undergoes initiation and proves himself as hunter and warrior. He then confronts the forces of nature in successive forms: fierce beasts, forests, and finally, mountains which threaten to overwhelm his village or force it into the sea. The encounter with the mountains is certainly his most daunting task. In one version of the myth the whole earth shakes as the hills advance and as the hero forces them back; in another, it is for this task alone that he must pray for supernatural assistance.

The myth is exceptional. Mountains commonly play a quite different role in world mythology. They are the "cosmic pillar" by means of which men or gods, for whatever purposes, can ascend to or descend from the sky. Sometimes this pillar is a magical tree, the World-Tree. Sometimes it is as insubstantial as a cloud. But often it takes the form of a mountain, whether familiar or legendary. It is the precursor of Daumal's Mount Analogue.

Most examples of the mountain as metaphor or symbol can be referred to these two mythic archetypes—the mountain as the ultimate hazard and the mountain as the religious pathway—and to their combination and elaborations. The mountaineer's traditional images of great ascents may also be related to these archetypes.

THIS ESSAY IS an attempt to account for the power of a strong new image directing modern mountaineering. We begin by considering the historical imagery of mountains and of man's relationships with them. These images often have their origins in the mountain's suitability as a metaphorical vehicle capable of carrying such concepts as eminence, grandeur, transcendence, aloofness, isolation, danger, struggle, perseverance—the list could easily be lengthened. Metaphor shifts easily into symbol and may be extended into allegory or parable. It is not useful, here, to spend time rigorously separating these categories and the approach must be restricted by excluding some metaphorical levels or directions. I will not elaborate upon the fancies mountains have provoked in those attempting to convey their appearance: the Matterhorn was a pyramid for Martin Conway and an obelisk for Sir Joseph Fayrer; it was a rearing horse for Ruskin and a stranded Greek galley for Hopkins. Alpine literature has been combed relentlessly for such figures of speech, most notably by Sir Gavin de Beer. But these visual comparisons the mountain brings to mind have little content; they lead to a dead end. They say nothing about the nature of our experience of the hills. It is something else that we seek here: the greater concepts the mountain can stand for; the meaning the mountain may hold for us.

Our language is rich in metaphors joining the world of mountains with the world of men and to document their varieties would be a major undertaking. However, a few locating points will indicate their scope. To begin with, we can summarize the whole human adventure: Darwin's *The Descent of Man* looks back to the past; Bronowski's *The Ascent of Man* works toward the future; as for ourselves, we rise or fall in the world. These usages resemble exhausted metaphor, but they are easily revived. For example, the concept of the Fall of Man (assimilated into most of the world's languages without apparent difficulty) takes on new resonance in William Golding's novel, *Free Fall*, simply through a neat conjunction with the concept of Free Will and a casual reference to the argot of the modern rock climber or sport parachutist; in passing we note the novel's hero is named Mountjoy (Mons Veneris), and the prison-camp interrogator who nearly destroys him is Dr. Halde (Dr. Slope). Turning from the serious novel to a universal art form, modern popular music groans with metaphors of climbing and falling. Yet, even in the 1970's, Melanie Safka has been able to draw upon such metaphors to produce curiously original images in her lyrics. In ordinary thought, the force of climbing as striving or risking, of the summit as difficulty or aim, seems to make sense to everyone. And if we try to find a substitute family of metaphors, we discover that nothing—not even the strong idea of the journey—has quite the same resources.

In order to see something of the mountain metaphor or image in transmission, here are two examples, transects of Western culture. The first illustrates whole peoples handling particular images. The second shows individual writers exploring a specific idea.

The ballad numbered 243 in the Child collection has been known by many names, among which "James Harris," "The Daemon Lover," and "The House Carpenter" are the most widespread. It tells how the ghost of a former lover entices a married woman from her husband and home, and how the phantom finally reveals his unearthly nature. In what is probably the best-known of the early printed versions, that appearing in the 1812 edition of Scott's *Minstrelsy of the Scottish Border,* the pair are crossing the sea when the woman learns her destiny in a chilling exchange:

> "O what hills are yon, yon pleasant hills,
>   That the sun shines sweetly on?"
> "O yon are the hills of heaven," he said,
>   "Where you will never win."
>
> "O whaten a mountain is yon," she said,
>   "All so dreary wi' frost and snow?"
> "O yon is the mountain of hell," he cried,
>   "Where you and I will go."

Then, effortlessly, the demon destroys the ship and all aboard.

A substantial work might easily be written on the origins and development of this ballad, which first appeared in broadside versions. As for the two stanzas quoted (which do not, in fact, appear in all the texts), one writer has found their source in the Mountain Otherworld of the Norse imagination; another argues that the hills should be traced back through *Thomas Rymer* and *Thomas of Ersseldoune* to medieval vision literature. The ballad's different forms were recorded in Britain from Cornwall to Southern Scotland and had taken root in the Appalachians and were spreading steadily through the Eastern and Southern U.S. well before Scott's version was printed. But there are many striking changes in the American variants. Take, for example, one that has chanced to gain a contemporary audience of millions through the voice of Joan Baez. In it the supernatural content, as it relates to the returned lover, the sea, and the ship, has been entirely eliminated. Instead it is concentrated and made explicit only in the two mountain stanzas. These have been removed from their logical position and now end the ballad, left suspended as a ghostly echo after the ship has gone down.

> What hills, what hills, are those, my love,
> That rise so fair and high?
> Those are the hills of heaven, my love,
> But not for you and I.

Winter ascent, El Dorado Springs, Colorado. Photo by Peter Eichner

And what hills, what hills, are those, my love,
Those hills so dark and low?
Those are the hills of hell, my love,
Where you and I must go.

Why did unknown singers make these shifts of emphasis and displacements of content? Why, in America, have the pleasant, sunlit hills of heaven lost their sunshine and gained altitude? Why has the snow-covered mountain of hell been diminished and transformed into a line of low dark hills? To attempt to account for these changes would require specialized knowledge in many fields—in religious differences, in folklore and folk music, in population movements, in the phonetics of local dialects, and in the local geography of the Eastern U.S. and Britain. But what stands out clearly is the way in which the mountain image at once exhibits flexibility and persistence, in having survived transmission by word of mouth over a wide geographic area and through more than two hundred years of the English language—and very probably for a much longer period through other languages reaching back to Norse or Romance origins.

To turn from the oral tradition to the written word, one of the most remarkable pieces of mountain imagery in the whole of English literature is that in Hopkins's Poem 65—the poem introducing "the desolation sonnets." The passage can stand repeating.

Oh the mind, mind has mountains; cliffs of fall
Frightful, sheer, no-man-fathomed. Hold them cheap
May who ne'er hung there. Nor does long our small
Durance deal with that steep or deep.

Hopkins's manner, which reads somewhat oddly on first acquaintance, exploits rather than obscures the resources of this image. Professor W. H. Gardner, a principal commentator on Hopkins, treats these lines at length. Gardner looked first of all to the natural association of height and danger expressed by climbing; then he found an analogy of "the tension between the upward pull of high principles and aims and the downward pull of physical and moral weakness." The precipice was of a supernatural order, he decided, it might have held a lifeline to God; he was able to imagine "a daring climber who, his lifeline broken, is left clinging to the sheer cliff face with no help from above and certain destruction below." He related the image to the Jesuitical concept of desolation—"separation from God, the difficulty of maintaining the religious life."

For the mountaineering reader, a perturbing distraction is created here. Gardner understood the gulf as something utterly inimical and appalling, but for the climber Hopkins's lines hold no such horror. To the contrary, they evoke very powerfully the fascination and glory of the mountain experience. They have such force and presence that they sidetrack us from the direction of Hopkins's onward thought. The appropriateness of the image is unassailable, but its strength is such that it almost breaks the poem by turning the metaphor inside out.

Gardner, moreover, felt it was possible to work backward from the passage. It had as "underthought," he claimed, the stupendous cliff in *King Lear* on which Edgar deluded the blinded Gloucester: "halfway down, hangs one that gathers samphire, dreadful trade." He found support for his bridge to Shakespeare in Keats's appropriation of the same words to describe the hazards of his own occupation: "I am one that gathers samphire." But the letter in which Keats's assertion appears suggests that he probably intended an image of peril, challenge, and struggle since it also contains the remark, "I must think that difficulties nerve the Spirit of a Man . . . the Cliff of Poesy Towers above me."

Leaving Gardner's backward journey we could follow the Hopkins image forward. His lines have found a place in many an essay on mountaineering, and we might even look for more scrupulous uses of the idea, as in Elizabeth Jennings's collection of poems, *The Mind Has Mountains*, in which she treats the theme of nervous breakdown. We could look for other aspects of the same idea, such as the statement of another modern poet, Gary Snyder: "Outwardly, the equivalent of the unconscious is the wilderness."

Enough has been said to indicate the extraordinary fertility of suggestion, the haunting power, that literary images of the mountain may hold. But these remarks would be incomplete without a brief reference to the place the mountain often occupies in religious and mystical thought and to the importance of the summit as the stage for revelatory experiences. The subject has been treated endlessly, and illustrations can be drawn from most of the world's cultures and from earliest times to the present. Here it is sufficient to present Jan Smuts's conclusion:

> So it has come about that all moral and spiritual values are expressed in terms of altitude. . . . The mountain is not merely something externally sublime. It has a great historic and spiritual meaning for us: it stands for us as the ladder of life. More, it is the ladder of the soul, and in a curious way, the *source* of religion.

Bringing this discussion closer to the world of mountaineering and common experience, it must be admitted that the mountain, considered abstractly, and the halt at the summit do not often provoke such exalted claims in those who know them best. Bad weather, the risks of the descent, exhaustion, familiarity with the mountain scene, often take the edge off the culminating moments of a climb, and such moments have been derided by many climbers from Sir Leslie Stephen onward. There *is* a distinct experience, but it is usually less easy to categorize and more low key than the flatlander imagines. It is closer in spirit to that strangely charged sentence of Sir Thomas Malory, written five hundred years ago, of an ascent in a yet earlier and legendary time: "King Arthur yode up to the creste of the cragge and than he comforted himself with the colde winde."

Despite these disclaimers, a broad generalization about the central, traditional image of the mountain is possible: it offered an eventual goal or experience distinct in nature and superior in significance to the struggles, however great, that preceded or underpinned it. This generalization could at one time be applied as truthfully to mountaineering as to religious fables. Not anymore.

W E CAN NOW turn to modern mountaineering and consider a new emphasis in the activity. The expression, "big wall climbing," has come into use to designate vertical, multi-day climbs on which the bivouac positions are sufficiently precarious to allow no sense of relief from the atmosphere and hazards of the face. Climbs of this nature were achieved in the Alps well before the Second World War. But, as a genre, the big wall climb was only isolated and named when, through new techniques and equipment, the great faces of the Yosemite Valley became accessible. Outside America, the recognition of the distinctiveness of this type of climbing followed mainly from Tejada-Florès's essay, "Games Climbers Play." At the same time the work of a new generation of climber-photographers was providing the visual images which made the big walls real to all those lovers of the mountain scene who will only climb such faces in the imagination.

Yosemite walls, unlike some of their counterparts in the Alps, usually finish on the valley rim and require only a walking descent through the forest. During their early ascents, a custom evolved that parties of friends might wait at the top of the exit pitch to greet the successful climbers; food and drink would be provided, a winding-down celebration might develop, and assistance would be offered in carrying the loads down to the valley. While this tradition may appear to be on the decline as the same routes are accomplished with frequency, there is no reason to assume that it will disappear entirely from the scenario, especially with regard to the more sensational enterprises: after their twenty-eight days on Dawn Wall in 1972, Harding and Caldwell were confronted by the biggest reception party ever seen on the top of El Capitan.

This is clearly a new development, and it appears to be mirrored, surprisingly, in the Alps. Recently, there have been a number of instances in which, by helicopter, parties have been ferried up the glacier to the foot of the wall or lifted from the summit without need of a rescue. Whether this is reprehensible, acceptable, or whether it is even worth arguing about from the viewpoint of "climbing ethics" is not at issue here. What is interesting is that attention seems to be focusing more and more narrowly upon the wall. The summit has lost something of its significance. It is no longer a step into Another Kingdom, to be savored briefly before the climber makes his hazardous or, at any rate, lonely descent. The summit is only the point at which the climbing stops. And as proof of the richness of the experience (and, in passing. of the competence of the party) one increasingly hears it said, "We didn't want it to finish," "We didn't want to top out till all the water was gone."

Literature anticipated this change of emphasis, and I want to fix on two writings in which this focusing of interest is strikingly displayed. The first is Menlove Edwards's short story, "Scenery for a Murder." This difficult parable still awaits a plausible interpretation, and, although it taunts us with significance, forty years have passed during which no one has been able to say what that significance is. In fact, despite some provocative clues, two or three readings give the impression that its central meanings have been quite deliberately concealed. Here I need not weigh the inbuilt ambiguities of the story and will only refer to its brilliant centerpiece, the ascent around which the allegory is constructed.

In "Scenery for a Murder," Edwards presents a description of a north-face climb spun out in the meticulous detail and the scrupulous idiom of his own rock climbers' guidebooks. To permit sufficient emphasis of the climbers' difficulties, he is repeatedly forced to allow a brief easing of the technical problems in order to substantiate the severity of the succeeding obstacles without recourse to inflated language. From the beginning, hints are supplied that success is unlikely. A strong sense of the desperate nature of the ascent is rapidly achieved, and this atmosphere is sustained throughout: but by its extension the two climbers draw steadily closer to a summit which must end their struggles. Edwards therefore subjects them to a delaying process whereby the speed of the ascent is steadily decelerated. Eventually the adversities of circumstance compound each other in a way familiar to any mountaineer, until this tending-to-zero of movement arrests the party (if we ignore the conclusion and queries the author poses later) before the top is reached. While this long-drawn-out struggle on the wall is taking place, the narrator's anxious mind strikes weakly, and with equal hopelessness, to break through the walls of his own personality and to apprehend his companion's thoughts and nature. But he is trapped as inescapably within himself as upon the wall—or, as Continental alpinists would say, *in der Wand, en paroi: in* the wall.

It is worth pointing out that a noticeable proportion of Edwards's small output, whether relating sea or mountain exploits, was left unfinished. His characters struggle very purposefully, but the struggles are more important than any hypothetical outcome, which, one senses, would probably be irrelevant or misleading. Before Kafka had made his imprint on the English imagination, Edwards's creatures fought in a Kafkaesque manner toward a goal which was less real or meaningful than the ordeal itself.

In Jeffery Long's fantasy, "The Soloist's Diary," the big wall takes on fabulous proportions. Three climbers pass through a mysterious forest, find the foot of the wall, locate the primary crack, and begin the ascent. Days, months, and winters pass: "The ground is no longer visible and even the horizon is obscured by dense low mists. There are no sides to the wall. There is no summit. . . ." The possibility of retreat is blocked.

The wall is sparsely populated by other climbers, occasionally seen within hailing distance. It has a history, manifest in the evidence of those who have died on it and in their abandoned equipment. And it has a mythology, pieced together from old diaries and from messages left for those to come. There are rumors of an earlier climber who may have reached "*a summit plateau*"; and of a legendary figure, the Soloist, who may have attained "*a top*."

The story, as it appeared in 1974, is unfinished. From time to time the party drives on hard, spurred by a bout of enthusiasm: "That was enough, to believe there was a summit. . . ." But essentially it is clear that there is no chance of success, and the party admits this at intervals: "We climb because it's what we did." Like Edwards's climbers, these three fight to retain control. They hear voices and are visited by phantoms. But each comes to realize that he is externalizing what is within.

There are many reasons why people climb big walls and most of them are shared with other forms of rock climbing and mountaineering. But on the big walls the dizzy beauty of the situations, the fascinating problems of mechanics, the whole range of interpersonal transactions are displayed in their most extreme forms. At the same time, as Ellie Hawkins has let us know, given the right party and good conditions these adventures may remain "fun climbs." What stands out in the two writings mentioned as on any actual climb, whether of desperation or pure joy, is the existentialist focus on the present moment. This is It.

Of all the physical risks to which human beings are subject, the most immediate is the risk of falling. It is the danger toward which the body's motor systems are primarily geared. When we flinch to protect an eye, when we recoil to avoid burning ourselves, when we choke, the brain directs our actions almost instantaneously. But, uniquely, when we are about to fall, the brain is bypassed for speed of response, and the muscles, eyes, and labyrinth collaborate without their master. On the big wall the possibility of falling is set on the most dramatic stage imaginable, and it is extended through the longest time endurable. It seems to me that the power of the big wall image has so modified our concept of mountaineering that all forms of climbing have now come to acknowledge its central place. As his fingers are about to snap off, the boulder-problem expert is telling himself—"imagine you're solo, a thousand feet up"; meanwhile, the Himalayan expedition increasingly seeks to imitate the situations, to copy the inescapability and elegance, the verticality and continuity of the big wall. And just as the struggle has become a sort of permanent protest, a way of life satisfactory in itself irrespective of whether its outcome is success or failure, a further change has taken place. The transcendental reveries popularly associated with the summit have been displaced and must now be fitted to where in fact they are more likely to be experienced: in the dark and quiet of the hanging bivouac, in its waking moments or its long-drawn-out vigil. Perhaps the big wall can be read as an analogy of the precariousness of our hold on the planet. In its perfect pairing of outer hazard and challenge against inner tensions and drives it seems to make an apt metaphor for one view of the human condition.

Galen Rowell
Storming a Myth

J UST AFTER THANKSGIVING in 1958, a party of three climbers
reached the base of the summit overhangs on Yosemite's El Capitan.
Only a hundred feet above them a celebration was beginning. El Capitan
was about to be climbed by its 3000-foot south face for the first time. An
assorted group of friends, lovers, media people, and ambulance chasers
had hiked up the trail on the back side of El Capitan to greet their heroes.
A feast of food and wine lay waiting, but long hours passed without the
arrival of the honored guests. Someone grew impatient and threw a rope
down over the edge. "Here, Warren, just prusik up this rope and we'll get
on with the party."

Warren Harding was drilling. He ignored the rope. He wasn't about to
take the easy way out after spending eleven straight days climbing under
his own power. The summit overhangs were massive and nearly flawless.
He saw no continuous cracks in which to place pitons, so he was drilling
by hand with star drill and hammer straight toward the voices overhead.
Under ideal conditions he could drill an inch-deep hole in fifteen minutes.
Hanging in slings from the overhang, it was now taking forty minutes per
hole. On a tiny ledge below were his companions, Wayne Merry and
George Whitmore, belaying his safety rope and waiting patiently for the
ordeal to end.

Darkness fell and Warren continued to drill. When a hole was completed he would insert an expansion bolt, attach a sling to it, move up
five more feet, and renew drilling above. The night was marked by the
passage of bolts. Five bolts . . . ten . . . fifteen . . . twenty. . . . Dawn came
and the supermarathon of drilling was not yet over. At 8 A.M., seventeen
hours after he began, Warren Harding crawled onto the summit from a
sling attached to his twenty-eighth bolt. "It was not at all clear to me," he
later said, "who was the conqueror and who was the conquered: I do recall that El Cap seemed to be in much better condition than I was."

In the twenty years since that historic climb, many climbers have
criticized the final bolt ladder on El Capitan's Nose. They say it makes the
climb too easy. Novices can clip their way up Harding's bolts instead of
working with the rock to follow natural weaknesses off to the side; that is,
novices who have climbed thirty-three pitches of vertical rock to get into
postition to clip up the bolts. And they also say that, if they were presented with the obstacle of the summit overhangs, they would find a way
up without using bolts; and they would, because big wall climbing has
gone a long way since 1958.

I began climbing at just about the time the El Capitan ascent was made. Given twenty years of experience, I know I could bypass the bolt ladder now. But I remember a time when I couldn't; a time when that very "easy" bolt ladder was the most difficult obstacle I ever encountered. Climbing it in 1966 on the fifth ascent of the Nose provided the most dangerous moments I have experienced on any route on any continent.

Climbing big walls was serious business in 1966. On the way to the base of the climb I didn't look up. I was too scared. Several times before, I'd walked in the predawn darkness with big-name climbers who looked up for a few moments too long. They lost their nerve and made up an excuse to retreat: a telltale cloud, a runny nose, a worn haul bag, a missing piton—things that wouldn't give a moment's hesitation to the wall climbers of the seventies who have broken so far through the fear threshhold they aren't even aware it once existed. In 1966 we had no helicopters buzzing in the back of our consciousness; if we were in trouble, we were on our own.

Something more subtle entered into our fear of big walls. We tended to intellectualize and philosophize climbing. We never called it a sport; it was an art, or better yet, a Way of Life. We walked around assuming we were involved in something special. Debates about rating systems were far more serious to us than events in Vietnam. One climber backed off a half-day climb six times. When he finally made it, he wrote home, "I have mastered the realm of the Yosemite Grade IV."

"These guys can't even write third-grade English," Jim McCarthy recently told me, "yet they can climb things we never imagined were possible." McCarthy was the outstanding East Coast rock climber of the sixties and every bit as much an intellectual snob as we Yosemitephiles. He was referring to the top rock climbers of today, who aren't afraid to call climbing a sport, to train for it like football, or to use sheer guts and will rather than reasoning and logic to overcome what we pigeonholed by language as "impossible," whether we intended to or not.

Talking with McCarthy, it suddenly dawned on me why we had been so scared in the sixties: we believed the written word. When we read Royal Robbins's account of two long leader falls above horrible protection on the Arches Direct, we vowed never to climb that route, or any that remotely resembled it.

I now realize that the prime movers of yesterday were really the anti-intellectuals. It is no coincidence that, amidst a great reservoir of technically skilled Yosemite climbers, a hard-hat construction worker named Warren Harding made the first ascent of the face of El Capitan. Nor was it coincidence that my presence on El Capitan in 1966 was due to the push of a Colorado bricklayer, Layton Kor.

In the winter of 1965, the immense Kor made his annual pilgrimage to Yosemite with a scrawny six-four teenager named Tom Fender. Like his mentor, Tom laid bricks, drank beer, and climbed with incredible energy. One evening Tom and I were talking about the dreaded west face of Leaning Tower, a climb involving a severely overhanging 1,100-foot cliff that had been repeated only a couple of times by preeminent valley climbers. The first ascent party had ominously written that, since a normal retreat was impossible, future climbers should carefully consider the problems before committing themselves. Layton listened intently for a few minutes, stared at us, and said, "Bullshit. You guys can climb the Tower right now, no sweat, and when you get done with that you'll be ready for El Cap."

Tom and I made the first "podunk" ascent of the Tower a few days later. We found it strenuous, but well within our limits. Once we proved that normal nonsupermen could climb the Tower, there was a line-up for the rest of the season. Even with our success on the Tower behind us, we were intimidated by the idea of mere mortals venturing onto the hallowed ground of El Capitan. Early in 1966 we started out with a three-man party. A hundred feet above the ground, our third man's nerves turned to jelly and we lowered him, babbling, to the ground. A week later we came back in the early morning and snuck onto the face before the harsh light of day could strike fear into our hearts. To our surprise the climbing went well, and after two days we were nearly halfway up the wall.

We were climbing in perfect March weather. There had been no precipitation for forty-five days. Yosemite wall-climbing weather was legendary. One of the head gurus, Yvon Chouinard, had written, "Bad weather in California means hot weather . . . the threat of stormy weather is not serious." Naturally we didn't take it seriously when rain began to fall as I nailed my way past the infamous Great Roof. In the afternoon the rain changed to snow. We were enshrouded in a quiet mist of flakes. We thought about descending, but considered the seven pendulum traverses that we had made as probably irreversible, especially in bad weather.

Throughout the afternoon, our world changed. It tilted on edge when the vertical fall of the snow became increasingly horizontal in a growing wind. The coming of darkness was disguised, and quite suddenly we couldn't see to climb. We drove pitons into cracks and strung out hammocks for the long wait. I didn't sleep a wink; my hammock filled with snow that melted from my body heat and soaked me to the skin.

At first brush of light we were off and climbing. Snow pelted our faces and numbed our hands. The climbing itself was easy, so easy that I marveled at how simple big wall climbing really was. We were in a single crack system aiming for the summit. We moved, not like acrobats or athletes, but with the jerky, repetitive motions of common laborers. I would bang in a piton, hang a sling from it, step up a few feet, and bang in another. When I reached the end of the rope, I would tie it to several anchors and sit in a nylon seat waiting for Tom to jumar his way up. Then Tom would play sky carpenter for the next hundred and fifty feet while I tried to renew feeling in my hands. Throughout the day we alternated leads, each time eager for the switch, the leader always wanting to thaw cold fingers, the belayer always seeking movement to warm his chilled body core. Both of us reverted to minutes of involuntary shivering after stopping each lead. Had we been winter climbing in the Sierra or Canada, we would have come equipped with tentage, waterproof outer garments, and a stove to make warm drinks. But we had nothing except the sloshing clothing on our bodies and the wet down sleeping bags offering less loft than cardboard.

A hundred feet from the summit our crack system ended. We stopped and contemplated the summit overhangs from the same point that Warren Harding had eight years before. I breathed a sigh of relief. We had been moving for thirteen hours with the power of desperation. Now all that separated us from the top was an easy bolt ladder, a matter of clipping into existing anchor points.

Somewhere behind the clouds, the sun sank below the horizon and the temperature dropped rapidly. Our ropes, soaked from water running down the face, began to change from the consistency of spaghetti to that of steel cable. I started up the bolts attaching two carabiners to every other bolt for the safety rope, hoping to cut down some of the rope drag I would encounter when clipping into each point. Nevertheless, the rope drag became increasingly strong, the rope was freezing into position as it ran through each anchor, and it took all my strength to pull through a new hank so that I could move on. Finally, it wouldn't budge. Time was running out and darkness was near. Tom, shivering wildly, was urging me to move faster.

We had two ropes. One was now frozen into the anchors, while the other ran freely from my waist to a haul bag that hung from a piton next to Tom. In desperation I told Tom to tie all the extra equipment to the haul bag and to cut it loose. I then pulled the bag up hand-over-hand and hung it from my waist. Breaking every rule of climbing, I untied from the belay rope, tied one end of the haul rope to it and the other to my waist. Now I had a static belay with one hundred and fifty feet of slack. But I could move. Even with the ungainly weight of the bag tugging at my midriff, I was able to go much faster than before. Minutes later I stood on the last expansion bolt in the highest loop of my sling and my hands touched the top of El Capitan.

I had a rude awakening. Instead of being home free, I was hanging from the lip of an overhang with my hands in two feet of fresh snow that covered steeply inclined slabs. In summer I could have stepped onto the slabs and walked off; to try that now would have been fatal.

I was at the top of El Capitan, a life's goal, yet no friends greeted me, and no one was celebrating. I was in more danger than ever before in my life. A slip would mean a fall of over two hundred feet, very probably a broken rope, and another three-thousand-foot fall to the ground. The one bolt I was on was certainly not a place to belay, and I couldn't see any place above me to anchor. Digging through the snow, I discovered a shallow crack in which I placed just the tip of a small piton. Tying it off, I attached a sling and moved up another two feet, feeling even less secure.

Digging away more snow, I found that the crack continued, and for the next hour I nailed my way up a thirty-degree slab. Finally I was able to stand up. I walked toward a tree, but was caught short by the rope. Even by untying my slings, runners, and belt, I couldn't have gotten enough cord to tie to the tree. Then I saw the sapling.

A tiny Jeffrey pine stuck out of a crack within reach. It was three feet high and an inch in diameter above its lumpy, gnarled base. I could bend it to the ground quite easily with one hand.

A minute later I yelled, "Okay, Tom; you can come up now." For a long while I listened only to the whistle of the wind. The rope ran tautly downward through a groove in the snow. Untied from it, I was lying on a narrow ledge clutching the sapling just above its base so it wouldn't bend.

I heard Tom begin to moan and groan. "I can't do it. My jumars are slipping," he yelled. Then again all I heard was the wind.

I'm not sure how long I lay on the ledge holding the tiny tree with hands that could no longer feel. It may only have been minutes, but it seemed like hours. The teeth inside Tom's jumars were clogged with ice, and the gadgets would not work even after he laboriously tried to clean them. I was convinced that he would never make it. Even a short fall would probably jerk out the sapling and send him flying down the wall. I couldn't wait out the night where I was, and Tom's situation was far more desperate. I had the bivouac gear, food, and water. His only hope was up.

For five days my world had been three thousand feet of granite. At the end of each lead I had calculated how far I had to go. Here I was at the end of that world, yet in the middle of a fight for both our lives. The storm had worsened and visibility was only a few feet. The wind twisting over the summit created a ground blizzard. I wondered what I would do even if I abandoned Tom. Could I survive a night here? Could I walk seven miles through deep snow in the dark to civilization?

Suddenly the sapling began to bend. I held it more tightly and watched the rope quiver. A shadow appeared on the horizon. Tom was at the very lip of the overhang with his full weight on the rope. He had clipped up the bolt ladder without a safety rope, and now, at the end of the bolts, he had grabbed the rope with his remaining strength to pull his way up the final slab. I concentrated on holding the sapling until Tom's eyes met mine. He looked back and forth from me to the pitiful anchor point, but he didn't say a word.

We talked only about the future: what we would take with us and where we would head. El Capitan does not have a classic small summit. The top is a peninsula of granite jutting out a full quarter mile from the rim of Yosemite Valley. We left all our gear except clothing and packs, then walked in a straight line away from the cliff. Each step was a struggle against the elements. We were in the same realm as a powder skier, but without skis, in darkness, totally fatigued, and moving uphill. The elements were all one to us. The clouds, the air, and the ground were all composed of varying amounts of snow. We pushed forward until the mist strangely darkened and the wind hit us more from below than from the side.

Tom was leading the way. Suddenly he turned and grabbed me, shouting, "Jesus Christ! We're walking off the edge of the West Buttress!" Adrenalin shot through me as it never had during the climb. A roped fall is something a climber can deal with in his head, but not an unexpected plunge into darkness.

We once again aimed for the rim of the valley and pushed through the snow. Minutes later the darkness and change in wind came anew. We were now near the edge of the North American Wall. We tried again and again, sometimes finding our own tracks, but we were unable to keep a straight path in the darkness and the storm.

I collapsed in the snow, too tired to walk any farther. We gave up and tried to survive the night, lying inside haul sacks, bundled into sleeping bags that had turned into thin sheets of nylon occasioned by lumps of wet down. I'd never been so cold.

With morning came a brief window in the clouds. It began to snow again, but we were able to chart our course to the valley rim. From there we found it relatively easy to parallel the edge, although it was quite impossible to locate the summer trail. We wallowed through endless fields of manzanita, a masochist's delight were it not for the fact that we could no longer feel our skin being torn by the hard sharp brush. I thought about how smugly I had sat in living rooms of nonclimbers telling them that climbing was some kind of ultimate chess game played with mind and body. Pro football was more erudite than our descent from El Capitan.

I also had my first inkling of something that is now common knowledge to all experienced rock climbers: big-wall climbing is a dead-end gambit. Climbing the longest and steepest walls is not the essential fulfillment of the sport. I had just completed the goal of many climbers, yet the climbing itself was remarkably unchallenging. After a day on the wall, the routine became almost *easy*. Any reasonably fit person could learn enough to do El Cap after a few months of practice. Our greatest difficulties lay beyond the start of the bolt ladder that was supposed to have made the finish too easy. The very idea of wall climbing imparts a purpose to the activity that isn't really there: to get to the top by overcoming specific obstacles of steepness and distance.

Setting up situations where climbing offers rational rewards is simply an intellectual pose. Now, twelve years since my El Cap adventure, it is obvious that elevation, steepness, and distance have been conquered on most of the world's major mountains, from Yosemite to the Himalayas. What is left is style: the disciplining of a natural human act into a satisfying precise ability. The expression of that ability is not necessarily rational. The purpose of climbing is no more the conquest of summits than the purpose of a mountain stream is the eventual production of electricity, although calculating minds might belabor both points.

At the end of my El Cap climb I staggered into a waiting line of high-heeled women and sport-coated men at the registration desk of Yosemite Lodge. Leaves, blood, and rags covered my body. Muddy water ran onto the clean floor. I checked in to a room with one hand while I held my pants up with the other; I didn't know it yet, but I'd lost twenty-five pounds.

Tom spent the next few days sacked out on the seat of his aging truck. Then he headed for Colorado, worked construction, and began to raise a family, he stopped climbing walls.

My vacation was over. I returned to my automotive business in the city. I might never have climbed a big wall again, except for an invitation from Layton Kor the following spring to do another route on El Capitan. On that climb he shared with me his many doubts about what he was doing, year after year, climbing one wall after another. Our climb together was his last major effort. He surprised everyone with a sudden conversion to the Jehovah's Witnesses. I soon changed careers and became a full-time outdoor journalist, but I never wrote about either of my early El Capitan ascents. They were too far outside the confines of what climbing was supposed to be about. The first provided suffering; the second, relaxed joy. In neither case was the overall feeling related to the technical nature of the ascent.

Now I know that climbing is merely a vehicle, a tool, and the climber a tool user. As a tool, climbing can be used to overcome 5.12 cracks, the difficulties of a Grade VI wall, or an 8,000-meter peak. But held only to this narrow definition, it can eventually bring boredom and despair.

The climbing tool has a spiritual component as well. At the heart of the climbing experience is a constant state of optimistic expectation, and when that state is absent, there is no reason to continue climbing. "I have found it!" can apply not only to those who feel they have found God, but to those, like me, who continue to find Shangri-las where we experience fresh, childlike joy in everything that surrounds us, including memories that are the most long-lasting and intense of our lives. It was in this spirit that I first ventured onto Yosemite's walls.

Page 84: El Capitan. Photo by Ed Cooper

In the Khumbu Ice Fall. International Everest Expedition, 1971. Photo by
John Cleare/Mountain Camera

Man risking his life in perilous encounters constitutes the original definition of what is worth talking about.

— Paul Zweig
The Adventurer

Bernard Amy
A Poetics of Alpinism

Translated from the French
by Elizabeth Cartwright

FOR THE MOST PART, mountaineers are not very prone to intro-spection. Undertaking their "sport" in complete liberty seems to them the best way of explaining it or of avoiding largely futile analyses. Perhaps here lies the true meaning of Mallory's declaration that we climb mountains because they are there. Yet there have always been mountain-eers who carry their thoughts further and, in particular, compare alpinism with other activities which give rise to similar passions.

Defining Mountaineering

Beyond simple descriptions of techniques employed or of ascents made (how many technical manuals or histories of mountaineering have appeared in which writers attempt "to define" this sport?), beyond les-sons on how to climb mountains, one can generally classify every analysis and attempted explanation within certain mainstreams of thought, all of which show that mountaineering, even if a sport in technique, is also through the conception we may have of it "something more."

—Many mountaineers stress the aesthetic aspect of the activity. The natural beauty of the mountains draws them and fires their passion.

—For others the activity principally offers a particular way of life. The methods used by a climber in the course of his ascents and his com-portment in the mountains become a code of living which influences his daily existence and constitutes a true ethic. This attitude is especially apparent in those for whom climbing, because it provides success and a means of asserting oneself in the eyes of others, becomes the chief and sometimes only love.

—Others see mountaineering as an art, an activity which, when exam-ined, may be likened to all the classical art forms, most particularly to dance.

—Finally, for some, climbing takes the guise, if not of a religion, at least of a mystique.

Of course, it is not possible to limit mountaineering to any one of these definitions. It is a sport, an art, a way of life, and a mystique at once, though it may indeed be more of one than another according to the way in which it is pursued. On the other hand it is possible, in the light of these analyses, to effect a synthesis and to discover what links these different ideas, thereby bringing to light their common denominator.

One can see immediately that a statement on poetry by Alain Bosquet may be applied to climbing: "A kind of madness (a delirium, a dream, etc. . . .)." We will therefore begin by examining poetry in order to compare it with mountaineering, and we shall see that the two activities have in common an essential feature enabling us to account for, if not explain, their most remarkable characteristics.

Poetry and Poeticity

OF ALL ART FORMS, poetry is at once the most fundamental and the least susceptible to analysis. Fundamental, because it chiefly consists of speech and language and is therefore specifically human. Difficult to analyze, because it works with words and cannot be examined without using words. It is hardly surprising that from time immemorial poetry has been regarded as an extraordinary activity and has been the object of extensive study.

And what exactly is poetry? The answer varies with each century. From the seventeenth through the eighteenth centuries, Western poets and philosophers agreed to define poetry by the sum of its themes, an ensemble of traditional requirements: the moon, the lake, and so on. . . . And from this process emerged a collection of rules regarding writing, presentation, or diction. This definition made poetry a quest for imitation, a quest for pure description.

From the romantic poets onward, a need to call this classical concept into question became obvious. On the one hand, the scope of poetic themes was becoming limitless: for a modern poet such as Yves Bonnefoy, anything could be a source of poetic inspiration. On the other hand, nothing in the classical definition explained why written or spoken poetry immediately struck the student as privileged discourse. Why it was that "he who writes, he who speaks, is not necessarily a poet"?

Novalis must have been at the origins of this rethinking. His ideas, first taken up by Mallarmé, then by certain Russian poets, gave rise to the work of such writers as Sartre and then to a whole linguistic school led by Jakobson. The latter strove to apply linguistics to the special realm of poetry.

The new ideas are based on the following observations. A speaker or writer generally has a single aim: to transmit a message, to say something to someone. It is essential for him to make himself understood, and therefore at every moment he must use the proper word for what it is—a bearer of information, a sign used only to denote an object or a concept.

The poet follows a very different path. While his work similarly involves the transmission of a message, the message, rather than being delivered directly, is passed through a preliminary process which is sometimes significant enough to almost conceal the message itself.

This process is called by Jakobson "the design of expression in the message as such," and he notes, "The emphasis put on the message on its own account is what characterizes the poetic function, the *poeticity* of the language." The poet is primarily interested in the way he is going to say what he wishes to say. The writing and its process are inseparable from the meaning.

"The poet," writes Sartre, "is a man who refuses to *use* language. He has abandoned at a stroke the language-instrument, he has chosen once and for all the poetic attitude which considers words as things and not as signs. For the ambiguity of the sign implies that one can, at will, use it like a pane of glass and through it pursue the thing meant, or turn one's gaze upon its reality and consider it as an object."

Jakobson's early research led him to see in poetry this single aim of expression. But reducing poetry to this narrow definition amounted to making it art for art's sake, the simple reduction to aesthetic form of pre-established speech or of meaningless verbal material. Jakobson and his followers now recognize that poetry is something more and that the message transmitted counts for as much as the poetic technique.

The poem does not register within the perspective of a syntax or a rhetoric reduced to ornamentation. Beyond "poetic discourse" we have to speak of a "poetic message." And a poetic message exists when all the elements used in its transmission are necessary for our understanding of it.

Thus poetry seems to be the interaction between what one wants to say and the way in which one says it, an interaction which is complete enough to forbid us from saying that either dominates the other. This simultaneous presence of message and process leads to two realms of thought.

First, there is the action of the poem on the poet (the interior diffusion of the poem) and on the recipient of the poetic message (the exterior diffusion). The poet, because he sees words as objects before he sees them as signs, discovers a new vision of what surrounds him. He is acted upon. The challenge of the language, its reduction to "crumbs," leads the recipient to question that to which it applies. Through and by poetic discourse he is led to perceive language itself, and from that point to ask questions about himself and his own sense of things.

Second, the transmission of the poetic message occurs on two distinct levels. It is upheld both by the words and by the way in which they are used. It "says something" initially because it is discourse, but it broadens its message by the distinction it introduces in the use of words.

THIS DEFINITION OF poetic function extends to all the arts. "Painting," writes Jakobson, "is giving substance to visual material of autonomous value, music is giving substance to aural material of autonomous value. . ." To summarize what has been said about poetry: the poetic function exists in a given activity if, on the one hand, there is an apparent change of technique, an adoption of technique to use the materials and rules in a novel way, and, on the other hand, a transmission on

Generalities on Poetic Function

different levels of the information carried by this technique. The emphasis is placed on the skill of the method of transmission, skill which in its turn is utilized to transmit a further message. The apparent gratuitousness of poetic expression only serves to focus attention on its unusual aspect and therefore on the importance of the message.

But the poetic function not only serves to fix the message in the recipient's memory; it would then merely be playing a supporting role. When it predominates, when poetic discourse really exists, poeticity helps generate the message, prolongs it in an exceptional manner, and enriches it. There is a reciprocal movement between the message and the "words" and the precise point of their conjunction is the poem or, in more general terms, the work of art.

The Poeticity of Climbing

CAN THE NOTION of poetic function be applied to climbing? Is climbing a poetic activity?

First of all, is there "a misuse of technique," a use of a technique as an end in itself? The history of early mountaineering indicates such is the case. Mountaineering was born, really, at a time when a combination of actions and techniques, until then strictly utilitarian—used in hunting chamois, in collecting rock crystals, or simply in crossing the mountains— became the means for a purely gratuitous activity.

This transition from the utilitarian to the seemingly useless was not of course effected overnight. It demanded more than a century, from the first ascents at the end of the eighteenth century to the beginnings of the true alpinism with Mummery in the 1880s.

After the first ascent of Mont Blanc in 1786, mountaineering developed rapidly. But almost all ascents were less a question of reaching the summit than of placing a barometer or a theodolite on the peak. For many years scientific research was to remain the only admitted aim of ascent. Yet, without the idea having been clearly formulated, the state of mind of these gentlemen climbers was already beginning to change. In 1828 Captain Durant reached the second summit of the Pelvoux with a team of surveyors loaded with sighting and surveying equipment. A few days later he returned again, justifying the second ascent by saying that there were other measurements to be carried out. It was pure excuse, the mere pleasure of the ascent seems to have been the only real aim of the captain.

Toward the middle of the nineteenth century, climbing—already removed from chamois hunting and crystal collecting—gradually separated itself from science. The number of those who went to the mountains for pleasure was rapidly increasing.

From 1879 to 1893 Mummery, first by climbing the Matterhorn by six different routes, then by reaching the summit of the Grepon without a guide, became the creator of modern mountaineering. The summit, for him, was only a pretext. As for the barometer, it had long been forgotten.

What counted was the route taken, the pleasure of the climb for its own sake, the perfectly mastered technique backed by a philosophy selected and created by this technique. All the fundamentals which would allow Mummery's heirs to become true poets and artists had been gathered together. To restate in terminology already used, climbing a mountain became at this point what it is in fact today, an art in itself, the "aim" of an action as such, the giving of substance to the "gesture" material of the alpinist.

But according to our definition of poetic function, for climbing to be an authentic poetic activity it must also have a poetic message, that is, a will to express a message and a process which acts upon it. If we hold fast to this definition, many climbers are less than true mountaineers. For them, climbing remains an end in itself, an art for art's sake through which, rather than expressing themselves and communicating, they forget themselves and the world about them.

For others, to the contrary—and they alone are Mummery's true heirs—the style of climbing, its realization, serves to create a certain concept of mountaineering and, beyond that, a true philosophy. The love of mountains creates a new art of living, which, in its turn, puts technique in the proper perspective and makes of climbing what Mummery called "unmixed play." For these climbers the work of art, the poem, is quite naturally the line traced up the face or up a ridge. It brings material reality to their idea and to their conception of their own activity.

WHEN CLIMBING is undertaken as an authentic poetic activity, all the analyses made with regard to poetry may be applied to it. Consider in particular the process of creation of a new route up a mountain, and its ascent by other parties, and compare the pattern with the mechanics of a poem being written and then read.

The schema of poetic communication is sufficiently remarkable to distinguish it entirely by means of language from ordinary communication. This poetic communication is brought about in three ways. Originally, before becoming an exchange between the poet and his audience, the poem is a form of communication between the poet and himself or, more precisely, between the poet and something he senses in the depths of his being. The poet, then, turns inward and seems to isolate himself from the world around, transported by what we call inspiration. At that instant the artist conceives his work.

The second stage of poetic communication, even if it may become confused in time with the first, is no less distinct. It is the act of creation, strictly speaking, of the work of art, of the writing of the poem. It is at this stage that technique comes into play and takes on central importance. The beauty of the work and its impact on the recipient will depend upon it.

These two stages correspond to the planning and the first ascent of

The Ascent as Poetic Communication

Philip de Loutherbourg, *An Avalanche in the Alps* (1803). Courtesy of the Tate Gallery, London

a route. He whom we may call the "tracer'" because he traces the way, invents a route, imagines the most elegant way of climbing it, and then realizes his work of art. The greatest climbers, at the height of their art, when seen leading a first ascent, always give the impression of being "inspired." This self-immersion is necessary in the creation of a new route if one wishes it to fulfill certain aesthetic criteria, and it largely explains the infatuation of those who specialize in the art of first ascents.

It is at the level of the third stage of poetic communication, reading, that the great moment of the work of art, its fruition, is found. For the recipient it is no ordinary reading or assimilation of information but, rather, a reading which demands "creative attention." The reader of the poem re-creates not the poem but a new poem inspired by the first. The new poem is entirely his own and exists only at the moment of reading; it will be replaced in further readings by yet another poem and another.

The same may be said for the repetition of a route. Yet "repetition" fails to translate the re-creation of a route by a climber. It is obvious that mere imitation of the actions of the originator is insufficient to explain the passion climbers show for tirelessly repeating routes. Each of us feels in the depths of his being a need, developed to some degree, to create. It is the satisfaction of this need that climbers seek, often unconsciously, in the mountains.

I T REMAINS OBVIOUS that when we speak of re-creating a climb or a poem, there is no new *material* creation. The rock, the face, the ink, the paper, all remain the same. Words and actions remain unchanged. It is rather our way of seeing them that differs. And since a poem is a collection of words fixed in a certain form, the reader's creation of a new poem is an interior creation. The poetic process, and therefore mountaineering, be it at the level of the first creation or at the level we conveniently call reading, is always an inner adventure. This aspect in alpinism pushes many climbers toward either of two extremes. Some, denying all inner feelings, affect to see in their activity only a technical game, devoid of any spiritual connection. Others, engulfed in mysticism, become aloof in their passion and make of climbing an ethereal art completely detached from daily realities.

Real mountaineering is midway between these attitudes. How can we find it?

How can we create inner adventure out of external technique while keeping a delicate balance between the extremes of mysticism and frenzied materialism? Some climbers have found the solution in the works of poets and artists, and especially in the teachings of Far Eastern philosophies such as Zen Buddhism.

A True
Mountaineering-
Balanced
Passion

Climbing and Zen Buddhism

UNTIL THE APPEARANCE in Japan of the extraordinary impetus of Westernization, Japanese life was deeply marked by Zen Buddhism. Coming from China, where it was born in the juncture of Buddhism and Taoism, Zen quickly became a school of thought sufficiently powerful to influence all Japanese art.

But the influence did not stop there. Zen addresses itself directly to facts; it is not a method of conceptualizing facts. It teaches us to live the facts and not to become detached from them by a deceptive scholasticism. This essential feature of Zen has made of it a philosophy which, far from being limited in its application to the most intellectual forms of cultural expression, has long controlled the most trivial aspects of daily life in Japan.

"It must be said that almost every profession, every trade, is considered in Japan as a *do,* that is to say a Tao or a way, not without analogy to what was designated in the West under the name of 'mystery'. Each *do* was at a given moment to some degree a secular method of study of the principles incarnate in Taoism, Confucianism, and Zen, just as modern Freemasonry survives from a time when the Mason's trade was a means of initiation in a spiritual tradition."

All Zen teaching tends to show that "the center of gravity of life remains *immutable* and that, when one succeeds in understanding it, all life's activities, whether tranquil and studious or intense, may lead to a state of self-awareness which expresses itself perfectly in life and action." The ultimate aim of Zen is to lead, through a given *practice* (which may simply be the practice of daily living), to what we may call a state of grace in which no deity intervenes, a state of perfect communion with the whole world and in particular with oneself.

The highest inner adventure possible is that which many artists find in the effort of their work. Observation of the physiological and psychological mechanisms which allow us to come in contact with the outer world show that when there is no focusing of the will on what we would attain, the human senses are fully disposed to perceive the world, to receive it.

The perfect experience in Zen, the *satori,* like the mystical illumination of the great Christians, may only be achieved if one reaches, *without wishing it,* an absence of thought that liberates our being and opens it entirely to the world. Whoever has reached a high degree of skill in practicing his art has felt that total liberation which arises at certain privileged moments. When art becomes "an art without artifice," when technique is reflex, there may be a kind of inner adventure through which the creative experience is forever new.

Alpinism as Art of Living

"IT IS POETRY that defends us against automatization," Jakobson writes, "against the rust that threatens our formulas of love and hate, of revolt and reconciliation, of faith and of negation."

Climbing as a poetic form holds an important place in a society which, without really understanding it, acknowledges it to be a particularly enriching activity. But, as we have said, it is easy to be carried away by the poetic process and to see in the art of climbing nothing but art for art's sake: a possibility of escape, an obvious refuge to flee toward, to elude that which offends in everyday existence.

There again, Zen teaching joins the exhortations of many poets.

The aim of the mountaineer, if he wishes to be an artist in the full sense of the word, is neither escape nor "the search for the absolute" as some have claimed, but rather to seek that place where "the mystic remains silent and the poet *starts to speak, turned toward men.*" It is to take the place of the Zen sage who, having meditated on his mountain, returns home not to teach, not to convert, but simply to show that the man who returns is different from the man who departed. It is knowing how to be "slightly mad in order to avoid complete madness"; it is not the madman turned in on himself in dramatic conflict, but the madman turned toward the things of life, knowing that to write, to paint, to sing, to dance, and even to climb, is to live, to discover reality and not distort it.

Alpinism is a poetry. The ascent can be lived as an artistic experience. But on one condition: that of knowing that "its true greatness consists of recovering, seizing, becoming aware of that reality far from which we live . . . from which we move farther and farther away in proportion with the weight and impermeability of the conventional knowledge that we substitute for it, that reality we risk dying without having known and which is quite simply our life, real life, life discovered and illuminated, the only life consequently which is truly lived, this life which, in a sense, lives at every moment in all men as well as in the artist."

Pieter Bruegel the Elder, *The Tower of Babel.* Museum Boymans-van Beuningen, Rotterdam

What is there, then, in common between the atmosphere of pious communion with which the medieval dusk flooded the naves and that massive intimation of transcendence which is conveyed by the Egyptian architectural complexes — what is there common to all forms embodying an aspect of the in-apprehensible? It is their revelation of the presence of an Other World.

— André Malraux
The Metamorphosis of the Gods

STAIRWAYS TO ANOTHER WORLD

Over: A first ascent on Helsby, Cheshire. Photo by Leo Dickinson

Samuel Beckett

Fragment: The Ladders of The Lost Ones

THE PURPOSE of the ladders is to convey the searchers to the niches. Those whom these entice no longer climb simply to get clear of the ground.

*   *   *

FROM TIME IMMEMORIAL rumor has it or better still the notion is abroad that there exists a way out. Those who no longer believe so are not immune from believing so again in accordance with the notion requiring as long as it holds that here all should die but with so gradual and to put it plainly so fluctuant a death as to escape the notice even of a visitor. Regarding the nature of this way out and its location two opinions divide without opposing all those still loyal to that old belief. One school swears by a secret passage branching from one of the tunnels and leading in the words of the poet to nature's sanctuaries. The other dreams of a trap door hidden in the hub of the ceiling giving access to a flue at the end of which the sun and other stars would still be shining. Conversion is frequent either way and such a one who at a given moment would hear of nothing but the tunnel may well a moment later hear of nothing but the trap door and a moment later still give himself the lie again. The fact remains none the less that of these two persuasions the former is declining in favor of the latter but in a manner so desultory and slow and of course with so little effect on the comportment of either sect that to perceive it one must be in the secret of the gods. This shift has logic on its side. For those who believe in a way out possible of access as via a tunnel it would be and even without any thought of putting it to account may be tempted by its quest. Whereas the partisans of the trap door are spared this demon by the fact that the hub of the ceiling is out of reach.

*   *   *

SO MUCH for this inviolable zenith where for amateurs of myth lies hidden a way out to earth and sky.

H. Byron Earhart
Sacred Mountains in Japan
Shugendō as "Mountain Religion"

O N A NUMBER of occasions I have had the privilege of accompanying Japanese religious groups during their ritual ascents of sacred mountains. In this short essay I would like to share with Western readers something of the ethos of the sacred mountains of Japan; but in order to participate in this ritual ascent, even vicariously, we must expand our mental horizons to admit the notion of "sacred mountains."

There are important factors in modern Western civilization tending to preclude the very idea of sacred mountains—indeed, to make "sacred mountains" a contradiction in terms. The first factor is the cultural and religious heritage of the West. As Marjorie Hope Nicolson reminds us, "Human response to mountains has been influenced by inherited conventions of literature and theology, but even more profoundly it has been motivated by man's conception of the world which he inhabits."[1] The conception of the world in the West has been influenced decisively by the Judeo-Christian tradition. In the Christian tradition, in particular, there is a generally accepted hierarchy of God highest, man below God, and nature a poor third. In this tradition mountains were long considered to be warts and blemishes—deformities of the earth—and "also symbols of warning to ambitious man who aspired too high."[2] Nicolson has thoroughly recounted the language of "mountain gloom" with which Western poets for the first seventeen centuries of the Christian Era described mountains.

> Here learn ye Mountains more unjust,
> Which to abrupter greatness thrust,
> That do with your hook-shoulder'd height
> The Earth deform and Heaven fright,
> For whose excrescence ill design'd
> Nature must a new Center find,
> Learn here those humble steps to treat,
> Which to securer Glory lead.[3]

It was in this same vein that Petrarch in the fourteenth century commented upon his ascent of Mount Ventoux. When he reached the peak, he was at first filled with "delight and aesthetic gratification." But then "tradition conquered feeling," and, after he read from Augustine's *Confessions*, Petrarch reports that he "closed the book, angry with myself for not ceasing to admire things of the earth, instead of remembering that the human soul is beyond comparison the subject for admiration. Once again, as I descended, I gazed back, and the lofty summit of the mountain seemed to me scarcely a cubit high, compared with the sublime dignity of man."[4]

It was only in the eighteenth century in the West that "mountain glory"—the appreciation of the wild, soaring beauty of mountains—began to overcome "mountain gloom."

> Inmate of a mountain-dwelling,
> Thou has clomb aloft, and gazed
> From the watch-tower of Helvellyn;
> Awed, delighted, and amazed.[5]

This new perception and emotion Nicolson calls the "aesthetics of the infinite." To her exquisitely complete account of this change of values we add only one minor point for our comparative purposes: this new aesthetic could develop only in direct opposition to the long-standing religious tradition. (In part this is a theological reconception of God-within-Nature, rather than God-over-nature and God-outside-nature; but this reconception is in tension with the Old Testament view of Jehovah as a transcendent divinity denouncing all fertility cults.) This new aesthetic appreciation of mountain vistas with which modern tourists and picture-postcard painters are familiar is a rather recent addition to the Western scene and is not intimately blessed by major religious tradition.

The second factor which tends to preclude the notion of sacred mountains in the West is the prevalence of secularism. Generally, Western man after the Industrial Revolution has become increasingly alienated from nature, in the process of advancing urbanization and industrialization. Mircea Eliade reminds us that many primitive peoples built and viewed their dwellings as miniature versions of the cosmos, following sacred models. But modern man, he adds, quoting Le Corbusier, sees his house as "a machine to live in."[6] For most modern men, the earth and the moon are things to be exploited.

Few would deny that Western man generally conceives of a gap between himself and nature. Even Thoreau, one of the most sensitive of Westerners in his approach to nature, was consciously attempting to bridge that gap. This is not a criticism of Thoreau, rather it is a recognition of the fact that the Western cultural assumption of man-outside-nature affected even that great naturalist. The recent rise of the ecology movement in the West, it seems to me, is nourished by this very sense of a gap between man and nature, a gap now widening into a yawning chasm. As a result, we yearn all the more desperately for a reunion.

These remarks on Western views of the world and the mountains are sketchy at best, but they are meant to indicate the kind of cultural baggage that must be left behind if one is to scale successfully the sacred mountains of Japan. For in Japan the cultural tradition has since antiquity emphasized the sacred character of nature. The *kami* (divinities or spirits) could inhabit or even *be* waterfalls, trees, rocks, mountains. To put it negatively—in order to counter our Western sensibilities—there never was a religious prohibition against the sacred character of nature: cultural values did not presuppose a gap between man and nature and they imposed less distance between divinities and man as well.

In Asia there was no need to wait for the eighteenth century to find "mountain glory" praised in poetry and painting. J. D. Frodsham has fully documented the venerable "landscape poetry" in China that Nicolson found wanting in the first seventeen centuries of Christian Europe. Frodsham notes that by the late fifth century in China it was already taken for granted that love of nature was innate in civilized man. He cites a Chinese poet of that era: "Men have always spoken and will always speak of the beauty of mountains and streams."[7]

In Japan's first collection of poetry, the eighth century *Manyōshū*, mountains were often taken as the exemplar of natural beauty. A poem by Yamabe Akahito, "On a Distant View of Mount Fuji," may serve as evidence:

> Ever since heaven and earth were parted,
> It has towered lofty, noble, divine,
> Mount Fuji in Suruga!
>
> When we look up to the plains of heaven,
> The light of the sky-traversing sun is shaded,
> The gleam of the shining moon is not seen,
> White clouds dare not cross it,
> And for ever it snows.
>
> We shall tell of it from mouth to mouth
> O the lofty mountain of Fuji.
> When going forth I look far from the shore of Tago,
> How white and glittering is
> The lofty Peak of Fuji,
> Crowned with Snows![8]

This is a typical example of the Japanese affinity for mountains—more ancient and far less inhibited than that of the West.

By comparison, then, we see that the first factor operating against the notion of sacred mountains in the West—an unsympathetic religious tradition—did not exist in Japan. However, the second factor precluding the notion in the West—modernity and secularity, as corollaries of industrialism and urbanization—is now making severe inroads into Japanese culture. Skyways, cable cars, observation towers, and recreational playgrounds have recently made their marks on many of the holy mountains of Japan. (It is a sad commentary on such modern conveniences that, by rushing us to our destination, too often they at once damage our mental framework for approaching nature and despoil the natural beauty itself.) However, the surge of technological modernity has come later in Japan, and traditional culture is still admired. Most Japanese, even cosmopolitan urbanites, know very well what "sacred mountains" (*reizan* in Japanese) are.

A final word of caution before we make our ascent. As Westerners, our very language obstructs our approach. The mind is already perceiving, "Ah, yes, the Japanese *think* that the mountain is sacred"; "I see, the Japanese *deify* the mountain." As Westerners we must abandon our attitude of knowing the *real* (secular, impersonal, *reified*) world, which undercuts the cultural reality of the Japanese. For them the mountain *is* sacred; it is *kami* (divine).

This sacredness has been demonstrated in a number of ways. Even during prehistoric times, mountains were singled out as the holy land to which souls of the dead traveled. Contemporaneously, they were revered as the source of water and fertility for rice fields. But archeological discoveries of ritual tools seem to indicate that the mountains were venerated from the foothills rather than on the summit; that is, at about the beginning of the Christian Era they were not yet *climbed* in order to revere them. The sanction for climbing and dwelling within the mountains as a specific religious career came mainly from the Chinese influence which flooded Japan about 500 A.D.

Chinese influence brought to Japanese sacred mountains both Taoism and the Indian import of Buddhism. Taoism, expressing its penchant for harmony with nature, encouraged wizards or saints (*hsien* in Chinese, *sen* in Japanese) to live a naturalistic life in the mountains. (It is interesting that the Chinese ideograph for *hsien* is composed of two parts, one meaning "man," the other meaning "mountain.") That part of the Buddhist heritage which made closest contact with Japanese mountain worship was the use of the ascetic tradition to gain religious power. The mountains were viewed as the ideal "practice site" for ascetic and devotional exercises. Many great Buddhist figures "opened" mountains, as the first persons to climb these mountains and establish them as centers for religious practice.

The Tendai and Shingon sects played a prominent part in this "opening." In fact their preference for mountain headquarters has earned for these two sects the title of "mountain Buddhism." In 788 when Saichō, founder of Tendai Buddhism, climbed Mount Hiei (outside the contemporary Kyoto) to establish his monastic headquarters, he recited his own song of prayer:

> O Buddhas
> Of unexcelled complete enlightenment
> Bestow your invisible aid
> Upon this hut I open
> On the mountain top.[9]

Kūkai, founder of Shingon Buddhism, set up his monastery on Mount Kōya, and was careful to take note of the various spirits, benevolent and malevolent, whose residence at the mountain preceded him:

> All evil spirits and gods, who may be to the east, south, north, west above
> or below this monastery: you hinderers and destroyers of the True Law, hie

you seven leagues hence from my altar! If however there be any good spirits and gods who are beneficial to the Buddhist Law and protect it, you may dwell as you choose in this Monastery and protect the Buddhist Law.[10]

Kūkai praised mountains generally as places for meditation:

I, Kūkai, have heard that where the mountains are high the clouds let fall much rain, thus nourishing vegetation, and that where drops of water accumulate fishes and dragons breed and multiply. Thus it was that the Buddha preached on steep Mount Gṛdhakūta [in northern India] and that Avalokiteśvara manifested himself on Mount Potalaka [in southern India], whose strange peaks and precipices face the shores. Indeed, these mountains have evoked their presence. Students of meditation fill the five Buddhist temples on Mount Wu-t'ai [in northern China], and friends of concentration crowd the temple on Mount T'ien-t'ai. They are treasures of the nation; they are like bridges for the people.[11]

He went on to declare Mount Kōya an ideal site for Buddhist practice:

According to the meditation sutras, meditation should be practiced preferably on a flat area deep in the mountains. When young, I, Kūkai, often walked through mountainous areas and crossed many rivers. There is a quiet, open place called Kōya located two days' walk to the west from a point that is one day's walk south from Yoshina. . . . High peaks surround Kōya in all four directions; no human tracks, still less trails, are to be seen there. I should like to clear the wilderness in order to build a monastery there for the practice of meditation, for the benefit of the nation and of those who desire to discipline themselves.[12]

These several traditions viewing mountains as religiously significant—from the prehistoric age and early historic poems to the influence of Taoist naturalism and Buddhist asceticism and meditation—interacted freely. In folk religion alone, there was such a proliferation of beliefs and religious rituals associated with mountains that they came to be called generically "mountain beliefs" (*sangaku shinkō*) or "mountain religion" (*sangaku shūkyō*). The folk tradition of sacred mountains is an interesting subject in its own right;[13] but we pass over it in order to concentrate on the major religious organization centered on sacred mountains: Shugendō.

Shugendō absorbed the ancient Japanese tradition and blended it with Taoist and Buddhist conceptions. The term *Shugendō* means literally "the way of mastering ascetic powers," but it is understood that these powers are gained by practices performed within the mountains. Indeed, the usual name for such practitioners is *yamabushi*, "those who lie down (sleep) in the mountains." The legendary founder of this tradition was one En no Ozunu or En no Gyōja. By the eighth century he is cited as a precursor for practicing Buddhism within the hills. He is reported to have gained his magical powers on Katsuragi, and thereby to have gained control over people. A later tradition gives a more full account of his achievements:

Every evening he entered a five-colored cloud and flew beyond the sky, associated with [Taoist] wizards and played in the garden of eternity. He lay down to rest in the flowering garden, sucking up the spirit which nourishes one's character. Accordingly, at more than thirty [or forty] years of age he entered a rock cave, wore clothing of vines, and ate pine [needles], bathing in springs of pure water and rinsing away the filth of this world of desire. He practiced the magical formula of the peacock and was able to manifest wonderful magical arts. He achieved the ability to order about and use spirits and *kami* as he wished. He scolded the various devils [*oni*] and *kami*, and called a meeting, saying, "Make a bridge between the peaks of Kinpu [Kane no Mine or Kane no Mitake] and Katsuragi in the province of Yamato, and cross over."[14]

His magical powers frightened the emperor, who had En no Gyōja banished to an island. "In the day-time, in accordance with the emperor's command, he stayed on the island, but at night he retired to a cave of Mount Fuji in Suruga and practiced austerities. Nevertheless, he begged that the severity of his punishment be pardoned so that he might approach the capital, and he lay down on the blade of his sword and ascended to Fuji."[15]

The literary tradition of En no Gyōja is symptomatic of the increasing number of *yamabushi* who started to practice austerities in the hills. At the same time, emperors and the nobility began to make pilgrimages to these mountains as part of their religious devotions. During the eleventh and twelfth centuries, all aspects of mountain worship, from the literary traditions to the imperial pilgrimages and the *yamabushi* groups, became more formalized and more organized. In about the thirteenth century the more highly organized Shugendō headquarters began to appear on many mountains.

Eventually, as many as six hundred sites were occupied by some form of Shugendō group. There was great diversity among these groups, depending on the dominance of particular branches of Shinto or Buddhism. However, there were also a number of larger mountain headquarters which were centers of propagation for Shugendō, and these major centers tended to provide particular forms of organization. But this is not the place to recount a general history of Shugendō;[16] it will suffice to indicate the general pattern of life throughout its most flourishing period.

The ethos of Shugendō is the practice of ritual training and austerities in order to acquire transcendent power. Despite particular differences, all the features of Shugendō support and enhance this ethos. The mountains served as a holy land, a kind of other world in the present world. The summits were usually uninhabitable during the colder season of the year, but some *yamabushi* lived permanently in headquarters on the slopes or in the foothills. During the warmer season, itinerant *yamabushi*, or those with branch groups in surrounding areas, made lengthy retreats to the mountain headquarters. During the retreats they performed austerities, practiced ritual techniques, and made religious pilgrimages to the holy sites. In late medieval times, as travel became more common, ordinary people also made summer pilgrimages. Laymen did not undergo the lengthy and severe training of the *yamabushi,* but benefited from having the *yamabushi* perform rites for them and profited directly from their contact with the sacred mountains.

Between the mountains, and the *yamabushi* and pilgrims, there was an intimate and crucial tie. This was brought home to me in 1963, when interviewing a woman who had participated in a ten-day retreat on Mount Haguro. I was asking persistent questions about why she had participated in the retreat, and she was answering generally about her desire to be a part of a meaningful period of religious practices. When I pressed her specifically as to why she should practice these rites and austerities around Mount Haguro, since rites and austerities could be practiced anywhere, her reply was quite direct. "Because the *kami* are here. Because the *kami* have always been here."

This tie between the believer and the sacred mountain is quite explicit. While in the mountain headquarters or at the holy site, the believer worships the sacred power directly. The name of the *kami* is phrased most simply as *yama no kami,* the ubiquitous "mountain divinity." Or a specific *kami* from the Shinto pantheon may be addressed as the specific divinity of the mountain. Or the Buddhist title *gongen* (incarnation) may be applied to a mountain (Haguro Gongen) to indicate that this is the particular incarnation of sacred power at Haguro. Or a specific member of the Buddhist pantheon may be addressed as dwelling at the mountain. But these are not mutually exclusive possibilities—all four may be used to refer to the sacred power and spirit of one mountain, even by the same person. Several traditions have come together to describe a manifold but essentially identical power.

Most of the physical contact with the sacred mountains took place during the warm seasons, but this did not leave the people without spiritual sustenance for the rest of the year. The spiritual tie was maintained through a number of means. Formally, the local Shugendō branch temple was a minor repository of power; its resident *yamabushi* was able to administer effective religious rites by virtue of his training, initiation, and annual retreats. More informally, a local group of laymen might meet as a voluntary association to pay homage to the power of the mountain and seek its blessing. In Haguro Shugendō there are three sacred mountains, and to this day it is possible to buy from the headquarters an inexpensive scroll featuring these three and their respective divinities. The laymen would purchase such scrolls and install them in their homes; then when the voluntary association had its regular (often monthly) meeting, the members could venerate the divinities as part of their religious devotions.

The connection between the people and the mountain could be observed in several ways. Of course there was a physical contact at the mountain itself, but there was also a symbolic contact. While in their homes venerating the *kami* of sacred mountains represented on scrolls, it could be said that the people were doing one of two things: either they were invoking the *kami* and power to their homes, or they were symbolically transporting themselves to the sacred mountains. And probably the two possibilities were imperceptibly merged in the minds of most practitioners. At any rate, the phrase "bring the mountain to Muhammad" is an apt expression here. A sacred mountain's power was so great that it was invoked in the shrine and temple precincts of the surrounding area simply by means of bringing a stone from the mountain to the precincts and engraving the mountain's name upon the stone.

The tie between the *yamabushi* group and the sacred mountain was exhibited even in a calendrical sense. For at each Shugendō center there was an annual round of ritual festivals marking a complete religious year. Within Haguro Shugendō there were four seasonal festivals called "peaks." The winter peak was a hundred-day period of confinement for two ascetics, ending with a colorful festival on the last day of the year. The spring peak was a ritualistic celebration and blessing ceremony for the New Year. The summer peak was a one-hundred-twenty-day period of pilgrimage to and retreat within the sacred mountain. The fall peak was a more intensive period of ascetic confinement for the professional *yamabushi*. These ritual periods not only carried the name "peaks," but were actually conducted on and around the holy mountain.[17]

The preceding comments about Shugendō have been written mainly in the past tense, because the once glorious and powerful Shugendō tradition is now represented by only a few practicing groups. In 1872 Shugendō was proscribed by the new government, as part of its attempt to purify Shinto and separate it from Buddhism. Shugendō mountains, being a mixture of the two, were forcibly separated into Shinto and Buddhist institutions. Only since 1945, with the enactment of complete religious freedom, have Shugendō groups been able to operate under their own name.

Haguro Shugendō is one of a few such surviving groups. In the early 1960s I observed and participated in the remaining festivals of the four peaks, some of which are now carried out by the shrine called Dewa-jinja on Mount Haguro. The four peaks are now but pale shadows of a once magnificent tradition, yet even in their days of decline one can sense their former greatness. I would like to close this account of sacred mountains in Japan with some personal impressions of one "peak."

The fall peak in late August of 1963 was a unique and memorable experience. Rites at the temple headquarters at the foot of the mountain announced our death to this world and our conception as a fetus with a new life. Leaving the village, we crossed the "river of purification," and entered the otherworld of the sacred mountain of Haguro. We climbed the mountain by means of a three-hundred-year-old stone staircase flanked by equally aged towering cedar trees. The retreat was held in an old Shugendō temple called Kotakū-ji, located on Mount Haguro but some distance from the Dewa-jinja (now Shinto, but before 1872 a Shugendō institution).

For ten days we were in retreat within Kotakū-ji, living out the vestiges of a medieval regimen of asceticism and training. There were rules prescribed for eating, clothing, and for regular devotions to various divinities. In each recitation the *gongen* of the three sacred mountains were prominent. And although we were "confined," part of this confinement included ritual pilgrimages to holy sites and the performance of special devotions. The symbolism of the rituals was complicated, with frequent duplication and overlapping of important themes. And several dynamic processes were unfolding simultaneously. We were dead, we had been conceived anew, we were gestating within the womb of the mountains, to be reborn. The portable altar carried into the mountains, and temporarily enshrined in Kotakū-ji, was draped with a piece of cloth representing a placenta: thus, the symbolism of enfolding womb was portrayed by the mountains generally and by the portable altar specifically. We had left the world of desire, and were cutting off our defilement through penance and devotion. In terms of more explicit Buddhist symbolism, we were proceeding from hell to paradise, from beastly existence to the level of a Bodhisattva or saint.

The unfolding of each step was quite dramatic. Fortunately, Kotakū-ji was not provided with electricity; the faint light of kerosene lamps during the late-night and early-morning devotions provided a proper atmosphere for the esoteric rituals. During our practice, an umbrella-shaped decoration hung from the ceiling of the main hall. Red and white streamers of cloth and lengths of hemp had been tied close to the ceiling. Not until later did we realize that this decoration was to alter as our condition changed. One of the several climaxes was the outdoor fire ceremony on the concluding night of the retreat. This *goma* was carried out by a complex ritual burning of crisscrossed logs representing the bones of each practitioner: the use of fire to burn away evil desire and purify, the composition of the logs to represent the reconstruction of our bodies.

At the end of the impressive ceremony, we reentered Kotakū-ji to find that the umbrella-shaped decoration had been untied and now hung down from ceiling to floor. The red streamers stood for our arteries, the white streamers for our veins; the hemp strands were our bones: in short, another evidence of our spiritual reconstruction, and our ascension as Bodhisattvas from this world (floor) to the heavens (ceiling). Then, the next morning, on the way down the mountain, stopping at Dewa-jinja, we all squatted in front of the shrine, imitating a fetal position, and leapt to our feet with a birth cry: we were reborn from the mountain. A final test took place outside the temple at the foot of the mountain, where every participant jumped over a small bonfire, demonstrating the endurance of twice-born people.

The fall peak may be summed up as an intensive period of contact with and practice within the sacred mountains. I have tried to present something of the spirit and flavor of this ritual process, but know that as a Westerner I can only hint at mysteries.[18]

What significance does Japanese mountain religion have for Western man? After my return to the United States, it was something of a surprise for me to find that Shugendō in modified form is practiced in California on Mount Shasta.[19] But very few Westerners are likely to choose this route. For most of us it is a question of what we can learn by looking over the shoulder of the *yamabushi*. We began by noting the great difference between Western notions of secular mountains and Japanese notions of sacred mountains. The least we as Westerners can learn, vicariously, is the relativity of our own cultural perception of mountains and landscape, and the narrowness of our conception of "nature."[20] Although our tradition has not viewed mountains as sacred, that option may still be open for other cultures. We also may learn that the aesthetic and religious perceptions of mountains need not be so divided, as in our own tradition. The praise of mountains in early Japanese poetry served as the elite literary tradition for the more popular religious heritage of Shugendō.

Modern Western man is severely alienated from nature, often seeking a way to return to its womb while trying at the same time to advance to a transcendent, transhuman condition. Shugendō, by identifying an other-world within mountains, has been able to recognize the sacredness of the "natural" world, and to advance to a transcendent state by returning again and again to this natural womb. Even if Shugendō is a vanishing tradition in Japan, and one not easily transplanted to the West, it constitutes a cultural achievement worthy of our respect and serious interest.

Page 106: Gakuō, *Landscape* Muromcahi period, 15th century. Courtesy of the Tokyo National Museum and Mariko Togashi of the Zauho Press

Evelio Echevarría
The Inca Mountaineers: 1400-1800

Hailli (Triumph)

Hailli, little shepherdess!
You go to the hill,
where the condor hovers.

Hailli, little shepherd!
You go to the mountain,
where the hawk flies and flies.

Hailli, shepherds!
You climb to the ridges,
and leave the fleeting fox
trailing in your steps.

—Traditional song of the Kechua highlanders

FATHER PLACIDUS, THE Benedictine monk of the Grisons who conducted a sustained climbing campaign after 1788, did not belong to the "one man, one mountain" school that had hitherto prevailed. Perhaps this is the reason Sir Arnold Lunn named him the father of mountaineering. Two years before Father Placidus began his Alpine career, Mont Blanc had been won. Prior to this eighteenth-century, early-mountaineering period, a few isolated climbs on European peaks had been achieved: Mont Ventoux, Roche Melon, Mont Aiguille, Titlis, Dent du Midi, and Velan. But a much earlier and even more extraordinary event may have taken place with the ascent of the Mexican volcano Popocatepetl in 1521 by a handful of conquistadors. This ascent to 5,430 meters (17,815 feet) was thought for centuries to represent an altitude record.[1]

Perhaps Sir Arnold Lunn never knew that long before Father Placidus, Balmat, and De Saussure, and perhaps contemporary to Petrarch's ascent of Mont Ventoux in 1335, mountaineering on peaks much higher than Popocatepetl was taking place on another continent. Ancient mountaineers were climbing peaks in an area so desolate that even today it poses logistical problems to expeditions. The ancients encamped on the heights, built sacrificial shrines as well as rooms for permanent occupation, and on some occasions buried their dead on the summits as offerings to the mountain gods.

THE AREA IN WHICH these ascents took place was the Atacama region of the Andes of South America, which stretches from the neighborhood of Arequipa, in Peru, to as far south as the Elqui Valley in Chile. To the east, it reaches the slopes that rise above the jungles of Argentina and Bolivia and, to the west, the mineralized plains of northern Chile. The mountains of this volcanic section of the Andes are very high, in some cases over 6,700 meters (22,000 feet). Although the snow line is also high, averaging about 5,800 meters, there is sufficient precipitation to allow grass to grow in the high valleys, and to sustain small flocks of sheep and llamas. These are shepherded by three hardy races of highlanders: the Kechua, in southern Peru and northern Argentina; the Aymara, in southern Bolivia; and the Atacameñan, in northern Chile; some Aymara clans have emigrated to northern Chile and some Atacameñans have settled in northern Argentina. From these three races sprang some of the earliest mountaineers.

For good reasons, the first men interested in the existence of early Indian remains on Andean peaks did not record the story of their finds. They were treasure seekers or gravediggers who climbed to the peaks and camped there in order to carry out excavations. It was well known among the Andean peoples that the Incas buried their dead with an offering of gold and silver, and gravedigging, even at such an altitude, may have offered rewarding sport.

The first traveler to actually report a discovery was the Chilean explorer Francisco J. San Román, who climbed several volcanoes in his journeys (1883-1889) and recorded his investigations in his work *Desiertos i Cordilleras de Atacama*. A few years later Sir William Martin Conway reported an Inca burial site on Chachani, having heard of it while en route to Bolivia (1901). Little attention was paid to such accounts until 1954, when an Inca mummy was found near the top of Cerro Plomo, a 5,430-meter peak east of Santiago. This event aroused considerable interest among mountaineers of several nations, and a number of expeditions set forth with the declared intention of seeking similar finds.

Although in the past twenty-five years important discoveries have been made, no one has seriously studied the motives, other than practical or religious, that drove the Indians into such widespread mountain activities; it is hoped that this personal view will provoke further research and discussion.

The Yields

IN EARLY 1885, San Román found on the top of Cerro Chuculai (5,421 meters, 17,785 feet) in northern Chile a copper knife of Inca manufacture.[2] Surprisingly, he did not show much emotion when he recorded this strange event in the account of his expeditions. Does his indifference hint that a find of that kind was commonplace among the people of the areas he explored? Whatever the reason, it was the first recorded report of an Inca relic found on a high peak.

Shortly thereafter, while in Arequipa, en route for the Andes of Bolivia, Sir William Martin Conway reported the news of a second discovery: "... Mr. Wagner, of the Cailloma mine, ... informed me that he found among the old papers at the mine one dating back to the time of the Spaniards, which stated that the summit of Chachani was a burial place of an Inca.... After repeated attempts Mr. Wagner succeeded in reaching the summit ... he took some native workers up with him and made excavations on three different days; but it was evident that a previous treasure-seeker had been there, for the grave had been disturbed...."[3]

Chachani, at almost 20,000 feet, is located in southern Peru. Lord Conway's report raised the assumed "roof" of the Indian mountaineers and at the same time considerably enlarged the geographic area of their activities. Slowly, similar discoveries began to trickle in. But again no European mountaineers of that era expressed interest when Count de Rosen reported in 1901 the discovery of Inca ruins on the top of the 20,000-foot Nevado de Chañi in Argentina.[4] As it was, a half century was to elapse before the Europeans would travel to the Andes in hope of striking a similar find. Until then, nearly all discoveries were to fall to the climbers, explorers, and scientists of the countries that had inherited the mountain patrimony of old Incadom.

At first, these early discoverers, when stumbling upon Indian remains on a lofty summit, thought them isolated finds; their remarks were limited to the peculiar idolatry of the heathens who had chosen such unlikely places to pay homage to their gods. Only the Pole, Witold Paryski, who had climbed in the Atacama in 1937, tried to chronicle the Indian mountain ascents; but his writings did not appear until 1956.[5] The first discoverers did not attempt to conduct excavations. They simply reported their summit findings: a bundle of *tola* wood (collected in the upper valleys), or a *pirca*, a rock construction used as a cairn or as a shelter against the wind. Several travelers held the opinion that such remains belonged not to the Indians but to prospectors, who would do anything or climb anywhere "to strike it rich." Only in the last few years have South American mountaineers questioned such theories regarding the *tola* and the *pircas*: if they were indeed the work of prospectors, such men were not in search of mines, but came from a breed of astute people who knew the location of the Inca graves and the worth of the ornaments with which the Inca dead were buried. However, it is still not certain whether the wood found on the peaks was carried there by Indians or gravediggers.

Remains of *tola* wood and *pirca* constructions are widespread, and one or both have been found on or near nine summits exceeding 6,000 meters as well as on twelve other peaks of over 5,000 meters located in Peru, Bolivia, Chile, and Argentina. One peak, Salla, has traces of an Inca road crossing over the top, and another, Pichu Pichu, boasts of staircases on its steeper parts leading to the rock shelters on the summit!

Among modern mountaineers, it is uncertain who were the first to initiate excavations. Perhaps it was the members of the 1948 Argentinian expedition to Nevado de Chañi. The climbers unfortunately chose the winter months for their work and found that the summit ground was frozen. Textiles and ceramics were unearthed but in the process became torn and broken. The iced ground was reluctant to offer up the Inca relics, and after much hard work the task was abandoned. And so began in the name of science the very operations that the gravediggers had been conducting for centuries in the name of Inca gold. Satisfying returns began to follow. Ceramics and textiles, with richly designed figures indicating a preference for terra cotta and black coloring, were the booty. These first diggings took place only within the rock-wall enclosures. But one event was to arouse the interest of many mountaineers and would mark the beginnings of a kind of high-mountain archeology, to be practiced chiefly by mountaineers instead of archeologists: the discovery in 1954 of an Inca mummy on Cerro Plomo.

Cerro Plomo (5,430 meters, 17,815 feet) is an ice dome dominating the eastern skyline of Santiago, the capital of Chile. Beginning in 1923, local mountaineers examined the Indian *pircas* near the top and even uncovered a few Indian artifacts. But local hill people knew something that climbers did not: that the Incas did not build stone walls at such an altitude just for the joy of building. One afternoon in February 1954, a solo Santiago climber became intrigued when he saw two hill men carrying down, from near the top, a heavy and bulky bag. They were evasive and their sly smiles left him puzzled. Upon his return to Santiago a few days later, he was to learn that a mummy had been uncovered from under the floor of the rock enclosure in which climbers had been camping for decades. The hill men had sold the mummy to a museum.

Immediately after the news was publicized, local mountaineers set up an expedition that ascended Cerro Plomo a number of times, methodically surveying the ruins and conducting excavations.[6] The expedition was to set the style for future discoveries: a group of climbers would ascend a peak likely to be crowned with Inca relics and, upon verifying their existence, would return with a larger party and establish shifts to perform excavations at the most promising sites. The Chileans and the Argentinians were the most active of these archeologists, but among foreigners, there were small but select groups of Poles, Swedes, Austrians, and Japanese. A more scientific approach was developed to locate the potentially superior sites. The Chileans concentrated their efforts on high mountains that commanded a view over an entire area and which, at the same time, had been known to have Indian rock walls at their base. And wherever found, conical peaks, admired by all peoples throughout history, were a special target. The Argentinians on their side, particularly when led by Antonio Beorchia, chose the higher mountains that overlooked or were within a reasonable distance from the Inca road network. Recently, some climbers have begun to argue that more attention should be paid to Indian or Spanish names that may hint at the existence of an Inca grave in a given mountain: Incahuasi ("Abode of the Inca"), Cerro del Inca ("Mountain of the Inca"), Cerro Sepultura ("Burial Peak"), Cerro Indio Muerto ("Mountain of the Dead Indian").

The most valued trophy for these climber-scientists is a mummy. Only two have been found. The first, on Cerro Plomo, was an eight-year-old boy, richly dressed and buried with a headdress of condor feathers, an offering of gold and silver statuettes, as well as moccasins and seashells. The second was found on Cerro El Toro (6,386 meters, 20,952 feet): two climbers, who "knew we were going to find something," discovered within a rock enclosure a human head protruding from the summit ground. After the mummy was disinterred and taken to a museum in Mendoza, it was found that the remains were of a youth some twenty years old who had been intoxicated with a corn-brewed drink and who may have been murdered as suggested by a wound on the back of his neck. There was also a dowry of clothing and six pairs of leather shoes.[7]

No mummy has since been found. On Nevado Tambillos (5,800 meters) evidence indicates that a body once occupied a gravesite, but diggers apparently removed it and no records exist either in Chile or Argentina to explain the missing form.[8] The same appears to be the case on Nevado de Chañi (6,060 meters) in northern Argentina.

The richest high-altitude archeological sites in the world are very probably the peaks of Licancabur and Llullaillaco.

Licancabur (5,930 meters, 19,456 feet), "The Mountain of the People" of the Atacameñans, is a conical peak located on the Chilean-Bolivian border. In 1886, José Santelices ascended the peak and discovered statuettes and other Inca adornments; he also found great quantities of *tola* wood, which he estimated at some 4,000 kilograms, most of which he burned to signal his successful ascent. Later expeditions, particularly in 1955, surveyed the Inca-Atacameñan ruins:

> The climbers discovered at once that they were not the first to reach the goal. On the eastern rim of the crater they found stone walls that were the remains of three old houses or shelters, the largest about 15 feet by 5 or 6 feet wide. Each structure was open to the east side for its full length. The walls were a little more than 4 feet high, though caved in at places. Construction was the *pirca* type, in which unworked pieces are fitted snugly together with mortar but all joints completely filled with fines. Beside one of the ruins was a pile of wood about 10 feet across, much weathered and fragmented. One straight stick about 8 feet long, in fair condition, was off to one side of the pile.[9]

So far as is known, Llullaillaco volcano (6,723 meters, 22,055 feet) is the highest mountain conquered by the ancient Andeans; a similar height, incidentally, was not to be attained by white men until 1857 in the Central Himalayas. Llullaillaco (*lloclla*—hot, *yacu*—water) has yielded more relics than any other mountain, perhaps because it has been more methodically explored. The work began in 1952, when the Chileans, González and Harseim, ascended the peak "for the first time" and found on top, much to their surprise, a small rock wall and something that looked like a leather bag half-buried in the ground.[10]

Thereafter, the search and the booty grew: in 1955, Josin and Ravizza found at 6,300 meters hand-worked cactus logs, probably roof beams. A sunken room was also located at 6,650 meters; in 1958, at about 6,600 meters, Rebitsch uncovered lumber, ceramics, and remains of corn ears, as well as a path with rock supports on one side. On the summit he found the substructures of two rooms; in 1961, Diaz and Rebitsch dug out other rooms, which were apparently part of a hamlet at 6,650 meters (21,818 feet). They unearthed rooms for sleeping, a living room, an enclosure for llamas, and even a wood dump. In the main room they found a hearth, charred wood, fruit seeds, a corn ear, a shoe, pieces of pottery, a rustic cloth, and a woven litter. Another wood dump was discovered at 5,750 meters. On the summit they found a small altar, and, under the slab of this altar, a piece of finely woven cloth; in 1971, six Argentinian climbers explored the north side of the mountain and located at 5,500 meters (18,045 feet) six graves, which were marked by rock walls and contained skeletons and skulls of adults. A wooden bow was also at hand.[11]

AN OVERALL SURVEY of the geographical and altitudinal reach of Inca mountaineering leaves the modern mountaineer gasping. There is now evidence that thirty-five summits exceeding 5,000 meters were ascended, and they are widely distributed along a 1,500-mile segment of the Andes.[12] The period within which most of this activity took place is thought to have lasted from 1400 to 1550. But the list is by no means closed. Not only are new discoveries still a probability, but the ceiling of Inca climbing might very well be raised. Higher than Llullaillaco in the Andes are only Huascarán (6,768 meters), Nevado de Pissis (6,780 meters), Nevado Ojos del Salado (6,885 meters) and Aconcagua (6,960 meters, 22,835 feet). Huascarán, in northern Peru, is too glaciated and was outside the area known to Inca climbers. The other three mountains are within the Inca area but Pissis and Ojos del Salado are rather remote and are lost within a maze of peaks. There remains only Aconcagua.

If Aconcagua, the highest mountain in the hemisphere, stood within the Inca empire, could its prominence have at least tempted the ambition of the ancients? Altitude alone was no problem for these highlanders, but what about technical difficulties and the weather? The FitzGerald expedition, which climbed Aconcagua from the north, found the route technically easy; only the wind and the cold may have worked as a deterrent to the Indians. In 1947 the body of a *guanaco*, a ruminant related to the llama, was found just below the ridge that connects the highest peak with the lower (southwest) summit. There is no explanation for this astonishing discovery, and no expedition has properly examined the body of the animal, which remains where it was found.[13] The activity displayed by the Indians on the mountains, the altitudinal advantage of their civilization, their apparent predilection for high places, all seem to suggest the possibility that they may well have embarked on this culminating enterprise.

M OST STUDENTS OF Inca mountaineering have, without hesitation, assigned to it only religious and utilitarian motives. Either the gods had to be enshrined on lofty altars or lookout posts had to be erected on the peaks to warn the valley dwellers of possible invaders. Perhaps originally, in pre-Columbian times, the peaks *were* only ascended for religious purposes; and later, with the appearance of the white men who disrupted the organization of the Inca empire, they *may* have been used as lookout posts as well.

The Incas as Mountaineers

But aside from these very plausible motives, did the ancients feel a compelling urge to climb their mountains for other reasons? At that time, when white men did not raise their eyes to the mountains without fear or superstition, could the Andeans have experienced an impulse akin to the sportive-aesthetic feeling that has traditionally moved the modern mountaineer? There will never be a definitive answer to this question, but it is fitting, in a speculation of this sort, to draw attention to a unique aspect of the mountain civilization of the Andeans: the beauty, exactness, and abundance of their mountain names.

In *Berge der Welt*, Marcel Kurz remarked, ". . . in Peru und Bolivien sind die Bergnamen die schönsten Ortsnamen der Welt."[14] To illustrate, consider the name *Andes*. It derives from *anta*, "copper," but it does not allude solely to the metal, which is found only in locales quite far from the Andean foothills. The Incas always had the mighty chain before their eyes, especially when the sunset on the Pacific horizon would lift the mountains out of the night and dye the high snows with the reflection of the rocks. *Antahuara*, "of the copper sunsets"; such is the beautiful meaning of the name.[15]

And so with the names of particular mountains: Ancopiti is the "white dart"; Coylloriti, the "star of snow"; Chorolque, the "silvery snail"; Illimani, the "shining condor"; and Aconcagua, highest of them all, the "sentinel of stone." Legends and traditions are also represented in mountain names. Huandi and Huáscar were lovers from enemy tribes; as a punishment for their love they were left in the heights to freeze to death. Today, the waterfalls that feed the Santa River are the incessant tears of the two lovers, remembered forever in the grandiose peaks of Huandoy and Huascarán.[16] Other names are related to gods and titans. Tiquimani is the "condor of Tiqui," the Thunder God. The volcano Thunupa is named after a titan who had rebelled against a despotic overlord and was sheltered by the mountain, which opened its flank to receive the tortured body of this Andean Prometheus.

The Inca mountain names often suggest both a form of description and a note of beauty, revealing a unique interpretation of the spirit of the hills. In ascribing motives to the Inca's high-mountain ascents, it would be unfair to the ancient mountaineers to ignore that attitude as made evident in their names.

The Argentinian mountaineer-philosopher José F. Finó once noted that both aesthete and mountain climber nurture a similar love for the hills, but that the climber differs in that he loves the hills *actively.* So too, the Incas. Today, on several peaks along the Chilean-Argentinian border, an Inca *pirca* stands, close to the modern cairn that holds the summit register. There is something unique in these Andean Indian constructions. They tell of an achievement that antedated by centuries the deeds of the enterprising pioneer alpinists; they represent a culture that went to the hills when the most advanced civilizations feared them. The *pircas* were on the tops first, and they are still there:

> . . . still the ancient home stands fast
> and its walls to the summit cling;
> and the footprints stay on the narrow trails
> that high on the grim wall wind.
> When you and I have told our tale,
> shall we leave as much behind?[17]

Amos Tutuola
The Yoruba and the Hill Spirits
A Nonfictional Prose Narrative

AT PRESENT, IN Nigeria, there are about twelve states. The Yoruba towns are in the west. But in each state there are many, and the people in each of the towns speak different dialects. The traditions and the beliefs are also different from one another. For example, in my town which is Abeokuta, one of the biggest Yoruba towns in the west of Nigeria, and which is about sixty miles away from Lagos, the federal capital, we have strong belief that many mighty hills are the homes of spirits.

In Abeokuta town, one mighty hill is in the heart of the town. This hill is called Olumo. Several shrines are on top of it. The people sacrifice to the spirits who dwell in this hill and many people worship these spirits in a certain period of the year. But of course, in the past days or several years ago, human beings were included in the sacrifices such as goats, rams, cows, costly clothes, cola nuts, plenty of palm oil, and many other valuable things they were giving to the spirits of Olumo, the hill.

The first people who came to Abeokuta had no other place to live but in the cave which is in this hill. At last they found out that the hill was the homes of spirits. But as they had no other god to worship, they started to worship the spirits of the hill. Of course as time went on the people were increasing in large number until the cave could not accommodate them. They began to spread to the surroundings of the hill, Olumo. It was like that, they spread on and on until a large town was formed and then the Olumo hill was then in the heart of the town.

In those days, whenever the neighboring people beseiged them, the devotees of the hill spirits would sacrifice immediately to the spirits. They would ask the spirits to help them conquer their enemies, and unfailingly their enemies would be conquered right out. Not only that, when one was seriously ill, that person would certainly be well as soon as the sacrifice was given to the hill spirits. When one was in great burdens, his or her burdens would be eased as soon as the sacrifice was given to the spirits. When there were epidemics of such the sicknesses as smallpox, etc., etc., and that people were dying in large number or more than it should be, the devotees would not waste time to give the right sacrifices to the hill spirits in order to help to get rid of all these things. When one woman was barren more than it should be, she would become the mother of children soon after the sacrifices were given to the spirits. When the rain kept too late to fall on crops in the year, then the sacrifice would be given to the spirits in order to help them to cause the rain to fall, and in fact the rain would start to fall as soon as the sacrifice was given to them. Furthermore, special sacrifices were given to them when the people of the town wanted to choose a new ruler.

For all these reasons, the Yoruba people still respect the spirits who are dwelling in this hill, Olumo, till present time, and the devotees are still sacrificing to them.

Again, to bring more light to the belief which we the Yoruba people have that there are spirits in certain hills. Ibadan, the largest town in West Africa, and which is forty-eight miles from my town, Abeokuta, also has a mighty hill which is at the outskirt of the town. The people here also have strong belief that spirits are in their hill which is called Oke-Ibadan, meaning Ibadan Hill. The spirits helped them greatly in the past days to conquer their enemies, to help them to overcome all their difficulties, etc., etc. They sacrificed to them every time that they needed helps from them.

From the children and to the very old age, people join together to worship the spirits in the month of March every year. They all dance about in the town with great joy for about two days.

The people of Ibadan are doing so every year in remembrance of the great help which their hill spirits rendered to them in the past days and which they are still rendering to them at the present days.

Harald Sohlberg, *The Mountains of Rondane at Night* (1918). Nasjonalgalleriet, Oslo

Attributed to Chou Ch'en (fl. 1500-35), *The Haven of T'ao Yuan-ming*.
The Cleveland Museum of Art, Purchase Fund, John L. Severance

No two hills are alike, but everywhere on earth plains are one and the same.
— Jorge Luis Borges
Utopia of a Tired Man

William Doub
Mountains in Early Taoism

I N THE MOST GENERAL terms, Taoism sought to discover how the natural world worked and how human beings, a minor part of nature, could live in harmony with it.[1] Mountains played an important role in the tenets and practice of this Taoist quest,[2] and I will deal with some doctrinal and practical aspects of the mountain relationship with emphasis on what has not previously been treated in Western languages. I will focus on the "early period" of Taoism, generally before the beginning of the T'ang dynasty (A.D. 618).[3]

"The landscape took on a symbolic significance as a place of retreat from society, or even as a prototype of the natural *way* of life."[4] Although there is no mention of mountains in what is probably the oldest Taoist text, the *Tao Te Ching*, the gradual development of the concept— that some sort of involvement with a natural landscape is an important way to be natural—appears as early as the third century B.C. in the *Chuang Tzu*.[5]

Probably the earliest example of this retreat from society, this identification with landscape, is found in the annals of the mountain recluses. Within the Chinese eremitic tradition (which goes back almost to the tenth century B.C.), not all motives for withdrawal from society can reasonably be called Taoist; but it is the Taoist perspective which reveals itself as the most natural and spiritual. Taoist recluses enjoyed living in natural surroundings. They relished the solitude, the simplicity, and the beauty of life in the mountains, unlike other recluses of the era who were only fleeing the cares and dangers of involvement in society.[6]

Although there was no unanimity on the extent to which one needed to rely on the mountain environment,[7] the celebrated Ko Hung (fourth century A.D.) declared that all who cultivated the Tao, or its variety of immortality rites,[8] had to go into the mountains.[9] These rites, which included meditation and fasting, were generally carried out in a Hut of Silence (*ching shih*). Revelations occured in which divinities instructed adepts to build such huts on a famous mountain or in a great marsh in a wild unfrequented place.[10] All those who were preparing special drugs and medicines (taken by many early Taoists to lengthen one's life or to become immortal), had to do so in the mountains.[11] The plants and minerals used to make these drugs were to be found there. The adept exhibited his love of the Tao and veneration of the divinities and immortals by renouncing the struggle for wealth and honor and by living among the mountains and forests.[12]

There are innumerable examples of mountain retreat. In the fourth century A.D., the famous Mao-shan sect medium, Hsu Man, secluded himself; when he found himself still disturbed by people and unable to concentrate on achieving unity, he moved to a more remote peak. It is related that he sometimes climbed cliffs to gather mushrooms and that whenever he happened to meet another lover of the Tao they would enter the tower where he lived and converse.[13] Chou Tzu-liang, an adept of the same sect who lived about a century later, decided to leave the mountain where he had been practicing immortality techniques and make a visit to the town. Having already received instruction from the divinities that he should not do so, the divinities again appeared and told him to return to the mountains to achieve peace.[14] A third Mao-shan adept, Hsü Mi, having made some progress in his spiritual quest, seemed unable to go further. But when he traveled to the peaks to seek solitude and to find silence he was able to break through to an understanding of the limits of words and to come close to reaching the Tao.[15]

Taoist techniques were developed for "mastering the mountains." Some of these appear to have been designed to protect the adept from the dangers of mountain terrain and from the fears it aroused. These early techniques revealed a contradictory attitude in that a fear of mountains and a love for them seemed to coexist; as time passed and the mountain scene became more familiar the apprehension generally decreased. An early example of unease is revealed in a poem in the second century B.C. anthology, the *Ch'u Tz'u*. The image conveyed in the poem, "Chao yin shih" (Summons to the Recluse), as summarized by Li Chi, is one of ". . . horror for the uncanny recesses of the mountains, the roar of the tigers and leopards, the treacherous waters of ravines, and the mournful cries of monkeys."[16] Similar fears were expressed by Ko Hung some five centuries later. He wrote of the danger to mountain travelers of tigers, poisonous snakes and insects, wolves, winds, damp, and cold. Evil spirits and demons of various kinds were ascribed particularly to mountainous areas, and bandits were also mentioned.[17] These and other dangers were sometimes viewed as tests set for travelers by mountain divinities, usually for religious purposes.[18]

Techniques for protection included recommendations for selecting when and where one should enter the mountains, what one could do before starting in order to ensure well-being, and how one should act while there. One chose only those months for entering the mountains, specifically the third and the ninth (approximately our May and November), in which they were "open"—meaning, apparently, that they were comparatively safe and hospitable. During those months, propitious days and times of day were to be chosen. If one's business was so urgent that he could not wait for another of the auspicious months, the best he could do was to choose an auspicious day and hour. In the case of the Five Sacred Mountains of China, there were entire years when those particular peaks were to be avoided, since during such periods the mountains suffered calamities such as harmful vapors and miasmas.[19] One of the major scriptures of Taoism, the *Ling pao ching* (Scripture of the Sacred Treasure), goes so far as to say that the traveler who enters the mountains on protected or proper days "will enjoy great good fortune," and that those who enter them on prohibited days "will certainly die."[20]

Probably the most complex and frequently mentioned means of protecting oneself while in the mountains was the use of talismans or amulets of various kinds.[21] However, as will be shown, mountain talismans had other uses, largely unrelated to protection during mountain travel. Protective talismans already existed in a rather well-developed form in the fourth century A.D., suggesting a considerable prior history. If Taoists seeking to lengthen their lives took appropriate talismans with them when they went into the mountains, they would be safe from tigers, wolves, diseases peculiar to mountain regions, and other dangers.[22] Certain mountain talismans could protect the traveler from evil or dangerous divinities and from mountain spirits.[23] The talismans were written on red silk, on peach wood, or carved in certain soft substances, and they were carried on a journey or placed a certain distance from a sleeping place or inside a mountain dwelling.[24]

The symbolism of many of these talismans, which were often named after famous mountains, is understood. Most of the earliest extant examples consist of a series of interrelated symbols or of greatly distorted Chinese characters conveying a short simple text.[25] Some, however, appear to have been accompanied by explanatory material. (There is strong evidence that a great many Taoist scriptures developed from the talismans or from their accompanying texts.[26]) It was common for the entry to a Taoist heaven or paradise to be indicated, for example, by the words "go up from here," and for the positions of retreat huts and the locations of immortality-aiding herbs and mushrooms to be indicated. A type of color coding was used; white or yellow for caves, red for water, and black for the mountain.[27]

Probably the best known of the religious talismans is that called "The Chart of the True Form of the Five Peaks" (*Wu yüeh chen-hsing t'u*). A great deal of information contained in both primary and secondary sources centers about this or related talismans of the Five Peaks.[28] The religious characteristics and effectiveness of these particular talismans appear to have been based on their use as symbols to aid such practices as meditation, which would bring one closer to immortality, or to establish contact with divinities who could help one become immortal.[29] The use in the texts accompanying some talismans of such terms as "mysterious observation" (*tung kuan* or *hsuan kuan*) seems to indicate a practice of meditation in which the Taoist adept saw through or transcended the symbolic representation of the mountains to their "true forms": probably their role as the abode of those who had reached the realm of the "true" (*chen*), the term often used by Taoists to refer to the state of being immortal, and, by extension, to a place where immortals existed.[30]

One talisman, called "The Chart of the Form of the Human-Bird Mountain as Originally Observed" (*Yüan-lan jen-niao shan hsing t'u*), was quite explicit in describing the religious purposes and uses of these "true form" mountain talismans. Its accompanying text reads in part:

> Each of the numberless heavens has a human-bird mountain. These mountains have a human image[31] and a bird shape. Their summits and cliffs are so extraordinarily steep that they cannot be described.... [There are places there] where divinities live. The trees, minerals, fragrant blossoms, fungi, and herbs all [yield] drugs which [in the form of] liquid extracts bring deathlessness. It is ... difficult to describe it completely. Describing it would not help those who study as they must themselves respond and concentrate their search on achieving unity. This [text and talisman] is a written indication which gathers together subtle essences into written characters. It has been written by writers of sage-like skill in order to transmit it to superior students and not to reveal it to those of intermediate abilities. The characters representing the subtle essences have the shape of mountains. The exterior expressions of them take various forms, and the traces[32] of them are seen in different kinds of appearances, all of which are the subtle essences, the transformations of which are complete therein. With thoughts which are mysteriously penetrating, close your eyes, and you will see it. Look all around, and it will be complete. Continue to do these things for a long time, and you will have evidences of it. The subtle essence will descend into you, and your corporeal body will be able to fly. After long practice, you will achieve the subtle state. You will be rid of the corporeal and be completely subtle. Your soaring will be like that of a bird as you go out roaming beyond the Three Realms....[33] [A person who has reached this state] is called a human-bird. Those who study this roam in the mountains, and when their reaching of the Tao is connected with the mountains, the state they have gained will be constant forever.[34]

Note the explicit identification of the mountain of the talisman with a place where divinities live, as well as the emphasis on meditationlike practices, apparently using the mountain talisman as some kind of object of or aid to meditation. The state of being immortal is symbolized by the ability to fly and by the subtle essences replacing the material body.

Among other uses of mountain talismans, they were sometimes employed as an aid in contacting or communicating with divinities, often but not always related to the search for immortality. Ko Hung tells us that when superior practitioners entered the mountains carrying "The Chart of the True Form of the Five Peaks," they could summon the mountain divinities.[35] With the aid of a text closely related to the mountain talismans, it was also possible, after purifying oneself and fasting for a hundred days, to summon various powerful divinities. One could then travel among the Five Sacred Mountains and the Four Rivers where the divinities of the local temples would reveal themselves. One would then be able to ask each divinity various questions about his locale such as what is auspicious or

Chorten and prayer flags at Thyangboche Monastery, Nepal. Photo by
John Cleare/Mountain Camera

inauspicious, what is safe or dangerous, what are the causes of local diseases.[36] Possession of a set of twelve texts and talismans including "The Chart of the True Form of the Five Peaks" gave one the power to be respected and welcomed by the myriad divinities and spirits as one traveled among the mountains and streams.[37]

All of this not only indicates the frequent involvement of Taoist adepts in Chinese popular or folk religion, but also points to the probable origins of the cult of the Five Peaks and their talismans in early, probably pre-Han, Chinese popular religion. Although we are not concerned here with popular religion, a brief reference to those origins may be in order. The Taoist specialists themselves appealed to the divinities of the Five Peaks and their subordinates for guidance in such matters as spiritual cultivation, dietary restrictions, and the performance of magic. The common people sought the aid of these same divinities when they asked for repentance or made offerings.[38] The origins of the beliefs in the Five Peaks as well as the continuing importance of popular faith as part of these beliefs is suggested by one of the earliest accounts of them in the *Tso chuan*. A group of leaders take an oath to behave well and cooperate with each other. The oath appeals to the divinities of famous mountains and rivers to destroy the person, family, and country of any who breaks the oath.[39] This appears to be an early example of the role of mountain divinities in enforcing good behavior among people.

A further influence relating to the development of the Talismans of the Five Peaks was the use of a system of certificates of authority by local officials and couriers of the postal relay system during the first and second centuries A.D. In a number of cases, the terms used to refer to these certificates were identical to those applied to the mountain talismans a few centuries later. Furthermore, many local officials and some cooperative institutions, such as the postal relay system and the inns for travelers, contributed to the development of various aspects of the Taoist religio-political movements of the second century and thus to the formation of religious Taoism.[40] There was further interrelationship in the similarity of these terms and concepts and those used in the agreements or contracts made between individual Taoist adept-mediums and the divinities with whom they made contact.

In summary, the role of mountains in Taoism was probably least central in the earliest Taoist writings such as the *Tao Te Ching* and *Chuang Tzu*, although the ideas expressed in such writings about man's place in the natural world provided a rich foundation for later Chinese thought. During the Han and Six Dynasties periods (about 200 B.C. to A.D. 600), a tradition of appreciation of the mountains and a desire to live among them emerged. This tradition was motivated in part by a love for the beauty of nature, mountains serving as the most prominent natural feature, and also sprang from the Taoist urge to identify with and live in harmony with it. The practice of reclusion, either for a few years or for a lifetime, was the most obvious manifestation of these concepts. They also gave rise to the practice, probably from the third or fourth century A.D., of taking shorter trips into the mountains and writing descriptive or impressionistic essays, called *yu shan chi,* about the experience, and there are great numbers of them extant from nearly every period.[41] Such essays were still being written at the beginning of the twentieth century.

The Jugal Himal from lower Belphi Khola Valley. Photo by John Cleare/
Mountain Camera

If among the objects of the world of the spirit there is something fixed and
unalterable, great and illimitable, something from which the beams of revelation, the streams of knowledge pour into the mind like water into a
valley, it is to be symbolized by a mountain.

— al-Ghazali (1058-1112)
The Niche for Lights

KINAESTHETICS

John Gill

Bouldering: A Mystical Art Form

THE WORLD OF mountaineering abounds with a variety of climbing pursuits, reflecting a society richly diverse in temperaments and interests. At one end of the spectrum, large-scale expeditionary groups attack increasingly precipitous and perilous flanks of the world's most awesome mountains, while at the opposite end, bouldering, a heretofore amorphous and suspect recreation, assumes a more definitive form, gaining substance as it is measured in new philosophical dimensions. Once considered merely training for mountaineering, bouldering has evolved into a microcosm, a glowing nucleus encapsulating the essence of those athletic and mystical elements found in the climbing dimension.

To most devotees, bouldering consists of free climbing short routes of substantial difficulty ranging in height from perhaps three to fifteen meters. Added to this apparently objective definition are a diversity of gamelike restrictions, frequently drawn from the larger world of climbing, and devised to establish a hierarchy among the participants. "On sight" ascents and unprotected soloing are fashionable criteria representing, to many, the most admirable styles of contemporary climbing. Thus, one may initially perceive bouldering as a miniaturized portrait of "outer" climbing, short and vivid strokes of the brush revealing a highly competitive and totally demanding social atmosphere.

There is much that is favorable to be said for this interpretation of bouldering, including the observation that it may ultimately lead to "inner" aspects of the sport. Even the most casual appraisal of bouldering cannot fail to recognize that it is the quintessence of the physical act of climbing. Whereas longer rock pitches may require creativity and endurance, bouldering routes require a concentration of power and insight under remarkable control. Maximum physical tension is generated, but its presence is frequently masked by an attitude of calm determination, indicating a certain inner relaxation. Showmanship pervades the sport, as is evidenced by a greater aerobatic flair and sense of drama than is found elsewhere in the climbing kingdom. Indeed, bouldering is the wellspring of the romantic physical essence of rock climbing.

Among most avid boulderers the competitive spirit is as great as it is in any sporting activity, and this commitment to competition can lead to breakthroughs in teachnique and intriguing refinements of style. Although classical climbing techniques are applied regularly to such routes, bouldering displays dynamic, acrobatic moves not seen elsewhere, perhaps indicating a future trend. Free aerobatics, graceful and precise refinements of the familiar lunge, are not universally accepted, but are being applied even to traditional climbing routes with increasing frequency.

The puzzle factor represents another enticing facet of the bouldering experience. Boulder routes are often referred to as "problems," emphasizing the necessity of intellectual analysis as a prelude to physical gymnastics. However, the intellect is bound inseparably with instinct and physical skill, and cannot operate in arid academic isolation. This forced integration of capabilities contributes to the wide appeal of rock climbing in general and of bouldering in particular. A primordial interplay of these characteristics is reestablished through accumulated experience, as the artificial barriers between them melt away. We find ourselves inspecting a potential route intellectually, and then suddenly "feeling" the climb in its entirety—not following through in an exhaustive formal analysis.

Our relationship with a particular route is subject to change, however, for a bouldering problem has a fluctuating nature and is more alive as a shifting and illusory conceptual image than as a fixed physical pattern. A certain stability can be achieved by repeating ascents—"wiring a climb" in current vernacular—although many climbers reject this practice as reducing climbing to gymnastic exercise. There is a compelling reason, however, why one should not condemn such an approach: repeated ascents allow the isolation of a near-mystical element of the climbing experience—kinaesthetic awareness.

Allow me to depart from the conventional definition of bouldering and instead describe a personal perspective of the sport that has evolved over the past ten years. Turning inward, the primary goal of bouldering may be considered as the attainment of kinaesthetic awareness during demanding technical moves. The boulderer, then, is an artist who seeks self-realization through kinaesthetic awareness. When intellectual analysis is past, and pain and fallibility have receded, there remains this intoxicating and fundamental quality of inner climbing. Agony and uncertainty play only a preliminary role in bouldering; if one never proceeds past these barriers, no matter what the limits of one's technical competence, the ecstacy of artistic fulfillment is never captured.

The acceptance of this metaphysical definition alienates one to some extent from the mainstream of climbing. Unfortunately, this is necessary if one wishes to internalize bouldering. Even so slight a concession as the use of a common classification system has the effect of suppressing creativity and discovery at a fundamental level, although it may enhance innovation in technique and equipment. The use of terms like *5.10, XS,* or *B-1* forms an invisible, but nevertheless powerful bond between climber and the contemporary climbing community. Pressures, exerted through this bond, will inevitably affect style, technique, choice of climbs, and basic goals. In fact, the climbing community is so strong that it creates a paradigm in which the climbing experience is interpreted; consequently, progress is measured in a very rigid manner.

Difficulty is clearly a relative concept, and the very use of the word induces an obstacle to the internalization process, for we are conditioned by our peers to associate a fierce competitiveness with a route so described. As outer climbers, we hope to deviate from the norm to the extent that the description is accurate for others, but not for ourselves. This sort of goal allows a sharpening of physical skills, but philosophically leads away from the more delicate and mystical aspects of climbing. To a large extent, the prevalent concept of difficulty is an illusive physiological metaphor, an artifice forced upon the consciousness by a competitive environment. By a conceptual adjustment, difficulty loses its association with outer competition and becomes a measure of the degree to which we sacrifice ourselves in the quest for an inner mystical and artistic satisfaction.

The search for kinaesthetic awareness, then, requires a refutation of and a detachment from the current climbing community. The internalization process flows most smoothly in isolation, so that bouldering should be a solitary activity, removed from the pressures that would keep one at the periphery of the inner bouldering experience.

Other internalizations of the sport are possible. Extended, strenuous, repetitive pitches occasionally produce an apparent separation of I-consciousness and physical body, similar to the experience of some long-distance runners, where the mind seemingly soars above the automaton-like running form. What is especially appealing in climbing, however, is not a separation *from,* but an intense realization *of* the climbing experience. To saturate the mind with kinaesthetic awareness is to enter a state of reality in which grace and precision define the world. During those brief seconds, cosmic chaos assembles in a sharp and meaningful design, inseparably combining climber and rock in an interlude of destiny. To practice such art in solitude is to protect and prolong the impressions of this acutely intense state.

Over: Wall meditation. Photo by Si Chi Ko

Al Chung-liang Huang
Return to Inner Mountain

THROUGHOUT MY CHILDHOOD, the mountain was always a part of the T'ai Chi experience. The morning practice would take place on the nearest summit. Our master's words would echo in the morning mist: "The air is clear and thin. As you climb, breath easily and make the natural adjustments in your body. Feel the slow change in yourself. Think of the climbing up as a downward flow, without strain. . . ."

When we reached the top, we would sit in silence. We would look down into the smallness of the valleys and fields, to the river of cloud floating about the landscape, then up into the vastness of the sky. From time to time we would shout uproariously with outstretched arms only to find our voices muffled and our bodies dwarfed. "Do you feel small and humble?" our master would ask. We would remain silent. "Then we shall begin practice."

It became more clear each day that the power of T'ai Chi centralizes the ego-mind in climbing the mountain. As our T'ai Chi energy became vitalized and our sense of the universe opened, we became more truly aware of ourselves. Our mounting strength, by the end of each practice, would carry us into powerful Kung-fu motifs. Our master would remind us: "Don't try to fly away, or punch holes in the sky. Compared to the sky, you are nothing. Take this dynamic sense within you down the hill. Flow down. Hold the mountain and carry it home. Return. You have known the outer mountain, experienced it. . . . Now, take it home, return, return to your center, your lower base, your *tant'ien* . . . return to your own Inner Mountain."

The Chinese written character for mountain, *shan* ( ), shows a picture of three peaks and two valleys as a unit. It tells us that mountains have outer bodies and inner ones as well. With the figure-ground depiction of peaks and valleys, we perceive at a glance the Yin-Yang polarity of the mountain, its convex-concave, solid-void, and upward-downward essence.

Flowing with the Tao, particularly in the art of T'ai Chi, all body movements fall naturally into circular patterns. Everything curves. The up motion inevitably circles back down and then curves up again. And the most basic motif in T'ai Chi Ch'uan, Embrace Tiger-Return to Mountain, illustrates this simple form beautifully: both arms reach outward from the spine to gather in the all-pervasive energy (Ch'i) and to connect the central pathway of our *tant'ien,* allowing it to ascend, descend, purify, and crystallize. Finally the arms circle back to the stillness of our earth base, the Inner Mountain.

From the *I Ching,* we learn that the fifty-second hexagram, *Ken*(☶), represents a mountain, majestically moving above and massively still below. Its ridge spreads out like the spine of a dragon, sometimes concealed, sometimes apparent. The mountain's attribute is twofold: both active and passive, like the Yin and Yang of T'ai Chi.

Moving bodily through the six lines of the hexagram, we experience, from toes to calves to thighs to loin to torso to jaw, the essence of the Inner Mountain. From our roots we absorb the energy of the earth that nourishes us. Our feet are our starting point. Toes are the feelers and moving antennae of the stable sole. Toes symbolize movement while the sole represents rest and repose. We are aware of gripping toes, the ground contact of the ball and heel, the hollow space under the arch.

As we continue to move up through the six lines, we discover the importance of keeping movement still and stillness in motion. Our understanding of this depends on an inward sense of settling. The muscles do not reach out to clutch. They make harmonious connections to coordinate inner and outer energy forces. The body experiences itself as part of the total consciousness of the universe.

The *I Ching* comments: "Ken (mountain) means coming to rest in motion. When the proper interplay of stillness and action is understood and practiced, the path for progress is bright and glorious." Restful stillness of the mountain means stillness in its proper place, the center. As we contemplate the outer mountain, let our inner mountain confirm this knowledge. The knowledge is within the human body.

The old Chinese proverb reaffirms this: "Man is heaven and earth, in miniature." Let us soar high with the heaven spirit, like the dragon. Yet, let us keep constantly in touch with our earth center. Often, let us return to Inner Mountain.

Dancing on hillside. Photo by Si Chi Ko

Mount Kailas, South Face from above Darchen. Photo by T. S. Blakeney

... the Earthly Paradise on a mount so that none can gain access; the wall shines in the sun like a star.

— *Gandharva Tantra*

THE JOURNEY IN THE MOUNTAIN EXPERIENCE

Two Tibetan men on a road. Photo by Michael Tobias

T.S. Blakeney
Kailas: A Holy Mountain

THE AESTHETIC APPRECIATION of mountains takes many forms. It may center on some particular aspect of artistic elegance, such as the beauty of an ice formation, or on the striking majesty of a mountain or a range (as, for all that they are hackneyed, the Matterhorn from the Riffelalp and Kangchenjunga from Sandakphu), or on the challenge to skill and daring that a great climbing problem may present. Related to such aesthetic evaluation, though differing in style, is the awe and reverence, perhaps not unmixed with superstition, that to which at varying times and places the mountains have given rise.

Sir Arnold Lunn observed that it is entirely fitting to worship among mountains, but that it is absurd to worship a mountain. Few would disagree, yet the distinction between a sense of awe in the presence of a mountain and reverence for the mountain itself has not always been easy to descry. There is nothing new about mountains being treated with reverence; the ancient Greeks took Olympus as the home of their deities, though Olympus is not a mountain of marked aesthetic significance. In the Far East, Fujiyama is a sacred place, though the delicate artistic sensibilities of the Japanese may account for their devotion to a mountain not strikingly dissimilar from other volcanoes.

The huge extent of the Himalayas naturally provides further examples of sacred mountains: Gauri Sankar has long been revered by Hindus, and one recalls that Charles Evans's party on Kangchenjunga in 1955 was required by the government of Sikkim not to tread upon the highest point. But Kailas, in Tibet, though separate from the Himalayas proper, has traditionally been regarded as the holiest of all mountains, being in its time sacred to both Hindus and Buddhists. Hindu mythology wove numerous tales about Kailas: it was the handle by which Brahma, the Creator, lowered the earth from heaven; it was the birthplace of Siva, central figure in the Hindu pantheon. Buddhist tradition has it that on his death Gautama retired to dwell on Kailas so as to remain in the world to be of aid to mankind.

Pedantically, one might argue that Adam's Peak, in Ceylon, was even more sacred than Kailas, for it was at one time revered by four religions, Christianity, Islam, Buddhism, and Hinduism. The great feature of Adam's Peak is the famous footmark (about five feet long) on the summit. It was Buddha's or Siva's according to Buddhist and Hindu tradition, while Islam, for its part, held that Adam did penance by standing on one foot for a hundred years after being driven from the Garden of Eden. Christianity, not to be outdone, claimed that the footprint was left by Saint Thomas, the Apostle to the East.[1] But to leave a footprint is hardly the equivalent to having one's abode in a place; nor can Adam's Peak be regarded as comparable in appearance with Kailas, which is also three times as high. In South India, near Tiruvannamalai, on the hill of Arunachalam, rests another claimed footprint of Śiva, and patriotic South Indians have maintained that their hill is a southern counterpart of Kailas itself.[2]

Ascents in the 1930s of these latter and relatively accessible peaks and a visit during war leave in the Swat-Kohistan region to 13,374-foot Musaka Musalla (revered by Muslims because Moses is expected to land there on his return to earth, its name means prayer mat of Moses) fired my enthusiasm for the more distant goal of Kailas. But I had to await the end of the war before I had the time and opportunity to fulfill this ambition. In the meantime, I was able to gain information about the mountain from accounts written by earlier visitors. Following the Younghusband expedition to Lhasa in 1904, Captain C. H. D. Ryder and others traveled westward along the line of the Tsangpo River till they reached the locality, a region visited earlier by William Moorcraft in 1812 and by Richard and Henry Strachey about 1846. Sherring and Longstaff came within sight of the mountain in 1905,[3] as did Howard Bury, a future Everest leader, in the same year.[4] Hugh Ruttledge and Colonel Roger Wilson made the *parikrama* or circuit of Kailas during a visit in 1926,[5] and Sir E. B. Wakefield was also in the area in 1929.[6] An unauthorized visit was made by Heim and Gansser in 1936,[7] and an earlier Hindu pilgrim, Bhagwan Shri Hamsa, wrote a curious book on his visit to Kailas in 1908, during which visit he claimed to have encountered a hermit of very rare character inhabiting a cave on the mountain.[8] Heinrich Harrer also passed through the region.[9]

But the most persistent contemporary devotee of Kailas was Swami Pranavananda, who embodied the results of his geographical researches which commenced in the 1930s in several books.[10] He paid no little attention to tracing the sources of the four rivers—Tsangpo, Indus, Karnali, and Sutlej—that rise more or less in the region of the two lakes of Manasarovar and Rakas which lie south of Mount Kailas.

The foregoing no means exhausts the names of Western visitors to Kailas:[11] one has but to think of "classic" explorers like Sven Hedin. In 1945 on my way up from Almora to the Tibetan frontier, I met at Sirkha two American missionaries—a married couple named Steiner—who had both been to Kailas and made the *parikrama,* the full circuit of the peak, a matter of two or three days, crossing over passes running up to 18,000 feet. Considered a solemn pilgrimage for most Eastern travelers, the *parikrama* attracted sadhus and many others, the feeling for the mountain being manifest throughout India. Even Pandit Nehru, a Hindu of modern, rationalistic tendencies, once declared that something urged him to make the journey, though I do not think he ever undertook it. In 1945 I was told that an Indian prince so geographically remote as the maharaja of Mysore had contributed the money needed to repair a long stretch of the track from India.

The contemporary Western mind may find it hard to appreciate "sacredness" in a mountain, but the *fact* of such reverence cannot be disregarded and must be accepted if one is to travel to such places. We may remember, too, that it is not so long since Alpine mountains like the Matterhorn were believed to be the habitat of demons; in 1880 Mummery, on the Furggen Ridge, found his guides distraught at the prospect of being attacked by satanic powers.

TIBET IS a tableland averaging about fifteen or sixteen thousand feet in height, though falling away considerably in the southeast. The altitude of the region of lakes Manasarovar and Rakas is approximately 15,000 feet and Kailas itself rises to 22,028 feet, while Gurla Mandhata, southward, is 25,385 feet. To the east lie lesser mountains which contain the sources of the Tsangpo River; north of Kailas are the derelict gold mines of Thok Jalung and beyond them, to the northwest, lies the little-known Aling Kangri range, with heights of 24,000 feet.

Disregarding undulations and great individual mountains and ranges such as those mentioned, the thousands of square miles of Tibetan land may be judged comparatively level; it is barren and austere, yet has a savage grandeur of its own. Between the lakes and Kailas is a flat expanse, stretching east and west, which provides the trade route that runs from Ladakh in Kashmir to Lhasa. A provincial capital and trade mart, Gartok, lies to the west of Kailas, while Taklakot, near the Indian frontier, is a permanent trading center. North of the mountain there is a stony valley (where wild yaks used to be found) and the source of the Indus river lies there. Some bird life and wild asses (kyangs) may be seen; but apart from numerous Buddhist monasteries and an occasional trading caravan, there is little life apart from nomads—who may well be bandits. In the summer months sheep manage to thrive and, before the Tibetan border was closed, would be driven over into India before the winter, to sell their wool. A familiar sight in autumn, the sheep flocks would cross the passes into India, each animal carrying panniers of salt mined in Tibet. Over all blows the unceasing and penetrating Tibetan wind.

There are various routes into Western Tibet from India; Major-General Richard Hilton enterprisingly travelled from Ladakh with a party of smugglers in 1935.[12] Other passes are the Shipki, from Simla, and the Mana, Unterdhura, and Lipu Lekh from Garhwal. Tuling, close to the Indian border, was the site of a Christian kingdom in the seventeenth century, and at the extreme northwest of Tibet, at Rudok, a Jesuit mission existed briefly in the early seventeenth century.[13]

In 1945, toward the end of the war in Burma, my chance came to make the journey I had had in mind for years. I went into hospital soon after the fall of Rangoon, and was released in July, having been ordered on sick leave to seek a cooler climate. And as my demobilization was shortly due, it seemed a good idea to spend (and if need be, overspend) this leave on a visit to Kailas, assuming permission might be obtained from the foreign department of the government of India. I wished to do the thing properly and make the *parikrama*, but owing to the depredations of bandits in the area (control having presumably slackened during the war) I had to promise not to do so, and had furthermore to enter and leave by the same route. I wanted to enter by the Lipu Lekh pass and leave by the Shipki, but this was forbidden, so it became a matter of going in and out by the Lipu Lekh, which reaches about 16,750 feet.

I left my army base in East Bengal on August 1 and reached Kathgodam by the evening of the fifth, next day going by bus to Almora, where I had already arranged with the deputy commissioner to hire porters and to get my Inner Line permit for travel to Tibet. I had tents, but was able to book places in the forest-department bungalows along the road, as well as to make use of the Dak bungalows. The route lay to the west of the Kali River, the boundary with Nepal: I left Almora with a cook and twelve porters on August 10 and reached Garbyang—some 140 miles away—on August 25. Slow going, but the monsoon rains were still on, roads had been washed away in places, and there was a great deal of ascent and descent—Garbyang, at about 10,300 feet, being less than 5,000 feet higher than Almora. I was also rather lame from wartime troubles and did not want to walk too hard at first; in any case, the village or bungalow stops were about ten miles apart and the porters were disposed to regard these as sufficient daily stages—which, in pouring rain, is not unreasonable. On August 16 a message from Almora reached me that the Japanese war was over; we took a day off on the seventeenth, after re-sorting supplies, leaving some to be picked up on our return. At Balwakote, on the nineteenth, we joined a local celebration over the end of the war. At Sirkha, on the twenty-second, I stopped to pay a call on the Steiners, the missionaries who had been to Kailas; they were anxious about a South Indian Christian who was due back from a visit to the mountain, and I promised to look out for him. The day before we had met a Hindu sadhu from Kashmir, en route to Kailas; he had been eight months on the road, coming via Gangotri.

After leaving the Steiners we met an Indian and his wife from Baroda, coming down from Kailas and traveling in great style in sedan chairs carried by a host of porters. We also met the Indian Christian (named Edwards) on the twenty-fourth; he told us he had left South India eleven years before, traveling entirely on foot, and of necessity having to spend long periods working to earn a little money to carry him farther, since he could not rely wholly on begging. We fed him and sent him down with a note to the Steiners; he said he had had his only blanket stolen in Tibet by bandits. And some Hindu ascetics we encountered also warned us that there were a number of lawless parties about; fortunately, the sadhus could hardly be looted, as they appeared to possess nothing but a loin cloth, a cotton sheet, and a begging bowl, minimum equipment for Tibet.

Garbyang was the last place of importance before crossing the pass into Tibet; the Potwari was very obliging, the Dak bungalow a good one, and we had left the worst of the weather behind. Leaving on the twenty-seventh, we took two days to cross the pass and descend into Taklakot, the Tibetan trading center above which towers Similing Monastery. I had introductions to two leading Indian merchants at Taklakot.

Courtesy required one to pay one's respects to the Dzongpen, or local governor; by custom some sort of gift should be made (and is repaid). I had rather little to give; apart from a token scarf—almost any piece of linen will do—I had some sugar to present, having an excess over our needs. In return we received a present of spaghetti, the loan of a rifle (of a sort I would have hesitated to fire), and were entertained at a gin party. Neat gin at about 13,000 feet is heady stuff: my cook came as an interpreter, though being a Muslim he should not, strictly, have taken alcohol. However, he was not going to be left out of the party, and he was in sad form the following morning (I felt rather unwell myself.)

I paid a visit to the abbot of Similing Monastery, to obtain a blessing for the trip. This I did alone, as my porters seemed content to receive it vicariously: in any case, I suspect they had other assignments in the village. My cook came to help interpret, but naturally did not enter to receive the blessing himself, which consisted of being touched on the head with a prayer wheel. (Later, on my return from Kailas, I paid another visit to the monastery, at a time when a visiting lama from Lhasa—a sort of apostolic delegate, I gathered—was present. I attempted a photograph of the party, in their splendid robes, but unfortunately it was spoiled by a leak in the camera. Through an interpreter I told them that the war was over; they seemed to understand that a war had been on, but little else, and my incompetent efforts at explaining how the atomic bomb had hastened matters were not very successful. They asked me if we had [as they had] magic words that could divert bombs and shells from hitting one; here I had to admit that the West lagged behind Tibetan technology.)

An interpreter had come from Garbyang and he took charge of the Dzongpen's gun. Accompanying me was a lama-policeman, also armed, with a gun that required a ramrod; it had an inordinately long barrel, with ibex horns attached to act as a rest when firing. I saw it used only once on our trip, but always viewed it with some trepidation. We had been told, as the sadhus had, that it was a bad year for bandits, one ambitious party having captured the entire mule train, destined for the Gartok market, of stores from India. Various smaller parties were said to be about, one especially dreaded band rumored to be captained by a woman.

A number of my porters wanted to return to India, so I hired a driver with two yaks and a couple of donkeys in their place, and we left Taklakot on September 1 to cross a low pass, the Taluding, leaving the great mountain mass of Gurla Mandhata on our right. On the third day out we reached the lakes and followed the eastern shore of Rakas Tal (a hogback ridge divides it from Manasarovar), where we camped. The beautiful bright blue water of these lakes made a splendid contrast to the parched setting of the surrounding land; in the distance Kailas had come into sight, to be greeted with cries of adoration from the men. Fuel was obtainable very often from a bush that grew in this region and contained a good deal of oil, making its branches, even when freshly cut, quite flammable. Otherwise, as I had done a year before when traveling up the Lhasa road, we used dried yak dung, which was plentiful.

Reaching the northeast corner of Lake Rakas, we crossed the narrow stream, the Ganga Chhu, that drains surplus water into the lake from Manasarovar; the latter is a much larger lake and more revered. A number of monasteries dot its shores, and whereas in Buddhist thought the *parikrama* of Kailas cancels one's past sins, to bathe in Manas is said to cancel sins both past and future. However, Tibetans do not seem much given to bathing. For my part I drank some of the water of Manas and washed my face and hands in it, but in the already chilly autumn weather felt disinclined to take a swim. I therefore failed to get all the benefits I might have obtained, and since the government of India had forbade my making the circuit of Kailas, must reckon myself at best a sort of spiritual, failed-B.A.

Kailas itself was now more discernible; at that distance its snowy, cone-shaped southern face, rising abruptly out of very steep rock, resembled somewhat Tenniel's picture of Humpty Dumpty on his wall. I called in at a monastery near the Ganga Chhu; the monks were friendly and warned us of a party of bandits thought to be about in the stretch of country lying ahead. The monks seemed to be in considerable awe of the woman leader, about whom we had already been warned; she was said to have a virulent tongue.

Our next objective was Barkha, a staging post on the Ladakh-Lhasa road. The ground was covered very often in shallow water from melted snow, for there was little runoff in such flat country. At one place we spotted a kyang, and my cook tried his hand at shooting a duck, but without success. We also met a small caravan en route to Lhasa, a Ladakhi trader with his two small sons whom he was taking there to go to school. He dealt in cloth (he had several ponies carrying immense bundles) and traded black jade to Ladakh; the boys, I understood, were destined to remain at school about seven years and their father would see them on such annual or biannual visits as he paid to Lhasa. This was devotion to study indeed, but they appeared to be very cheerful; I gave the boys a rupee or two for pocket money, and took a photograph.

(Very different was a caravan we met thereabouts on our return journey; this was a grandiose affair, with armed outriders and people wearing armor and fantastic clothing—Marco Polo, one felt, might have seen just such a group. Meeting them put one in mind of accounts one has read of trading ventures in the Middle Ages, to the Levant or farther East—Constantinople, Aleppo, Damascus. And indeed in Tibet one felt one was back in the mentality of those times.)

From Barkha a day's journeying brought us on September 6 to

Darchen, at the southern foot of Kailas. The village, I gathered, was a Bhutanese enclave, and I had a friendly welcome from the head man, a lama, who invited me to visit him later in the year, when he moved to less rigid quarters at Khojanath, on the Nepal border. Alas, that I could not do.

On September 7, a splendid day; we went up to inspect the southern face of Kailas. We passed another monastery, Genta Gompa, on our way to a high ridge behind it from which we could look straight at Kailas, and down on a row of chortens known as Serdung Choksum. The ridge we were on appeared to merge into the snows of the southeast ridge of Kailas and would seem to offer an approach route to the mountain proper. With a camp on the southeast ridge, it would not be difficult to reach the summit, for the ridge was only steep in its upper part. I had no ice axe, no nailed boots or anything suitable to make the attempt: our highest point may have been 19,000 feet, but we had had no real climbing anywhere.

Looking southward over the route we had traveled was memorable. The brilliant blue of the lakes contrasted vividly with the bleak, austere landscape stretching for hundreds of square miles on either side, with the massif of Gurla Mandhata towering immediately behind; serving as a drop screen, we could view a vast extent of the Zaskar-Himalayan mountains— from Kamet and others in the west to (I presumed) Dhaulagiri and the Nepalese giants in the east.

The next day, the eighth of September, I left our camp with light loads, to go around by the west flank of the mountain to the Diruphuk Gompa on the north. Though forbidden to make the full *parikrama*, I felt it would not be stretching my permit too greatly to see the north face of Kailas, which, from Ruttledge's photograph and others, I knew to be striking. I salved my conscience regarding my promise to the Indian government by returning to my base camp from Diruphuk by the same route, though my policeman-lama asked permission (which of course I gave) to complete the circuit and so gain the blessings to be derived.

Leaving the cook, who was feeling unwell, at the Darchen base, the policeman and I had no problems in reaching the Diruphuk Gompa, but the weather broke giving us sleet and snow on the way. The steep black rocky northern face of Kailas proved fitfully visible and very impressive. After a noisy night in a crowded caravanserai, we left early the next morning to visit the valley running up to the north face; but snowfall and cloud prevented us from reaching the true foot of the mountain. The policeman-lama then left me, indicating that traveling alone and fast (though he begged me to accompany him), he reckoned to do the two-day trip over the 18,000-foot pass and by the Zunthulphuk Gompa in one long day—as indeed he did. That same evening I went out from my base camp, eastward along the path to the last-named Gompa, and met him coming down. On our return by the road from the Diruphuk to Darchen we passed a *shapje*, or holy footprint, of some saint.

I found my cook suffering from a touch of fever. Perhaps the height affected him somewhat, for he was not a young man; and on our way back to Garbyang, I put him on a yak that was carrying stores, and then on a pony to take him over the Lupu Lekh Pass.

In due course we came upon the tents (or *yurts*) of a group of nomads, whom the policeman said were the bandits of whom we had been warned. They all came out to look at us, and I scanned them with interest searching for the lady with the long tongue. I concluded that she was the one who stood at the door of the largest tent, with her arms folded and a lowering look about her (as much as to say, "We don't want to fight, but by jingo if we do . . .") seeming to mark her out as a person to treat with respect. My policeman, however, was made of sterner stuff than I; he harangued the party (his gestures were amply eloquent, even without an interpreter of his words), telling them that I was an army officer, had brought up a machine gun, and at the slightest sign of trouble would open fire and mow down men, women, and children alike. It was hardly my idea of the honeyed word, but it worked excellently, thanks to the small boys present, who obviously thought it one of the funniest things they'd ever heard. They clasped their sides and stamped about, shouting with laughter, and for the life of me, I could not help bursting out in laughter too; after that, all went well—in any case, our little caravan was clearly not worth looting. The innate hospitality of the Tibetans asserted itself, tea was produced, and I gave them some of my surplus sugar. Sugar was in short supply in Tibet, they managed without it. But it was acceptable, and mothers and babies soon came along for handouts. Tibetan tea is not everybody's choice and I cannot say I ever managed to like it. When yak butter and salt or soda is mixed in, it is very unlike tea as we know it; I found it best to regard it as a sort of soup. But good relations were established with the nomads, though I fancied the boys were perhaps a little disappointed at no machine gun being produced. I daresay one might spare an uncle or two for the pleasure of seeing a machine gun in action.

I looked in at the Chhu Gompa on the way back; the people were as friendly as before and I found a hot spring nearby, but though gas was escaping I failed to make it light. There were some quite heavy falls of snow higher up, but not too much with us. On September 12 we camped at the southwest corner of Lake Manas, having followed its western shore. I then walked up to Thugolho Gompa on the southern shore because I had been told at the Chhu Gompa that Swami Pranavananda was staying there. The swami, as already mentioned, was an authority on the whole district, and we had a very pleasant talk. He agreed that for an ascent of Kailas the east ridge seemed the most likely line of approach and he did not think that the local people would object to the mountain being climbed, although there had been objections made when someone wanted to boat on Lake Manas. He himself had made no attempt to climb Kailas, though he had traveled up the northern valley (which I had only partially entered) in order to lay his hand on the mountain.

His opinion on climbing the peak agreed with what my policeman had said when we were inspecting the mountain at close range from the south. When I asked him if he thought it would offend religious opinion to go to the top, he said no; and when I said that perhaps the monks might object to the home of Buddha being trodden upon, he replied seriously that no harm would result, but—"of course you cannot see Him."

The remainder of my journey back to India calls for little record. It was interesting to note how different were the reactions of villagers on the way down since they had dismissed my chances of ever getting to Kailas. Now (my cook must have kept silent about my incomplete circuit of the mountain) I was treated with something like reverence; I did not need a good deal of my rations, being treated to a number of meals in the villages. During one day we trespassed into Nepal, traveling down the other side of the Kali river and crossing back at nightfall into India. This was just for the satisfaction of entering Nepal; it is difficult today, when visitors and tourists abound in that country, to realize that as late as the 1940s one could almost dine out on the strength of having set foot in Nepal.

I got back to Almora on October 4, to find I was already late for demobilization from the Indian army; so I had to wind up the expedition and left for Ferozepur on the ninth. I had entertained hopes that, the ice having been broken with the foreign department of the government of India, I might another year make further and more extensive explorations into this region of western Tibet: visits to the gold mines of Thok Jalung, to the Aling Kangri range, and to Rudok, the remote trade mart at the extreme northwest of Tibet. Such lavish ideas, however, were cast into oblivion by the Chinese invasion of Tibet. And, in fact, I was never to see the Himalayas again.

LOOKING BACK TODAY to these events of three decades past, one can think of things one wishes one had done, and at the same time be glad that one seized some of the opportunities one did have. In 1944 I think I might have obtained leave from the British agent, Sir Basil Gould, to visit Lhasa, only a week or so's journey from Phari Dzong, the limit of my trip that year; and now I dearly wish I had. But to give myself a further two or three weeks' leave from the Fourteenth Army, when the Burma campaign had still a year to run, would surely have been unwarrantable. In 1945 I was handicapped by a late start, August, and I had of course no seasonable clothes; jungle battle dress was to prove chilly covering in the winds and storms of Tibet. It would certainly have been practicable, as my lama proposed, to complete the *parikrama*, but though it could not be known till much later, the "grapevine" in India might have carried the news and I would have been faced with the disagreeable task of attempting to excuse the wanton breaking of the undertaking on which my permit to travel had been based. Trouble had, I think, arisen over Heim and Gansser's visit in the 1930s, and something of the same had happened after the 1924 Everest expedition, when a breach of regulations by one or two expedition members not only black-marked one of them with the authorities, but led to a ban on any Everest parties for nine years.

The changes that followed Independence in India in 1947, and the Chinese occupation of Tibet a few years later, would have made further travels difficult to carry out. Although for a while Indians were permitted to visit Kailas, as Mr. Gurdial Singh found in 1954,[14] the agreement with China soon broke down. One must be glad to have caught a glimpse of a Tibet that has probably now largely disappeared.[15] That it was a backward country in many ways is no doubt true, yet it was making progress of a sort, in its own time and in its own way. The blessings of Western civilization when transported into widely different settings have not always been very obvious, and we have yet to find out whether modern Tibet is a real improvement on the old. Tibetans of bygone times managed to survive in a harsh setting and an exacting climate, by finding a working balance between human requirements and nature. Tibet's curious, theocentric civilization had doubtless become arrested (like others named in Toynbee's *Study of History*), cut off as it was from so much outside influence, and tending, like all theocracies, to become petrified. Yet travelers and students have found in the people a basic charity, a likableness, a cheerfulness that inclined me at any rate to think of them as fundamentally a happy people, in contrast to the people of India who I could not think of as happy.[16] People as varied as Sir Charles Bell, Basil Gould, Hugh Richardson, George Patterson, and Heinrich Harrer have warmed to the Tibetans in their homes. Although, like other races, they had their bad points, in at least one respect they were superior to almost all other races; they did not covet other people's lands, they only asked to be left alone. And when they were overrun, the world did not lift a finger to help them.

Despite the severities of their climate, they appeared as healthy as they were hardy; a doctor who was on one of the early Everest expeditions told me that, venereal diseases apart, the main disability he found was a tendency to pyorrhoea, due to deficiencies in diet. Anyone crossing over from India into Tibet would be struck by the change in appearance of the people, not least of all the children: in place of thin and weakened bodies one found rosy cheeks and robust appearance; and the womenfolk were far from being the downtrodden result of the caste system found across the frontier.

By our standards they were certainly unbathed, but it is to be kept in mind that cold heavily reduces perspiration and the altitude ensures the rapid evaporation of sweat. Bathing is therefore less of a necessity than in warmer climates; Dervla Murphy was struck by the fear of water among Tibetan refugee children that she saw in Indian camps, for it was something not normally much in use.[17] On the other hand, dehydration at their altitudes was general, hence the large intake of liquid in the form of tea. In many respects their diet was well balanced: the tea gave them liquid and warmth; the yak butter provided fat that helped retain the warmth; the *tsampa* (a lightly roasted flour) that they might mix in with the tea provided the four essential vitamins. The better-off people might eat meat; although as Buddhists they were forbidden to take life, they were not so foolish as to waste the carcass of a yak or a sheep, the meat of either being welcome. My party bought two or three sheep to provide meat for the porters and myself; the Garhwalis had no objection to slaughtering sheep, and as for a yak, nothing was wasted—flesh, hair, tail, horns, and so forth, all found a use.

The land had produced the people and it was a hard, exacting land. "Expansiveness" seems to be the word that most naturally comes to mind as descriptive of it. Just as nature on the grand scale, though it be only a vast expanse of ocean, or a limitless spread of desert, is impressive, so, too, is the landscape of Tibet, carrying with it (at least in the regions I have visited) the additional dimension of height in the great mountains. It is not difficult to understand how a traveler like Sir Francis Younghusband, after his great journey from China to the Karakoram and beyond, was never quite the same man again. As a result of the impressions burnt into his mind during the days and nights spent in the wastes of the Gobi Desert and elsewhere, he was to become something of a religious mystic. Sheer scale provides us with an aesthetic pleasure that mountaineers are particularly able to appreciate; it is something more than just elegance or artistry. The traveler in Tibet is conscious of this sense, and the presence of a significant mountain like Kailas tends only to accentuate the emotion. Those of us who have been able to look upon the great central Asian plains of which Tibet is so important a part are fortunate indeed.

Over: Yuan Chiang, *Carts on a Winding Mountain Road* (1694). Courtesy of the Nelson Fund, William Rockhill Nelson Gallery of Art, Atkins Museum of Fine Arts, Kansas City, Mo.

William M. Bueler
Hsu Hsia-k'o: Middle Kingdom Mountaineer

I N THE LITERATURE of traditional China one rarely encounters a scholar or official who did not at some time in his life withdraw from wordly affairs to find repose in the mountains—or at least dream of doing so. Yet among all the glowing passages about mountain scenery there are very few which reflect any of the joys of climbing or of genuine exploration; Chinese travelers—at least those capable of recording their impressions—were, in truth, little inclined to leave the established trails. Hsu Hsia-k'o, who lived from 1586 to 1641, was an exception.

Hsu occupies a unique place in the history of Chinese mountain exploration, and he can with justification be called the first true mountaineer of the Middle Kingdom. He began his travels in 1607, and in the next twenty-nine years visited almost all of the important mountains of eastern China—the relatively low but often precipitous peaks which really do resemble those depicted in traditional landscape painting. Perhaps no other traveler ever knew these mountains better or loved them more, but his mind was filled with visions of greater mountains rumored in the west, and it was his lifelong amibtion to make their acquaintance. Finally in 1636, at the age of fifty, Hsu began a four-year journey to those mountains, during which he wrote the extensive, detailed diary which was to give him a place among the handful of most important explorers in Chinese history.

In western Yunnan Province Hsu explored the upper Yangtze, Salween, and Mekong rivers, which flow through some of the deepest gorges and wildest country on earth, and his diary contained the best information on this region available until this century. He is credited with several geographic discoveries, the most important perhaps being the fact that the Chin Sha River is the true source of the Yangtze.

To fully appreciate the accuracy of Hsu's descriptions of routes and topographic features would require a familiarity with the vagueness and flowery language that pervades most classical Chinese descriptions of nature. Geographers of this century have had little difficulty in retracing Hsu's routes on the ground. Hsu compiled a lexicon of topographic terms which made clear distinctions between peaks, ranges, cliffs, ridges, plateaus, pinnacles, passes, gorges, and valleys—in sharp contrast to the way in which most Chinese writers played with such terms more for euphonic effect than for geographic precision.

But Hsu Hsia-k'o was not only a geographer and explorer; he was also a climber. He did not of course make any ascents of the great snow-capped peaks of western China, but it is clear from his writings that he reached hundreds of lesser summits, that he reveled in rough travel well off the beaten path, and that he did not shy away from an occasional cliff problem. Illustrative of the kind of enthusiastic detail that fills his diaries is this passage describing his search for a small pond called Wild Goose Lake, which Hsu had been told was located near the summit of a high, rocky ridge of the Yen-tang Mountains in Chekiang Province. He and two servants were following the ridge, Hsu wrote, when,

> The ridge became increasingly narrow, and we seemed to be walking on a knife edge squeezed up from the earth. Blades of rock rose in angry forms all along the crest, and we seemed to thread our way through a maze of knives and swords of rock.
>
> Up and down we went, over three distinct spiny summits, along this crest with barely room to walk. How could a lake be up here? Suddenly we came to where the mountain seemed to have been split asunder. We had been frightened by the sharpness of the knife edge, but now there was no edge at all! We stood perplexed above the drop-off, reluctant to return by the route we had come.
>
> Under the cliff, to the south, we saw some "steps." The two servants removed their leggings made of strips of cloth and, after tying the four of them together, we dropped our cloth-rope over the precipice. One servant went down first, then I followed, hoping to find a continuation of the route.
>
> At the bottom of the cloth-rope there was a ledge with barely enough room to stand. Below our feet was a drop of a hundred *chang*. We thought to return to the top of the drop-off, but the rock overhung more than three *chang* and it was impossible to fly back up.... After several attempts we succeeded in looping the cloth-rope securely, and using all our strength, pulled ourselves back up. We thereby regained the ridge crest and extricated ourselves from the dangerous impasse.
>
> When we returned to the Monastery of Repose in the Clouds, the sun was setting in the west. The clothes and shoes of master and servants were in shreds.

Hsu never found the lake on that visit, but some years later he returned and reached it from another direction.

That Hsu traveled with servants is not surprising; he was a man of means. But on his great western trek his servant deserted him and he had to complete the journey alone. He was repeatedly robbed and was saved only by the generosity of local officials he encountered. In one case he is said to have written a careful topographic description of the land of a tribal chieftain in order to earn the funds to continue.

Once during his western venture Hsu spotted an intriguing cavelike opening high on the side of a precipitous peak. His description of his efforts to reach it provides a rare instance in Chinese literature of what might be termed incipient rock climbing:

> I gazed up at the high peak before us and was struck by its unusual form. I walked about its base and it seemed to have step-like cliffs on all sides. I went eastward then turned north; suddenly I spotted high up among the cliffs a cave that opened toward the east. I wanted to climb up to it but saw no route. I suppose I should have given up the idea, but that I couldn't do either.
>
> So I told the servant to wait with the luggage by the side of the path, and started the climb. After half a *li* the ground became too steep for secure footing, so I grasped some roots to pull myself up, but soon the roots proved inadequate. Just then I reached some rock which seemed firm but unfortunately was not; when I stepped on a rock it would crumble and when I grasped one it would break off. Only occasionally was the rock firm enough for me to plant my feet and hook my fingers. I was plastered to the rock like a bulletin affixed to a wall. I couldn't go up and I couldn't go down. Never in my life had I been in a more perilous spot. . . .
>
> Finally I managed to place all four limbs on firm rock. Then I extended one arm out over space to reach the next hold, then moved a foot. When these were steady, I moved the other hand and foot. Fortunately the rock now held. The strength was gone from my arms and legs and I felt as if I was about to fall; but somehow I managed to get up.

From such passages as this we can see that Hsu felt the peculiar fascination for exposed and precarious places that moves the climber of today.

Clearly the guiding force in Hsu's life was, as the editor of a 1928 edition of his diaries said, his "untiring intellectual curiosity and his passionate love of mountain scenery." That mountains filled his thoughts even when he was at home between journeys is indicated by the unusual names he gave his sons: Ch'i, Hsien, and Kou. In each case, in the Chinese ideographs, the left component is *shan* (山), which means "mountain."

Makalu. Photo by Matija Maležič

Jeffery Long
Makalu

T HE LAST OF THE CLIMBERS had come down for the last time. The
mountain was abandoned. There could be no going back. A little like
exile, a touch of hate and shame, a touch of relief, too, that we'd survived.
They began to drink. Oblivious to the cold, they sat on the frozen earth,
warmed by their internecine heat. By the time I arrived they were finished.

Fritz was slamming the empty bottle's throat onto a tent stake. Someone lolled against his leg. Elsewhere people crouched or clutched their
knees.

Rocking in the midst of others was Matija, swabbing his tears, elo-
quently demanding, "Four men, only four men in the world who have
harmony . . . no, just two men, we should climb this."

To his left Rodney was grinning; the whiskey, the altitude, a very
wide grin. He grabbed Matija's hand with fraternal concern and assured
everyone we'd fought the good fight, it was done now and we could forget
about it.

Fritz sullenly rammed the bottle's throat. Arnold stood behind the
group, watching their celebration as he puffed on his pipe with angry
bursts. He said nothing, limped away disgusted.

Charlie, whose medicine that whiskey had been, began to assert certain statistical facts in an effort to justify our retreat, seeming to say there'd
never been much of a chance anyway.

Matija thrashed about and sat upright. He pulled his hand from Rodney's, and ominously told the doctor to kick him in the mouth for speaking so, for he'd promised himself he wouldn't say a word about the expedition. But damn those statistics and numbers, it takes more, it takes heart
and soul to climb such a mountain as this. This was Matija's mountain,
he'd failed on its face twice now, a second exile.

On and on they wheeled about, huge men draped with parkas, sitting
in their circle as the colder night came on, with puffs of frost locating each
volume of words. A star came out. Matija rose up and wove in place, untouchable, sobbing. Down the valley and above us, the mountain shone
massively in the moonlight.

It was dinnertime. There would be no radio call this night. No one
to call, none of us left on the mountain. It was done, over. The softly
glowing moon began to illuminate the mountain. Avalanches rumbled
into the quiet night.

Not to forgive, not to forget, not to make ourselves common. Matija
was heartsick. Already the mountain was fading. Things were being for-

given and amnesia was closing. The feuds and hatreds of the mountain-side were gently dispersing.

The moon drifted higher. In his Yugoslav-English, Matija raved softly, tottering like a mooncalf. His accent and peculiar linguistic jerks formed a music of their own. Sobering climbers wandered away from him gradually. Matija's threnody was touching but useless. And it was dinnertime.

In the moonlight he became alone, gesturing and compelling himself and a ghostly few others back up to the higher camps for another try. At last he was led to a fire where the Sherpas tended him. He sat staring at the fire with rheumy eyes, mumbling. Not long after he passed out.

The Trek

FOR THREE DAYS we had camped on the grassy airstrip at Tumling-tar. During the day there were flies and the startled clucking of hens being mounted. At night jackals yapped and belched. The police-housing barracks, mud and stick affairs, flanked our camp to the south. Throughout the day their women passed in and out, largely ignoring us as they cleaned pots and tended children. One of them had huge breasts, one several pounds heavier than the other and dangling inches lower; both breasts hung below her blouse. As I recall it she had only one eye or maybe it was just her teeth that were a chaos.

One of the locals entered our camp. He began to tinker with equipment. After authoritatively peering through the wrong end of our telescope, he accidentally upended its tripod. Since the scope was down now anyway, he tried to pull off the lens. This went on for a while. His hoodlum insolence was more trying than his clumsy curiosity. At last Nima Sherpa told him to leave. A crowd developed, fast words, shoving. Nima pulled a knife. Three of the locals brandished logs. It was a macho charade, no blood, no blows. The fight was dispersed.

Next morning a small squad of police arrived to take Nima away. Two of yesterday's stick-wielding locals were policemen. Nima refused to go, certain they would beat him in the jungle. We threatened to inform our friend King Birendra of this outrage. The bluff worked. Much later the assistant police inspector rode a horse down from the headquarters at Khandbari. He wore the costume of a military leader: sunglasses, a swagger stick, a holstered pistol. Always a step behind him was a barefoot soldier with what was possibly the district's only carbine, an ancient giant.

Charlie had earlier treated the assistant inspector with placebos for his hypochondria. Smiling, apologizing, poking around our campsite, the assistant inspector casually dismissed the charges against Nima.

I SETTLED INTO the loft of an empty house. There was fading linear script, muted Sanskrit, on the wooden slats of the wall. I discovered this as I socketed my candle in its wax and leaned the flame close to the structure.

Drunk. Stumbled to the outskirts of the village, rebounding from voices and flashlight beams, bounced to the ground. Lay still on a hillock.

Somewhere the nasal singsong of All-India radio. It died away. In the silence another sound appeared. A buzzing drone. It was sporadic at first, but steadily grew more frequent. Where? I sat up, trained my ears in different directions, then gave up, couldn't say. Lay back. The drone continued, humming. It could have been chanting in someone's dark house, or a sick animal groaning, or the buzz of a nocturnal airplane, maybe far away music or insects. I remained attentive. Not long after, the sound was punctuated by a squeal and a grunt: some farmer balling his woman.

SMALL GRAY PUPPIES, ribs like sticks, stood death-still, almost transparent, vulnerable to small winds and children's screams. When they've finished living they are left in the ditches and gutters. I've seen children with sticks run alongside a dying dog, teasing a piece of gut that swung from its belly, flicking it with long twigs, the dog in a mad horror to escape. At last it lay down in a posture of submission. The children converged.

A NUMBER OF our porters were women. They sweated and strained under big loads all day long, padding barefoot behind other bare feet. After setting down their loads, the women and girls would preen, adjusting skirts and belts, tucking strands of hair back into coiled braids.

One of the women was truly beautiful. Her features were clean and contained whatever proportion it is that imparts beauty. But she was self-consciously marred, imperfect. Her hands and feet boiled over with heavy flowers of wart tissue. It shamed her. Even her perfect face was spoiled by that. She would sit apart, patting and rubbing her warted hands on her warted feet.

WE PASSED THROUGH Jile where it was rumored the citizens would kill lowland folk, split them open for meat, then throw their bones into outhouses. It was Jile too where a farmer gathered his friends and neighbors one night and caught two lower-caste men between his daughters' legs. One of the men jumped out the window and escaped. The group surrounded the other and with their long heavy knives played with him, nicking and slashing his body. A peace-corps volunteer told me he saw the man next morning when they carried him out. The face was gray. The daughters were beaten.

ON THE ARUN RIVER a bloated thing rode the swells of water, barely visible for its muddy color, but explicit in its surrender to the lazy motion of the flooded river. This brought to mind old stories I'd read: stillborn children and murderers, the unblessed dead that is, are tossed into the rivers to go unburied, unburned. Their bodies never settle, their bones float detached from the earth to far away.

IT TOOK MORE than half a month to trek from India's border northward to Tibet's. We came to identify certain places with particular buildings or insects. We all remember the schoolhouse outside Dhankutta; at Shershon, the yak herder's hut. Near Chainpur there were swarms of dragonflies hovering like tiny helicopters. At Leghua Gunth the fireflies were so thick and so bright they inhabited their own illicit constellations. Hururu and Nun Ridge came to be known as Leech Ridge, and Utishecame as Leech City.

Below Jile I encountered my first leech. At first I was horrified, later just annoyed. They made my clothes bloody and my feet ache; their bites ulcerated and wept for days. The locals mix a leaf, or perhaps hashish as they claimed, with a pinch of salt. They wrap this mixture into a ball of cloth and attach the ball to the end of a stick. A slight tap with the ball of moist cloth and the leech contorts in agony.

THE NIGHTS were hot and often beautiful but monstrous sounds threaded the air. The monastic murals of Buddhist hell . . . I'd wake to the noise made by gangs of hogs rutting and biting each other, grunting ferociously, trampling their piglets. And dog packs cannibalizing, tubercular coughs, water splashing in hard jerks onto cobblestones. That or some night thing's nausea, vomiting bowels amplified by some far wall . . . formulating words, trying to bracket and drop it all into oblivion, to sleep.

Makalu nights were different. The smooth rumble of avalanches. That was all. The glide of stars. Silent clouds. No other sounds.

The Mountain

AT TIMES it was a stark and miserable idyll, but nonetheless an idyll. An easy existence. We suffered, but our pains were immediate and touchable, and not so terrible at all. No one was killed. No one was mangled or deformed by the mountain. Moreover we had the luxury of a concrete purpose, the summit.

The gigantic world societies dimmed and fell away. We were left to fashion for ourselves a solitary home on the strata of earlier myths. Makalu tempted thoughts of an abandoned civilization: it had ruins and heritage, a grave marker, legends, all the trappings of a place once in time . . . now, deserted, a catch for wind and prayer flags. We calmly inhabited it. We made our own laws. We came to understand who was friend or just another climber. We became acquainted with the mountain. We shared, and that alone simplified our lives for a little while.

We'd come to climb Makalu. Assured by Fritz that its south face was the most sought after route in the world, our attempt was made somewhat holy and blessed with relevance. Some of us went up and lived on the mountain, climbed, ate, slept, laid about. Memories faltered, dreams collapsed. Slowly the mountain reduced us to filaments of itself. After a little while, having sucked at the thin air too long, we tired and became stupid, drifted down to Base Camp, exhausted. Others replaced us. Then we replaced them.

WE LAPSED INTO a pack of ugly men. Desiccated hands, hoary masks for faces. Our cheeks scabbed and our lips swelled. Scars purpled in the intense sun. Solar lepers. We haggled. We bellowed, prattled, pronounced, sometimes pondered by ourselves, or again giggled collectively at tribal jokes.

For months we rose at dawn, each day hoping to penetrate the rhythm of possibility, slipping all the matrices of our social existence toward that one point, the summit.

We clustered upon the steeps of Makalu. Our words were our gift to ourselves. Given time and children our cluster would have deviated into a secret ancestry, and our words into a lost and changing literature. We came from somewhere.

Matija showed me a flat Russian-made piton which had been with him to the highest point men have yet reached on the face. He had brought it down two years before when he was forced to retreat from the wall. He carried the piton in his pocket. "It is my talisman," he explained.

WALKING ALONG the flat and sandy path I saw an occasional rusted can. Jepa unearthed an old metal connector for a French oxygen system. Our little party advanced along the suggestion of a trail used by only a few men before our time, toward a semifabulous island camp pieced with old and odd remains. We passed a view of Everest hunched at the tip of the valley. Crossing a river we touched upon our mountain.

Seven hours later I reached the site for Camp I, a plateau at 19,000 feet. A stone ring had been piled as a fence against the west wind. Here and there were flat areas tiled with stone for tents; others had slept here. I found an old tube of Austrian shaving cream, and a weathered bamboo wand once used to mark crevasses. Over the east edge was a garbage dump with cans and a few scraps of cloth. That was all that remained of earlier expeditions.

Four of us huddled at the porch of Fritz's tent, gobbling small portions of lukewarm stroganoff. It was snowing thick sloppy flakes. My seat was wet, my parka was half soaked. I had roundworm cramps. There was no sugar for the tea. I felt my discomforts and wanted to crawl into a tent and be warm.

FOR THE FIRST TIME we passed through them; glassy undulations, frozen, broken, brittle columns shattered into anomie. All around us were snowy pods growing shapelessly on top of themselves, plates and shields of hot ice, avalanche scars. We kickstepped our way up a ridge of snow to drop suddenly into a scanty bowl that overlooked the Barun Valley. There Matija found, tucked within a cave of ice, the impacted remains of his old Camp II.

Like a ghost it surfaced to welcome him back. The Austrians had apparently bypassed the Yugoslav site during their attempt last spring, for the camp was intact and unruined. We sat in the snow panting for air, blankly staring at the forms that stuck out from the solid ice. There was the silhouette of an erect tent locked inside.

Matija began to exhume the camp faithfully. Twenty-one thousand feet. With a weary exuberance he chipped and chopped free a shovel, a pot, then exposed the skin of two weather-beaten tents and several sleeping pads. On the second day he made his crowning excavation: six candles and two butane gas stoves. He carefully revived one of the stoves and held a match to its burner head. Without the slightest falter of age it lit. We cooked a pot of celebration tea over its flame.

The ice cave still required work. In the coming days, while Matija and Fritz climbed and fixed ropes toward Camp III, Arnold and I dug deeper. Icicles hung like bars throughout, and the entire serac had filled its pockets with solid ice. The two tents were like iron, like mummies which are mineralized inside and out with amber perfumes. We ripped and tore at the fabric, then chopped out the frozen viscera. The scraps were committed to a garbage crevasse.

Finally the cave was deep enough to set up our tent. We used the Yugoslav sleeping pads to pave the cave floor, and tied the interior strings of our tent to cords and shreds that hung out of the ice.

A REST DAY. We sat around fiddling with crampons and boots. Three of the climbers were conversing in choppy English. Their talk was of filthy India, of beautiful India, of the Sikhs, of the coming mail, of pieces of Makalu that reminded them of other countries. As the palaver burred on, Fritz began stirring a pot of snow and canned jam together attempting ice cream. The attempt failed and he ended by heating the mixture into sugar soup.

A CIVILIZED URGE, some would say, to touch the warm guts of a freshly slaughtered animal, attempting to bode what fate might lay in store. Similarly, with unconscious seriousness, we scrutinized our feces, forcing a meaning from color, texture, and firmness, almost mystically attending this refuse from our guts, delving into the future our own bodies might unveil. Our divinations were not so much a preoccupation with forecast as an innocent wonder, a primitive shuffling of every piece of this new life on the mountain.

We gathered once. Each of us took his pulse. We wondered aloud about blood pressures, anxious to plumb the meaning of a heart's beat. There was fumbling to find an artery, to count and clock it at the same time. Our session muddled on. Like a coven of invalids we pondered our bodies.

The eventual concern was with psychosomatic illness. The matter of hypochondria was first brought up by Fritz, who swore by natural medicine, a good diet, proper exercise, lots of sleep. It was his firm conviction that most ill people are mere hypochondriacs, victims of doctors and their drugs. Fritz's belaboring induced in at least a few of us the possibility that our ailments might be the product of a negative mental state. I came to fear a demon that was making me seem sick when in fact I was quite healthy. During the last weeks I couldn't dream. The slightest nightmare threw me into fits of gasping. To exorcise this fiend I composed rebel fetishes; I drank unpurified water, threw away my weekly malaria pill, ignored headaches, endured sleeplessness, struggling to explore and undermine illusion with superstitious fervor.

Our bodies survived. We stared at crude mirrors scattered among our everyday objects. We found our shaggy heads reflected in the pits of our tea cups, the freakish gleam of our faces in the bowls of spoons or in the dim brown lenses of our snow glasses. But these offered only a poor suggestion. The real treat was a genuine mirror. Down at Camp I there was a small signal mirror for flashing up to higher camps. One by one each was given his turn to examine the sun wounds, the scabs and bloodshot eyes. Each climber would twist and turn the mirror to encompass every side of his portrait.

JEPA STROLLED from the cook pit. At its entrance roosted the skinned head of a sheep, its glassy eyes socketed above the flayed muzzle. Jepa padded about in his long cotton underwear printed with purple, yellow, and green stripes. Finally he noticed me down at the far end of camp. I was shaving; pulling off beard and underlying sunburn scabs with each scrape of the blade. Jepa watched me for a moment and suddenly, as if just coming awake, hurried over to urge me not to shave my face, not to wash, not even to touch it until after the expedition was done. To demonstrate his meaning he pointed to his own unwashed mask. It was painted white with a crusty zinc shell. He obviously meant what he said. With a dignified flourish he indicated the sheep's head in the distance as if to finalize his precaution against the brutal sun that was frying even the brain. To appease Jepa I shaved only my neck, waiting until the next day, when he'd left, to finish exposing my flesh.

THERE WAS immense mirth. Someone was splitting with laughter. I could hear the sounds, obviously Fritz's hoarse bellow, through a whole line of tent walls. In the morning he told us Rodney had eaten his hemmorrhoid cream, mistaking it for the tube of white chocolate Fritz had assured him it was.

RODNEY POPPED a recording of electric rock music into his tape deck. The tunes wound out. Fritz began to cha-cha; Andre's head appeared from a tent, mouthing words, clapping his hands; Arnold shook his hips in the semblance of imagined American bacchanalia. Soon he was leaping and heaving about, a huge thick mountain man, unconstrained dense motions. Nima began writhing with the beat. More sedate Sherpas politely watched.

KARMA SHERPA showed me. Maybe twenty yards south, among all the fractured stone, a huge boulder. A grave marker. A chiseled inscription:

RND Jan Kuoncky
x 25 XII 1939
t 26 V   1973

Makalu is the grave. He wasn't brought down. Karma gestured toward a cloud on Makalu. Up there.

AT DAWN would come a frail, antique grayness spreading through the valley. Its origin was not the eastern rim; the pallor diffused evenly and seemed to come from everywhere at once. The skins of different tents drew at that light, coloring but not charging the embryo each tent shell enclosed. Within the high-altitude tents there would be a plum-red light, a frigid lapis lazuli within the dome tent, a grisly earthen light beneath the cook pit's smoky plastic tarp. In the distance boulder and snow webs began to rise from darkness into distinct minutiae. After a time jaundice ran along the skyline, the sun.

At first light a flock of quail would begin gabbling, rushing about on the ground and in the air. Their insane, loony giggles usually awoke me. By the time I could get out of the tent they were always gone. They were holy, I was told, or at least they were charmed. A liaison officer, a Nepali official, on an expedition several years ago before, had shot one of the flock with a rifle. Soon after, the officer was dead.

Up higher, on the mountain, I saw strange bird things. Liquid wings casting unreal progeny: two birds dipping low over a field of snow, and by their quivering shadows becoming four birds. And branchlike bird tracks in the snow suddenly blossoming into boot marks.

MATIJA TOLD ME STORIES. He talked about Serbians, Montenegrans, and Slovians. Of languages, that English is too harsh, French too affected, but that Russian is fine and soft, even more beautiful than Serbo-Croatian. And about Yugoslav writers; a favorite playwright. That his parents were freedom fighters. And of Ljubljana: he described castle walls he and his friends climbed in early morning and he asked about the rock in Colorado and Yosemite. Avalanches rumbled below us, the mountain unknitting itself.

I asked Matija about the mountan. "Tomorrow the seracs and crevasses, not so bad." But the Czechs, theirs had been a terrible route. Through the icefall a long, long way just to reach their ridge, and then near the top their leader's death, a broken spine and five horrible days of waiting for him to die, at last to bury him somewhere up there, up around 8,000 meters, in ice. "Those Czechs are kamakazi."

WE FOUND BRUCE outside the line of tents early one morning. He'd spent the night meditating there, sitting in what seemed like the sepulchral wraps of his orange sleeping bag. He sat there coated with frost, his eyes closed and his head bent. What little of his expression that showed through the wrinkled hole around his face. . . was weary. In groups of two and three we watched him from a distance. I was reminded of the mariners' awe of Queequeg. The sun came up. At its first touch Bruce roused himself.

Coarse, grating tones ruptured the radio call. . . a fiend or some high-altitude monster, or Fritz with bronchitis. The latter.

WE HONORED the upper mountain with the august strains of classical music. The rich sounds dipped and rose in tiny swells between tents, competing only with the wind and snow slides. Tchaikovsky and Beethoven were our favorites. Electric, blues, and vocal musics were left to the lower camps. The thin air made us mindless enough I suppose, without having choral and acid-rock repetitions steal away what few strings of words and fantasy we were able to hold on to. We endured a certain starvation of the mind, a bankruptcy of vocabularies. Attention to thought became a matter of task.

Andre shucked Teilhard de Chardin. Fritz quit a work on Alexander the Great. David failed to penetrate *The Origin of the Mind*. Instead of Proust and Milton we were soon discussing the merits of *The Warlords of Time* and *The Tightrope Man*. Science-fiction, detective thrillers, animal stories: we fed upon these as we languished at the upper camps.

THE SUN WAS BRIGHT and hot, perfect visibility, no wind. But it turned the snow to mush, and the nearly vertical trail refused to hold its shape. Again and again the steps would collapse and leave the climber dangling from fixed rope. And just as he recovered from a broken step a noise like an arrow would invariably originate high above in the avalanche chute, whine past and diminish, then another, then a fist of ice would finally slam home. After once being hit, each fresh piece of ice, even each imagined piece of ice, caused a desperate flinch and cringe. I was most afraid my eyes would be hit, that the snow glasses would splinter and blind. I halted every few steps and allowed myself no distractions so that the faintest whistle or buzz would alert. After the avalanche chute I flinched even at the sound of birds.

It was no wonder Fritz balked. Arnold and I hung below him, waiting for him to evacuate the snow ledge. For almost an hour Fritz would false start, then retreat, then almost go. Finally he set off. Upon entering the chute, he was struck. Swearing his Munich curses he looked back at the protected snow ledge, but continued.

The sun had us sweating. My candy bar had melted. While Arnold and I balanced on the ledge, we prepared ourselves: having no helmet, I packed Arnold's stocking cap, some gloves, and a pair of mittens inside my wool cap, thus padding my skull. We drank the last of the sugar water, resting, gathering energy for the sprint. The buzz of speeding ice withered our resolve. We pulled ourselves out onto the face.

It took two hours to traverse the ice chute. Fritz was knocked out, revived, was hit again in the groin. I was hit. Matija was hit in the neck. Then Arnold on the arm. Then me on the knee, knocking me down. Finally we found a slight shelter from the nightmarish day.

A voice called down that Arnold and I should come up. We didn't want to. We stayed behind the rock. listening to ice and stones shoot past us and over us. Finally we resigned ourselves. I entered the chute and within five steps my knee was struck again. This time I lay still, raging, my hands over my head, hiding from the sounds. Arnold came out and shielded himself below my feet. He talked to me. I tried to stand but kept collapsing. It was the bad knee I always favor. It felt chipped or cracked. I couldn't kick hard enough to get a toehold. Arnold sank his ice axe in the snow for me and held its spoon steady as a step. Each step with my right foot and Arnold would relocate his ice axe a little higher. We climbed like that, ascending the rope, finally reaching a lip where we could see Fritz. He was crouched beneath an overhang. We stalked up the rope, slamming Jumars higher until we arrived at Fritz's hideout. Matija was above us, leading to place a last rope to Camp III. The fears and pains were numerous. It's easy, maybe too simple, to dramatize climbing.

BRUCE HAD KNOWN HIM. He was a doctor in the Netherlands. Down at Base Camp, I heard stories about Avalt. He was tall and thin, draped with cameras, very gentle. The Dutch expedition had passed through the valley to reach their mountain farther up. Avalt, so it was joked, had almost not made it. Really looked sick. How could he climb?

Avalt had given Bruce vitamin tablets. Every day Bruce drank water laced with them. The taste of ascorbic acid was strong.

We climbed on our mountain. A few hours away the Dutch climbed on theirs. Once in a while we would have visitors from their camp. They brought cigarettes to Rodney, Arnold pipe tobacco. Over lunch there was discourse, pleasantries. Two communities exchanging. They took back with them chocolate bars, some batteries.

Near the middle of October we heard. Avalt was gone. There had been three of them at the camp. They went to sleep. Two days later two of the climbers awoke. Avalt was missing, drawn from his tent during unnatural sleep. They found him in the snow.

L AY AT CAMP IV all afternoon. My day was done, I'd carried up a rope, some food packets, cylinders of gas. Two climbers were up above, setting ropes to Camp V.

I rested in my sleeping bag conversing with all sorts of people. I can't remember who exactly. They were friendly, anxious to mumble kind though incoherent things. Some of them resembled old friends or old voices. Others were precisely as I remembered, past lovers and friends.

After we ate I found myself alone with Arnold and Matija. It was dark outside. Early night. Arnold was already complaining of frostbite, worried about the climb as he rubbed his feet together. He lay bundled in his sleeping bag.

We surrendered the night to dawn. Scant sleep. Matija was drowsy. His lips were blue. Arnold kept shifting his feet. We all stayed in our sleeping bags. Ice pelted the tent. The wind blew. No one moved to go outside. Time passed. The sun crept out onto the face. Matija began melting snow over the stove. We ate something, I forget what. Finally I rolled my pad and slipped my boots out of their plastic bags. Squeezed out and buckled on my only surviving crampon, pissed over the ledge, hunted down my snow glasses. Before leaving I knelt half inside the tent and wished Matija good luck. Arnold got out.

It was finished for us both. Arnold had frostbite, I had lung trouble. Matija told us to go down. Arnold said no, he would stay, but Matija swore at him. Several hours later we were at a lower camp. The wind wasn't fierce anymore. The slope relented and we no longer had to rappel.

T HERE WERE NO soliloquies, no histrionic prologues to our retreat. Matter-of-factly we asked each other if this was worth a life or even a limb. Down lower, among warm and sunny forests, or drinking beer or wine around a fire, the poets and priests can advocate or denigrate man and the mountain, the creature-aspiration-object dialectic, the sacrifices, romanticism. To commit a life or limb to a mountain when you're nowhere near the mountain is a clown's game. On Makalu that was too much. Maybe climbers are getting softer, maybe it's just the climbers I know. Herzog threw away his hands and feet to Annapurna, and possibly would again, but at Makalu no one considered a limb, or even a single toe or finger worth the summit. There was no oratory or opinionating. No fanaticism on that order. I felt myself alive. It wasn't a grand and transcendent feeling at all. I was just alive and wanted to keep on being alive.

CAMP II WAS MESSY and squat. Cans lay strewn about, positioned with hasty purpose. Some were color coded for meats, fruits, and vegetables, some were stripped of their labels and held water or ice. Ropes lay piled in transitory postures, soon to be hauled high. Red stuff sacks were pyramided or loose: they contained wind pants, down sweaters, personal gear. The snow was dirty with food scraps, jelly cups, wet chocolate wrappers, and was colored with spilled tea, soup, urine. Flung debris that had missed or fallen short marked the mouth of the garbage crevasse.

The ice cave was located upon a crevasse that was gradually convoluting, the tent inside was moved. A box tent nestled nearby in its own space. Helmets, crampons, carabiners, hammers, and harnesses hung from its corner rings. Some of the gear was iced with rime: disuse. A jar of wheat germ lay where it had been cast away.

Objects were in tired transit. The camp itself was a mere station, impermanent. In three, maybe four days of abandonment it probably became a wreck.

FRITZ AND MATIJA decided to go for it. The route would be complete if they could exit left off the face onto the French ridge. No one else would be up there to help them on the upper mountain. They would be alone and beyond rescue.

I'm told that just before they left Camp I for their bid they locked hands, spat in mock team spirit, then broke their two-man huddle and surged away, two men diminishing on the giant mountain.

In the coming days, days above, they became motes shifting on the mammoth face. As motes they described tiny lines on the face, the pattern of our route. As men they suffered the wind and altitude. They found Camp III destroyed by weather. One tent was shredded by the wind, useless. The other tent's zipper had ripped open and spindrift had impacted the tent with hard snow. They cleaned out the tent.

Down at Base I looked toward Fritz and Matija as toward a concept, no longer as people. They were a small point of dynamism, barely distinct from that single massive element, the mountain. They sank from us, became voices on a small, cold radio, and when the radios finally stuttered into static void I wondered what they would be. No longer voices even, they'd have gone beyond all presence. We sat about in the dinner tent, morose. Fritz and Matija weren't even ghosts, just names. Not the slightest substance to them anymore it seemed. And above us, all the time, they kept sinking farther into disappearance. I was unsure if they'd ever come down again. We were too weak to go up.

Through the telescope I could see the ice-tattered rain fly at Camp III as it shook thunderously in its hurricane, but miles away I could hear nothing of its thunder. The sun was shining. Not the slightest breeze. As I watched, a tiny bulb appeared, then shoulders, a protuberance on the tiny tent's edge, then quickly it disappeared back inside the tent. Hours later someone announced that two figures were descending, not rising on the face.

DAWA HELD THE ROPE. The animal's legs were spread, a log set under its neck. Charlie held its hind legs. Nima swung. The head popped off, opened its mouth. The body leaped and collapsed, epileptic in the dirt.

There was a small audience of members and Sherpas. We clapped, told Nima good job. He grabbed the head and shook his knife in the air, danced a moment. While Nima was gloating, Dawa slit the belly and started to shave away the skin. There was no regard for the pelt. There was no way to cure it.

Later Kipa sat with the head between his knees, carving off the skin. He sliced off the lips, pulled the nostrils away. Like a trophy, the muscled, grimacing head was mounted at the entrance to the cook pit. It was the fourth such skull.

By the next morning Nima was feeling penitent about his bloodlust. He grew subdued when the murder was mentioned. Asked when the next and last sheep would enter our stewpot Nima launched into a mercy plea. It was too skinny and too young, still just a baby; it would have no meat. We agreed happily, enough killing.

Our last sheep was blessed by Jepa, a lama, and Passang, a Sherpa shaman. A yellow prayer flag was tied to its side. There is a term for this that I needn't relay; it means the sparing of a life. Once consecrated the sheep would go untouched for the rest of its natural life. Previously skittish and half wild, Luke domesticated with incredible speed. Karma Sherpa adopted him, fed him, housed him in a plastic tent on the trek out. When we left him at Sedua, Luke bawled. I have no doubt he was later eaten by the Seduans. The idyll had ended.

Page 173: Climber on Makalu. Photo by Matija Maležič

Philip Temple
The Isolated Mountain

AFTER THE MISERIES and confusions of adolescence, rock and ice gave parameters to thought and action, and mountains became an obsession. Pain and joy were no longer the product of dimly understood human conflicts. They were the gall and fruit of endeavor in a world in which the consequences of decision were always sharply and certainly revealed. A child in a garden of mountains. And nothing seemed more virtuous or valuable than to explore and understand the face of a high landscape. Here were the answers to life, and I was enthralled by their simplicity.

Beyond this first euphoria I began to understand that mountains were an unyielding environment for the exploration and definition of self. In the test of physique and mentality, survival was founded on the recognition of weakness and an awareness of capability. In the mildly competitive world of New Zealand face climbing in the early 1960s, I pushed hard to convince myself that I was both capable and willing to foot it with the best. I was neither, and acceptance of this discovery was hard. Even then I was lured by the isolated mountain, the one that stood apart, distinctive in character, dominating the valleys and glaciers of the range, remote, demanding a journey and particular homage. It required a different commitment. In 1961 I attempted the first of two such mountain journeys. The Carstensz Pyramide of New Guinea seemed to me then the epitome of the isolated mountain: distant, sequestered by jungle, swamp, and primitive peoples, unclimbed, high enough to hold ice in the tropics, at 5,040 meters the highest peak in the Pacific Basin.

At first the commitment proved too much. Twenty-five-kilo packs in knee-deep mud, a flurry of ambushing arrows, obstructive missionaries, timid airdrop pilots. Symbolically, an ice-axe shaft was broken among the roots of the moss forest. In the persistent rain one had to concentrate to conjure any vision of the mountain. But, though we failed, there were compensations enough to bolster faith in eventual success, including the first sight of the objective which had occupied my dreams for more than a year.

So in the beginning there was the mountain. It exerted an influence over thought and action that flowed not from its eminence as a peak in a great range but from its dominance of a unique and isolated landscape. The longer it remained unclimbed, the more time there was to unravel the mysteries of the strange and uninhabited plateau that was its plinth.

After our first ascent of the Pyramide, Heinrich Harrer said, "The

Heinrich Harrer scouting the Carstensz Pyramide (1962). Photo by Philip Temple

We are doing what we came into the world to do. We are affected not only by the beauty or majesty of our environment, but . . . by a total something in it, which has been calling to us from all time.

— Wilfred Noyce

climb was the last of its type—similar to the original climbs of the Western Alps." But success was disappointment. Those two years, filled with energy, dreams, and hopes centered on one goal, had dwindled to a vanishing point on the summit. There was no answer at the apex of that cloudy mountain: simply more questions arising from the experience of the journey. It was some time before I understood that climbing was actually a motive for exploring the qualities of both a natural and a personal wilderness.

After the Pyramide, I indulged in six months of traveling in the ranges to the north. Harrer and I were the first to witness the manufacture of stone axes in West New Guinea; and traveling alone, I was the first white man to explore valleys which until then had been vague lines on aerial maps. Later I returned to the Carstensz, employed as a scout for the U.S. Army in the grisly business of recovering human remains from a wartime plane wreck. More important, my interest in mountain bird life led to the capture of a rare bird of paradise which, in turn, led to eighteen months' work as a zoological collector throughout New Guinea and the Solomons. I exploited the wilderness to the full!

The other mountain was cleaner in its lines. There were no trappings to Big Ben, no jungle or primitive people, no exotic animals. He rose whitely and roughly from the coldness of the Southern Ocean. Unclimbed, he stood five hundred kilometers distant from his nearest island neighbor. After months of simmering in the tropics, the prospect of ice held unusual appeal. I cannot answer now whether any ice would have done, or whether again the idea of an arduous journey to one of the most remote spots on earth was the irresistible lure. Certainly, in time and planning and effort, the journey was the thing. We were to sail our twenty-meter schooner sixteen thousand kilometers over a four month period. And I had never sailed before.

New Guinea had been a selfish experience: traveling with a single companion or alone, I was a twenty-two-year-old working out his problems through what to most outsiders was an outlandish, even useless, enterprise. But on a small boat in the Southern Ocean, ten men needs must find each other. Ten days out from Sydney in November 1964 I felt that we had hardly begun: the steady strain of keeping watch and catching up on sleep did not cultivate the formation of a club. I felt this was a good thing: it would be longer before we became sick of each other.

The real achievement of the expedition was that we never reached that point. And for the first time I learned what could be achieved by cooperative effort. There was no option; one could not descend to base camp to quit the strain of personality frictions. One's individual worth was placed in real perspective against the timeless stoicism of our skipper, H.W. Tilman, and the inspired sagacity of our leader, Warwick Deacock. He wrote John Donne's verse on the galley bulkhead:

On a huge hill
Cragged and steep,
Truth stands, and hee that will
Reach her, about must, and about must goe.

Two months out of Sydney as our ship lurched through the near-freezing sea, Big Ben appeared in the guise of lenticular cloud rising through a low mass of horizon fog. It was monumental: twenty kilometers across, nearly three thousand meters of ice sweeping out of the water. The great white mass slowly hardened in shape, aloof above the querulous mists, wind snapping at its feet, a shrug of cold shoulders in the sky. The achievement of the voyage, a pilgrimage to that sight, was almost enough. But there could be no stopping, it was not yet time to go back, to start again.

I could not generate much enthusiasm for the climb of Big Ben. It was merely inevitable, success overlaid by anxiety. The days. following were troubled by perplexity about the worth of it all. We had climbed the mountain and had come down safely, but I felt this was insignificant as I looked along the shore we had named Capsize Bay. The surf beat as it did the day we landed and as it had done every day before and since. The prions mined in the azorella, the skuas stalked them, the penguins paraded and squabbled. The seals molted and slept, irritated rather than awed by our presence. Though we had laid claim to the land and the mountain, we were a rare, migrating species with a delicate grip on existence. They were the true children of the island.

The journey to the isolated mountain was, after all, an allegory of life. Once understoood, it could not be repeated, else one was putting off the longer journey in favor of an artificial reality. There came a time when what one had learned had to be translated into the more complex language of everyday life. To go back would be, at best, to take refreshment at original springs; at worst, blindness to the point of the exercise. The youthful drive to make journeys and achieve summits in the plain terms of climbing unknown mountains was a desire to capture truth "on a huge hill." But the metaphor could not be lived. Instead, those unforgettable treks and voyages gave me resource and skill for the longer journey on which one "about must, and about must goe," with no certainty of a summit.

Mount Brooks. Photo by Ed Cooper

Just go on and on. . . . Do you see the mountain ranges there, far away?
One behind another. They rise up. They tower. That is my deep, unending
inexhaustible kingdom.

— Henrik Ibsen
The Master Builder

Casper David Friedrich, *From the Summit: Traveler Looking Over the Sea of Fog* (c. 1818). Courtesy of Hamburg Kunsthalle, West Germany

PAINTERS AND POETS

Suiō Genro, *Han-Shan and Feng-kan*. Courtesy of the
New Orleans Museum of Art and Dr. Kurt Gitter

Han-Shan
Six Poems

Translated from the Classical Chinese by Burton Watson

At my ease, idle among white clouds—
do you have to buy a mountain to enjoy it?
Going down the steep spots, I use a stick;
climbing the crevices, I hold tight to the vines.   **I**
In valley bottoms pines are always green;
streamside rocks have patterns of their own.
Though I'm cut off from friends and companions,
when spring comes, birds chatter chatter away.

Level fields, water stretching wide,
Cinnabar Hills linking up to the Four Bright,
city of the immortals, the highest peak,
clusters of crests ringing it like green screens.   **II**
Far far off I spy it in the distance,
soaring soaring in shapes of a greeting,
alone, this mountain at a corner of the sea,
here and there flashing its message of good news.

A thing to be valued—this famed mountain;
how can the Seven Treasures compare?
Pines and moonlight, breezy and cool;
clouds and mist, ragged wisps rising.   **III**
Clustering around it, how many folds of hills?
twisting back and forth, how many miles of trail?
Valley streams quiet, limpid and clear—
joys and delights that never end!

IV

Yes, there are stingy men,
but I'm not one of the stingy kind.
Robe thin? I wore it full of holes dancing;
wine gone? I drank it all with a song.
Just so you keep your belly full—
never let those two legs go weary.
When the weeds are poling holes in your skull,
that's the day you'll have regrets!

V

Among folded cliffs,
plenty of clear breeze,
no need to wave the fan,
cool winds come through.
Bright moon shining,
white clouds all around,
sitting alone,
one old man.

VI

Master of Cold Mountain,
grows old like this,
living all alone,
no life-and-death for him!

Linda Siegel
The Riesengebirge as a Transcendental Image in Friedrich's Art

CASPAR DAVID FRIEDRICH was the greatest German landscape painter of the romantic period and the most interested in the mountain as a subject for art. In its broadest sense, art was seen by German romanticism as a fusion of nature, philosophy, and religion, a representation of the inner and outer life of man and of the finite and infinite. This multiplicity of concepts could be expressed through symbolism. "The artistic creation," wrote Schelling, "requires the presence of a symbolic world of poetic existence which mediates between the universal and the particular."[1] "Beauty," for August Wilhelm Schlegel, was "a symbolic representation of the infinite."[2] For Friedrich the landscape was always more than a representation of nature; it was a work in which allegorical symbols played a significant role in creating the ultimate vision of his heart and mind.

This salient characteristic of his style is well demonstrated in his handling of the Riesengebirge, the "Giant Mountains," which stand between Czechoslovakia and Poland. Formerly known as Silesia, in Friedrich's time this area was predominantly German. On the Bohemian flank the mountain slopes fall gradually, but toward Silesia they descend abruptly. In the romantic era the nearby town of Schmiedeberg, which afforded travelers an excellent view of the mountains, was a popular tourist attraction, as was the spa, Warmbrunn. The highest summit, the Schneekoppe, reaches 1,603 meters, and upon it today stand several lodges, the Laurentius Kapelle (a small chapel dating from the seventeenth century), and a modern weather station.

The Riesengebirge occupied a special place in Friedrich's life and art, and at least thirty-five of his works depict the range in various media. His treatment of other hills was quite different from that reserved for this favored place. His paintings of the Harz Mountains, for example, emphasize his fascination with height, and they thrust the viewer downward with frightening speed toward the depths of the earth. The same preoccupation with height and danger is evident in his well-known painting, *Chalk Cliffs on Rügen* (1818), depicting the scene of his youthful climbing exploits.

From 1810 to the end of his life he painted the Riesengebirge many times, and yet each study shows the mountain range as a heavenward striving force. The beholder does not look down, but upward.

Friedrich's interest in the Riesengebirge dates to the summer of 1810, when he journeyed to the range from Dresden with the artist, Georg Kersting, a fellow student with Friedrich at Copenhagen who was to remain one of his closest friends. (Kersting's *Caspar David Friedrich in His Studio* [1811] is one of the most important surviving portraits of the artist.) A drawing by Kersting (in the Berlin National Gallery and dated July 18, 1810) shows Friedrich with a knapsack upon his back. In the right-hand corner of the sketch he has written, "Professor Caspar David Friedrich drawn by G. Kersting, 1810, resting in Meissen on the journey into the Riesengebirge."[3] The sketches which Friedrich made during this journey were to form the basis of several subsequent renderings.

The Riesengebirge as a subject in German art dates back earlier than the seventeenth century. In the eighteenth and early nineteenth centuries the hills appear in the works of Anton Balzer, Christoph Nathe, and Adrian Zingg (with whom Friedrich studied in Dresden). Ludwig Richter, for a time a pupil of Friedrich, was also attracted to the range, along with Moritz von Schwind and Friedrich's close associate, Carl Gustav Carus. But a brief comparison of their paintings with those of Friedrich reveals how very individual was his feeling for the Riesengebirge. For Schwind and Richter it was the association with Germanic folklore that drew them to the mountain range, particularly the tales associated with Rubezahl, the legendary mountain spirit and weather lord, often depicted as a long-bearded monk in an ash-colored cowl. In the works of Nathe and Balzer the beholder confronts a panoramic view. The mountain range is depicted in the distance towering over a small town; one or two tiny figures are dwarfed by the immensity of nature. These paintings exhibit a certain picture-postcard quality in that no factual detail was omitted from the painting. Friedrich, however, developed his scenes to create some greater meaning. In the paintings of his predecessors the human figures were generally pictured with their backs to the mountain, engaged in their particular activity before a backdrop of hills. In Friedrich's portrayals, however, when human figures appear they are turned away from the foreground and look as with longing at the summit, thereby leading the viewer's eye to the subject of the painting. Friedrich does not clutter his mountain views with man or his buildings.

Friedrich's portrayal of the Riesengebirge can only be fully understood in the light of the German romantic literary descriptions of the range found in the works of Kleist and particularly of Theodor Körner, both close friends of Friedrich. It is here that we find that special transcendental imagery which characterizes Friedrich's paintings. Beyond the Schneekoppe, in these writings, lies that heavenly paradise for which German romanticism longed, that realm above earth in which the ultimate goal of human endeavor is achieved. For the first time in painting,

Casper David Friedrich, *Morning in the Riesengebirge* (1810). Courtesy of Walter Steinkopf

The Christian Church is chiefly a rebuilding of the sacred house erected to the worship of one of the Gods of Olympus.

— K. H. Bouman

Friedrich captured that heavenward striving in the summits while the mountain range itself came to symbolize his inner striving.

Morning in the Riesengebirge, his first important work following the journey of 1810, is at first glance a nature study, based, as it is, upon sketches made during the journey. But his initial view has been transformed into a powerful statement of the transcendental quality of the mountain range. The scene is viewed from the peak of the Schneekoppe, which emerges and rises out of fog-covered rock formations—a fog which hides the earthly world from view. The summit pushes above this mist with an overwhelming, inexhaustible energy, which was, the German romantics believed, the most prominent characteristic of nature. The sun, newly risen, stretches across the horizon like the entwined mountain chain itself, dividing the canvas into two distinct areas, a lighter clear atmosphere above the horizon (a heavenly paradise above earth), and a darker area not part of that realm.

The three figures Friedrich has placed on the summit are of great significance: a crucifix with the figure of Christ, a woman below in a garment of white, followed by a man clad in black. The female figure is assisting her male companion, and both are striving to reach the cross. The cross is the only figure to cut the horizon, linking the finite and the infinite worlds. The figure of the cross deserves special attention as it is one of the hallmarks of several of Friedrich's works. The placing of a cross upon a mountaintop was not in itself a new device in German art. Indeed many of Goethe's drawings portray a cross placed on top of a hill overlooking a small chapel. But in the sketches of Goethe, as in similar works of certain eighteenth-century German painters (Dietrich, Hess, and Zingg, for example), this rendering seems only to note the German custom of erecting such crosses and wayside altars. Friedrich's cross appears, rather, as a deliberate symbol of the hand of God, which will lead and transport the man and woman beyond the summit.

The role Friedrich has assigned to the woman is also interesting. This female figure is reminiscent of the German romantic idealization of the "ever womanly" maiden who leads man upward to the divine. This theme, which is related to the German romantic interest in the Gothic period, occurs in Goethe's *Faust* as well as in German romantic literature (Hoffmann's *The Mines of Falun*) and opera (Weber's *Der Freischütz*, Wagner's *Der fliegende Holländer, Tannhäuser*). Friedrich, incidentally, portrayed the same concept in the allegorical drawing, *Autumn* (1834). Here a young woman, one hand pointing to the summit, has begun to ascend a path leading to it, while at the same time trying to deter her male companion, whose hand she holds, from descending to the nearby town, which represents earthbound existence.

In *Morning in the Riesengebirge* the summit of the mountain also assumes the form and function of a cathedral, but it is a church in God's world. This imagery is suggested by Friedrich in many other works depicting mountains. In the watercolor drawing, *Group of Rocks in the*

Elbsandsteingebirge (1828), he has placed a tiny church high on a ledge of rock, the steeple drawing the eye of the viewer upward as the mountain and cross do in the earlier painting. It is also significant that the mountain dwarfs the human figures and even the cross. This imagery suggests the German romantic philosophy of Wackenroder that "nature is the clearest explanation of His being and His qualities . . . for it is infinite nature that draws us through the wide spaces of air directly to God."[4] Thus in the painting it is the mountain (nature) which is the link between man and God (the cross). Friedrich has accomplished in *Morning in the Riesengebirge* what Wackenroder also believed was the goal of art: "From the confusion of our lives," he wrote, "we are redeemed as with an omnipotent wand by art . . . it leads us to a land where the beams of light spread order everywhere . . . we feel ourselves and our worth with renewed vitality."[5]

Friedrich to the end of his life turned again and again to the Riesengebirge. But later renderings differ markedly from the youthful vision of 1810. In his last years he was beset by ill health and financial problems, and his importance in the Dresden Art Academy waned. In 1835 he suffered a severe stroke and his output considerably waned. *The Riesengebirge*, dating from the year 1835, is one of his last renderings of these hills. In this work we miss the hopeful enthusiasm of youth, the sense of imminent salvation. Night is falling and the weary traveler is far from the summit. As the sun sets the wanderer sits upon a rock longingly looking upward. The Schneekoppe in the background is illuminated by the last rays of the sun while the lonely traveler in the foreground is gradually enveloped in darkness. The wanderer is still shackled by earthly existence.

Friedrich is known to have placed himself in many of his landscapes, and it is quite likely that the traveler in this still and lonely scene is the artist himself. In contrast with *Morning in the Riesengebirge* there is a pronounced feeling of intolerable isolation—an isolation which Friedrich grew to know as the friends of his youth, the pioneers of German romanticism, passed from his life. In the distance the sky and mountains recede into infinite space. The climber, however, has not reached his goal.

I wanted to follow the craving of my heart,
I wanted to come closer to the holy heights,
I wanted to view the summit of the mountain,
But who could have been fortunate enough to have discovered it,
For it was hidden from my glance.

—Theodor Körner[6]

Eastern Sierra: Mount Morrison after a snowstorm. Photo by Ed Cooper

Reuben Tam
Three Poems

The glacier that scours the mountains
winds a long way toward muskeg.
Ice rounding the cirques and mounds
filters streams from blue caves.

On the mountainside, they said,
look for mastodon climates.
You'll find outcrops, shale on sandstone,
and layers of cinder in grantitic folds.
You could gather and divide the ages there.

When I arrived the peaks had turned
into jackstraw shadows.
I stumbled over boulders in dim ravines
and walked among dead spruce
that once might have touched stars.

Here in the low weather of the melt
the sky floats down in whorls of lichen,
gray clouds on gray rock.
Ice narrows past gravel and graywacke,
and a thin sun breaks in tentative streams.

In silt-blue eddies
crystalline stones turn and flash and turn,
like mountains,
like glaciers.

Yukon

The mountains were turned the other way
as if we had come up the wrong lake.
At the summits
hanging valleys funneled the sky down
but the falls were white pegmatite.

Rising or plunging
the verticals canceled
horizontal eons.
Glaciers cut across the programs
of geology.

Maligne Lake Mountains

A wind came down.
It shook our view
and turned the lake around
spilling it into another.

From the sedges a blackbird sang,
ringing its territory,
calling over the summer's nesting,
beyond the climates.

We walked into a meadow of saxifrage
where an ice age was ending.
Ice dripped down
to errant wildflowers.

Our world fell into place for a moment
with the song of a bird,
drift, silt, tremor, thaw,
note by note in jeweled cadence
imprinted in the beginning,
coursing down the intricate surfaces,
phrasing the wilderness.

Hawaiian Archipelago

I saw Niihau from the upland of Mana—
Niihau, half its hills drowned,
joined undersea to Kaula Rock, to Lehua,
to the bird islands beyond,

to Necker and Laysan, to the unnamed shoals,
to the last of the reefs, galaxies of darkness
clouding the blue ocean,
staining the eye of the frigate bird.

I once heard of an island spewing black ash.
The mountainside trembled in the channel.
The magma raged all night.

In vertical unease the wind-honed islands rise.
They spill their strata onto the coastal plain—
Kapaa, Kealia, Waipouli, Anahola.

The ocean floor bears the pattern
of drowned stream courses, as plovers
bear the veins of ancient flyways.

I have followed a stream to the sea,
to a reef the color of crabshell,
to my mornings, myself among ghosts of coral.

Above me, high across the span of glint
seabirds gather all the tilting sea.

Taktsang Monastery, Bhutan. Photo by Michael Tobias

He who makes the true ascent must ascend forever.

— Saint Gregory of Nyssa

AN OVERVIEW

Over: John Martin, *Sadak in Search of the Waters of Oblivion* (1812). Courtesy of the Southampton Art Gallery

Michael Tobias
A History of Imagination in Wilderness

THERE IS A FAMOUS early-thirteenth-century painting by the Chinese Liang-K'ai entitled *Sakya Coming Out of His Mountain Retreat.* The ascetic saint in this picture is a nobleman of the wilds. He is portrayed pondering a future, a descent into the real world. Standing on the edge of a brink, at the top of a trail, clad in an old robe with a cane in his hand, he is a supple mixture of grim trauma, accumulated fatigue, bewilderment, and spiritual calm. Behind him are the overhanging crags of a Chinese otherworld. The tension of the work accrues in mute irony which is our own vantage. He is caught, perhaps forever undecided: below him is a horizontal pantheon of commerce, pollution, and delights. Behind him, the pure world of nature. And where he stands is consciousness. In this combination of elements—the mountain, the mind, and society—exists a circumstance, an option, a fantasy which is ancient.

In a chronology of vignettes we wil' examine metaphorical and literal configurations of this circumstance. "The richness and variety of ascension symbolism may at first look seem chaotic," writes Mircea Eliade, "but seen together, all such rites and symbols are explained by the sacred value of 'height,' that is, of the celestial."

This spiritual immanence, a dazzling ledger of practices and philosophical adjuncts, will be our starting point in the historical eludication of a vertical aesthetic.

DERIVED FROM a Babylonian verb—*zagara*—meaning "to be tall," the ziggurat was *to be* a mountain, not just resemble one. In his book *The Birth of Civilization in the Near East,* Henri Frankfort writes:

> In Mesopotamia, the "mountain" is the place where the mysterious potency of the earth, and hence of all natural life, is concentrated... Our interpretation takes its starting point from the "mountain" not as a geographical feature, but as a phenomenon charged with religious meaning.

These ziggurats were constructed of five strata culminating in a heavenly level to accommodate the god. They were "local" mountains, "the marriage of heaven and earth," and in Sumerian and Akkadian seals, the god and goddess of sky and earth are exhibited incarnate in the person of a priest

Prehistory of the Symbol

and priestess joined in divine connubium on the summit. Writes Joseph Campbell in his book *The Mythic Image,* "The informing thought of the Sumerian world feeling is: 'What is above is below'; and from this, two directions of spiritual movement are projected: the Above comes downward, the Below mounts aloft."

In Ethiopic, *dabr* means both mountain and monastery. Although it is only an isolated example of the architectonic implicit in the religious phenomenon of mountain worship or habitation, is suggests a widespread pattern. "Altitude" is a universal symbol. In the history of Chinese landscape painting, it is represented by the merging of rocks and waterways in penetrable loci where the spirit is uplifted. Such terrain, in other contexts, provides access to sacred penitralia, as evidenced in the *"routes de passage"* throughout Anatolia (the caves of Cappadocia), France (the sites of Lascaux, the Dordogne, Ariège, and the Gironde), the Sahara, and Himalaya. The domain of reconnaissance of the labyrinth, of aerial mystery, it is the precinct of exile and ultimate contrast.

The journey upward is the significance itself, the physical component of spirituality. Lingering over the psyche like a far-off rumor, an atavistic scent, altitude—the cobalt night, the stars, the mountain leaning in—is our least domesticated symbol, mankind's oldest dizziness. These pre-Cortésian pyramids which Octavio Paz describes as always harboring other pyramids beneath them refer to this combination which is history and symbolic regeneration. At Arunachaleshvara in southern India, at Ankor Wat and Borobudur; in the examples of the Mexican *teocalli,* the Mayan temple at Tikal, the Toltec Temple of Quetzlcoatl, and the adobe Olmee pyramid in La Venta (the earliest known artificial mountain in the Western hemisphere, constructed about 800 B.C.); in the Egyptian pyramids; and in the myth of the Titans piling Mount Pelion on Ossa—in all of these examples, the same vision is readily discernible. The Tower of Babel motif presents a tantalizing spiritual metaphor of ideographic applicability. The aspirations of our epics, the architecture of urban colossi, and their implicit juxtaposition which is ascension, are neatly affixed to a universal impulse that even Gauguin, writing in *Noa Noa,* commented upon when he whimsically described the Marquesans energetically climbing their palms. Much earlier, Herodotus asserted that the Babel ziggurat in Babylon was visited by God. Archeologists know of at least twenty-five Sumerian, Babylonian, and Assyrian pyramidal temple towers averaging 125 by 170 feet in perimeter built of sun-dried bricks. They were constructed to be climbed.

While there is no mystique, certainly no religious orientation, to the construction of our skylines, it is interesting to note that a *Newsweek* reporter hailed a young Yosemite climber a "national folk hero" when he ascended a 110-story World Trade Center tower. There is no doubting the claim that rock has provided a unique medium for millenia—a vehicle for physical and mental expression. "It's not the height which is terrifying," wrote Nietzsche, "but the cliff." The examples are legion. MacCullough and Tancrède have explored the role of sacred mountains, and there is con-

Left: Stele commemorating a victory of Naram-Sin of Akkad (2159-33 B.C.). The Louvre, Paris. Photographie Giraudon

Below: Sun-god Ascending the World Mountain, Akkadian cylinder seal (c. 2350-2150 B.C.). Courtesy of the Director General, Baghdad Museum, Iraq

Icon after Saint John Climacus and the Ladder to Paradise. Saint Catherine's Monastery, Sinai Peninsula, Israel. Reproduced through the courtesy of the Michigan-Princeton-Alexandria Expedition to Mount Sinai

And he dreamed, and behold a ladder set up on the earth, and the top of it reached to heaven: and behold the angels of God ascending and descending on it.

— Genesis 28:12

siderable material in the *Motif Index to Folklore* as well as in the multi-volume *Sacred Books of the East,* edited by Max Müller. To draw some examples:

Pausanias tells us of the "territory of the Lycaean Zeus," a region located on the highest peak of Arcadia, which became the site where the "high cult" and the "tree cult" originated. The Japanese Ainus were known to perform the Iyamande Ceremony, in which a captured bear cub was nourished on the breasts of village females and then returned to its mountain in maturity, the ceremony implying that the mountain was a territory for "completed" beings. In the *Eighth Ode of Kau* (sixth century B.C.), King Mu is described as sacrificing to the spirits of "Ho and the highest hills" after overthrowing the Shang dynasty, believing that if those spirits are satisfied with him, those of all other mountains will be so as well. Bodhidharma, an Indian by birth and the twenty-eighth patriarch to succeed the Buddha, came to China in 520 A.D. and became the father of Zen. He meditated wordlessly for nine years facing a rock, and the tradition, now widespread among Buddhist sects, is called "wall meditation."

The earliest known representation of a mountain god is the Naram-Sin stele from Akkadia (c. 2150 B.C.). Naram-Sin, a king, is portrayed climbing a mountain with his people beneath him. It is a political celebration. A similar event takes place on a rock shrine from Yazilikaya, a Hittitian center. The relief portrays King Tudhaliya IV (1250-1220) standing on a summit.

But perhaps the first true mountain invocation in the West occurred with the cult of the great mother Kubila, or Cybele. Later known by the Lydians as Agdistis (she of the rock), her consecration spread throughout Anatolia commencing around the ninth century B.C. and reached Rome in 204 B.C. Her greatest shrines were at Pessinus in Galatia on Mount Dindymus. Her attendants were Corybants who performed Bacchanalian orgies on the mountain peaks dedicated to her. Apollonius said that as a child the goddess was exposed on a mountain, nourished by beasts, and accompanied by satyrs during her mountain wanderings. She was said to issue from the bare cliffs, and the rivers of her peaks were said to inspire lunacy. She was equated with Pan and Rhea and mentioned in the writings of Lucretius, Catullus, Cicero, Livy, Virgil, Horace, and Ovid. Her cult spread to all of the Roman dominions.

The density of sacred mountains is most pronounced in the Middle East, in China, and in Japan. Robert Cohn has traced the contagion of proverbs and mountain imagery in the Old Testament. Religious association is made with Zion, Nebo, Tabor, Moriah, Peor, Mizpah, Gibeah, Ophrah, Ebal, Gerizim, Gilead, Carmel, Hermon, the Mount of Olives, and Sinai. In Muhammadan cosmology, the *Qāf* is the earthly mountain boundary figured topographically as Mount Safa and Mount Marway in the Koran. Dante's teacher Brunetto Latini visited Spain in 1260, studied the legends of the *Mi'rāj* (Muhammad's ascent), and undoubtedly contributed to the image of ascension in his student's *Divine Comedy*. The Koranic term for paradise refers to the highest part of a garden, and classical Islamic architecture tends to stress an anticipation of the mountain-hereafter by endowing building space with the transcendental attributes of ethereal height. This religious impulse for sacred immediacy is the underlying assertion of both ziggurats and spiral mosques like UcSerefeli and Samarra.

The essayist Edmund Burke (1729-1797) wrote that a level stretch of land will never excite us as much as the vertical. In their book *Balinese Character*, Margaret Mead and Gregory Bateson compare the differences between the Balinese highlanders and plain dwellers, but no one has yet attempted an overview which cross-culturally delineates the topographic-specific characteristics of mountain peoples (i.e., the Nuba, Sherpa, Navaho, Basque, Appalachian, Takhali, etc.) as compared to flatlanders. There are particular problems inherent in such a study. The Egyptian Semites knew of El-Shaddai, the Israeli YHWH, a mountain god. But Egypt has few mountains. The South Dakota Lakotan Sioux worshiped the Black Hills and Crazy Horse hung a stone from one ear and repeatedly told the tribal elders he would return in the form of a stone; but the Sioux were Plains Indians. They rarely set foot in their sacred mountains on the western horizon, only doing so during times of drought or dwindling buffalo supply.

What then is the single thread, if any, marking man's relationship to mountains prehistorically and in the modern world? We have skimmed the architectural analogues and mentioned a few religious examples of invocation. To say that height merely excites us is to say very little. An exclusive relationship must be drawn from the superabundance of data and it must illuminate a consistent orientation toward the alpine environs.

Is there such a unified strain of perspective? Not everyone finds mountains beautiful, and certainly the mountains of Moab or Saudi Arabia *do* differ vastly from those of Korea or Grindelwald. Even Sir Leslie Stephen commented on his own preference for the Alps over the Himalayas. Those who love the mountains, for whatever reason, constitute an amorphous elite. And any forced sociology is bound to miss worlds-within-worlds of tradition and understanding. The Iranian mountain farmer, the Spanish gypsy, the eastern Tennessee mountaineer, the Ladakhi monk, the Bolivian coal miner, the Caucasian shepherd, the rock climber—if there is one conceivable encompassing link it is rural resolution, an apotheosis of mountain privacy, though even here we risk anachronism and cultural-conceptual trespassing. The rage for "personal space" is a relatively modern phenomenon. Medieval Europeans for the most part lived walled up in congested towns. The forests, those scrub-strewn collines of shepherds' huts, crumbling limestone, and juniper, were dangerous haunts of robbers. While such wilds were no less intimidating in seventeenth-century America, the difference was an evolving concept equating freedom with frontier vistas. The mountain has always provided people a paradoxically unpeopled dimension. During the late Paleolithic period, the inner sanctum of a mountain was the hermetic ritual site for a veneration of nature.

A poetic intuition—of these beginnings in nature—haunts, indeed precipitates, much of modern self-reflection. To enter this mental and physical wilderness, this Nature of history, is to streamline consciousness, to propel it toward that convergence of experience which is at once familiar and mysterious.

Wilderness transcends temporality. Man, ancient or modern, finds communion in the hills. In so doing he courts invigoration, wilfully unleashing the physical upon the symbolic. Thoreau believed that wilderness exists *inside* the person. Lao Tzu said it could be found in one's backyard. Paraphrasing Dōgen, one might conclude there is a wilderness of the mind, and a wilderness of the body. The mountain spirit harbors perhaps the clearest similitude between them.

The Ascetic Revelations

CONVERSIONS OF EGYPTIANS by Greek-speaking Christians began sometime in the early third century A.D., and within a matter of decades the first ascetics made their solitary ways into the deserts of the lower Nile, of Scete, Chalcis, of the Thebaid, Arabia, and the Sinai. Christ took his body unto himself. The "spiritual body" (as it is described in the Testament of Abraham, the Ascension of Isaiah, the Assumption of Moses, the Book of Enoch, the Apocalypse of Elijah, the Transitus Mariae, and the Lucan and Johannine Ressurection narratives) is a physique that has tortured itself. Honed in the bleached rubble of sand dunes and scorched terrain, such a body was conceived to be pure for ascent into heaven. Saint Gregory of Nyssa said that "he who makes the true ascent must ascend forever, and for him. . . there will never be wanting a wide space in which to pursue this divine course." Gregory, who lived in the fourth century, composed the *Life of Moses* which outlined in extreme detail the mystical ascent of the soul.

Saint Paul was the first hermit to live near the Red Sea in disciplined retreat. He was visited by Saint Anthony shortly before his death in about 340. Anthony remained at Der el Memum carrying on the Pauline tradition, and later moved to Der Mar, an oasis at the foot of a mountain near the Gulf of Akaba. He died in 366, having emerged as the father of Middle Eastern monasticism. His precepts for ascetic life were compiled by Athanasius in the *Vita Antonii*:

> After leaving his Pisper companions Anthony stopped on the Nile bank with no clear notion where he would go; and suddenly he heard a heavenly voice telling him to make his way to the inner desert. Some Bedouins were passing at this moment and he followed them coming eventually to the Eastern bank of the Nile near the foot of Mount Colzim by the Red Sea, at the Eastern end of the mountain chain known today as Gebel-el-Galaza. There when he had reached the height of meditation as well as the summit of the mountain [and it is not a play on words for the parallel between material ascent and spiritual elevation is maintained throughout *The Life of Anthony*,] he decided to stay for the rest of his days.
>
> [Lacarriere]

Saint Paul described such a Christian as an athlete striving for a heavenly prize. And Saint John of the Cross in his *Ascent of Mount Carmel* would equate that treasure with knowledge.

Aaron, David, Elijah, Paul, Muhammad, Christ, Moses, Aias, Biarke, Siegfried, Oiagros, Werther, Chiwantopel—all were called into the wilderness. The ascetics were inconsolable wanderers, holing up in caves awaiting visions, surviving on meager staples, drinking tepid water, walking ceaselessly and barefooted through the arid landscape. Such exile offers a variety of interpretations.

There is Nietzsche's condemnation of the civil world looming over the ascetic in the personage of Zarathustra who retreats to his mountain precipice. Or Aeschylus' Prometheus shackled to an outcrop in the Caucasus which, in a sense, the rebellious protagonist craves. Describing mountains, the Sung dynasty painter-poet Kuo Hsi (fl. 1060-1075) wrote:

> Inexhaustible is their mystery.
> In order to grasp their creations
> One must love them utterly,
> Study their essential spirit diligently,
> And never cease contemplating them
> And wandering among them.

Three interpretations: the solitary, embittered self-exile; the political rebel; and the mountain poet. Swamped with the word of a wrathful god, ascetics of the Augustine era were no doubt motivated by all three claims on the soul. In the lyrics of the *Apophthegmata Patrum,* the writings of Basil, Gregory Nazianzen, and Ausonius, we are given a matchless display of starry nights and rocky expanses. In John of Ephesus' *Syriac History of the Eastern Saints,* such feelings for landscape are rendered in words which "hiss and gasp."

The *Conferences of Cassian* and the *Lausiac History of Palladius* provide accounts of hundreds of monasteries in Anthony's Egypt. By 500, when Saint Benedict hid himself in a cave near Subiaco in the Sabine Hills, there were five prominent types of ascetics: the sarabites, consisting of small groups of monks living together; girovagi, wandering hermits who roamed together; cenobites, who lived in large monastic communities; and eremites and anchorites, who were generally solitary.

These monks (*monachos*—man alone) prescribed ghostlike vigils over their own bodies which could last a century. Their legendary stamina is unrivaled. They relished their ghastly bouts of austerity, their frantic wrenching in the night, as only Émile Cioran has described in his *Short History of Decay.* Pachomius of Tabenna in the Nile Valley had seven thousand men and women living together in cells cultivating these orgasms of delectable torment. During the "Era of Retreat" (fourth century), there were five thousand monks on Mount Nitria and ten thousand in Arsinoe. Reports in Palestine and Egypt at the time noted that the desert-mountain monasteries and hermitages boasted of populations exceeding those of neighboring towns.

And there were the competitions: Saint Thalelaeu spent ten years in a suspended tub; the Boskoi sect near Nisibis lived on grass; Acepsimas never left his cell for sixty years; the Syrian Sisoes lived standing up on a cliff ledge, never sleeping; ascetics in Ethiopia placed spears around themselves so that sleep and subsequent angulation of the body would be fatal. The most famous, Symeon Stylites, chained himself atop a column forty cubits high for thirty-seven years. Known as "the most holy martyr in the air" when he finally died in old age, a long succession of other saints paid tribute to their aerial master by locking themselves in small palings on pillars. For centuries the pillar cults were popular.

WHEN THE EASTERN TSIN dynasty made its capital at Nanking in the fourth century A.D., the region of the T'ien-t'ai Mountain was explored. Its karst formations were celebrated and imbued with supernatural legends. Its overhanging rocks, its creamy waterfalls, the "Natural Bridge," and "Jade Terrace" were poetically commemorated in feverish delectations whose philosophical rudiments were divided equally between the canons of Buddhist meditation, *shan shui* (mountain-water landscape painting), and ascent. Ko Hung's *Pao-p'u-tzu* was written in this period, and the association between mountains, mountain climbing, and Taoist immortality was widespread.

The monk T'an-yu built a monastery on the peak subsequent to the explorations of Wang Hsi-chih and Chih Tun. The poet Sun Ch'o introduced the mountain to China's literati with his "Fu on a Visit to T'ien-t'ai," in which he praised it as being divine:

T'ien-t'ai Shan

> Once in view of the peak's Red Wall and Cascade, the mountain climber
> is already within the realm of Taoist immortals.
>
> [Mather]

By the sixth century, this mountain, known as the most sacred to Chinese Buddhism, gave its name to the prominent T'ien-t'ai sect. While the mountain was not to remain the most sacred, it acquired an unprecedented reputation for the times.

The first major Taoist temple had been erected on the mountain in 239 A.D. and was known as T'ung-po tao-kuan. Hsieh ling-yün (fourth century A.D.) climbed it and most of the other difficult peaks south of the Yangtze. For that purpose he invented the first climbing boots and crampons with removable studs. In Li Po's poem relating his own ascent to one of the Taoist earthly paradises in Chekang on T'ien Mu Shan, he says that he wore "Hsieh's climbing shoes to ascend to the rocky stairway through the clouds." J.D. Frodsham sees ling-yün's mountain climbing (*dharmata*) as a "devotional practice" which would have brought him "into contact with the 'Body of Dharma' itself." Hsieh writes:

Try living by the Method of which I speak.
I climbed these crags to build a secluded cabin,
brushing aside the clouds I rested at Stone Gate.
Who can walk on these slippery mosses here,
or clutch the dolichos plants to keep from falling?

One of the most popular immortalist folk legends, the "Liu-Yüan" tale (in which two men who go searching for herbs lose their way amidst the rocks and clouds only to find themselves in paradise), was also engendered on T'ien-t'ai. But the mountain's greatest fame came by way of the three T'ang dynasty hermits: Han-Shan, Shih-te, and Feng-kan. Han-Shan ("Cold Mountain") scribbled out some three hundred poems on bark and on stones and monastery walls. His verse recommends a life style of complete and casual mountain disappearance. Like Hsieh ling-yün, Han-Shan was a climber, a contemporary of the Japanese Shugendō mountaineers.

In his book on the Haguro Sect, H. Byron Earhart introduces a revealing lexicon of ancient Shugendō mountain words. While they stem from a somewhat different religious tradition than Han-Shan's loose Taoism, their meanings promote some appreciation for the mountain-ascetic lore symptomatic of both Chinese and Japanese mountain hermits of the period. I quote some of the more appropriate terms: *ubasoku* (mountain magician), *sendatsu* (a completed mountain guide), *sangaku shinkō* (mountain worship), *yama-biraki* (the ceremony of opening a mountain), *nyūbu* (entering the mountain), *ennen* (ascetic practice of pleasure), *nōdarani* (lifetime mountain ascetic), *suzukake* (ritual lowering of a *yamabushi* over a cliff for the purposes of enlightenment), *sangaku tōbai* (climbing as an act of worship), *sangaku rengyō* (ascetic confinement in mountains), and *shintai-zan* (mountain of worship).

John Climacus and the Ladder to Paradise

THE SYMBOL OF HEIGHT is most easily achieved in the logic of a ladder. Religious history—emphasizing heaven and the divine—invariably projects its moral injunctions in the guise of a journey, of aspiration. The ladder has frequently satisfied the metaphorical demands of such a journey.

The *Egyptian Book of the Dead* provisioned Ra's ascent into heaven upon a ladder, known as the Maquet, which was engraved on numerous tombs during the Old and Middle Kingdoms. Plato's *Symposium*, Plotinus's *Enneads,* and Porphyry's *Commentaries* all utilize the image of a ladder as a convenient means of detailing the astral progress of the appetites. In a variety of cultures, a village shaman is called upon to assist the passage of the dead via the use of a bridge, or, more regularly, a ladder. In the allegories of the Symplegades, the rocks of Scylla and Charybdis and the Straits of Messina are Homerically anointed as the earth-heaven passage.

The *sakhra* or Minbar on the summit of Mount Moriah (now the floor

Pol de Limbourg, *Eden and the Expulsion,* from the Très Riches Heures du Duc de Berry (c. 1515). Musée Condé, Chantilly. Photographie Giraudon

in the Mosque of Omar in Jerusalem) was the original location of Muhammad's trajectory. The religious thrust, the imagery of the vertical, was associated by Euripides with the Pillar of Atlas. Proclus, Heraclitus, and Anaximenes argued over its height. The ladder represents the passage to paradise in the *Hortus deliciarum,* in the third-century Vision of Pepetua, and in the twelfth-century Vision of Alberic. But there is no more graphic portrayal of the religious function of the ladder than in the book of Saint John Climacus.

Abbot of Mount Sinai, Saint John wrote his treatise *The Heavenly Ladder* in the late sixth century. None of the existing early copies of the work antedate the ninth century and they are written in Syriac, Latin, Arabic, Armenian, Greek, Russian, and Spanish. (One of the first books published in North America, *Escala Spiritual de San Juan Climaco,* was printed in the sixteenth century and finally translated into English in 1858.) Saint John wrote his treatise in the shadows of numerous two and three thousand foot granite walls. The work attests to a jubilantly physical mechanism driving his spiritual theories as it did for Anthony. To this day the dozen or so monks of Saint Catherine's Monastery regularly hike up the mountain as a religious component of their Byzantine orthodoxy and the "scala santa" is the embodiment of psychosomatic ascension whose ethical delineations were applied by Aquinas and Dante to the many layers of the Renaissance Empirium.

Climacus utilized Jacob's Ladder (Genesis 28:12) as a prime motif to intellectually engage the awesome granite-domed desert environment in which, during forty years of solitude, he evidently occupied his time through prayer, writing, and climbing. He considered himself the second Moses, and his book explicitly states that to ascend the ladder is to ascend Mount Sinai, which is equivalent to attaining enlightenment, paradise, Christ.

This functional attainment is the characteristic message of most sacred mountain-monastery configurations. The Chinese sought self-revelation on the slopes of Hua Shan; Spanish monks hike up the precipices of Montserrat; Greek Orthodox priests scale Mount Athos; Russian Orthodox adepts dwell on the cliffside of the Mount of Temptations overlooking Jericho. At Bhutan's Taktsang Monastery, and throughout Western Tibet, Chile, the Pyrenees, and Switzerland, the religious ascent is via this path, this ladder made flesh. The Arabic ḥajj pilgrimage is celebrated annually at the holy mountains of Arafah. The Jains go to Mount Ābū. The sadhus to Mount Kailas. In Japan, mountain pilgrimage has been outlined for centuries in the *Kojiki.* Throughout the Middle Ages and the Renaissance, pilgrims, such as the famous Felix Fabri, made their peregrinations to the Holy Land, and an arduous and risky journey awaited them in the hard deserts leading to Mount Sinai.

Climacus's book is divided into thirty chapters, or rungs, as he calls them. Each step is designated an accompanying praxis. Of the illustrations, the most common image takes the form of a diagonal ladder upon which numerous monks are grappling. Christ is leaning over the top to assist them in their final efforts. Some of the monks have lost their footing and are plummeting upside down into hell—not exactly the Blakean ladder in which Beatrices, long-robed and sinewy, strolled happily into the stars.

In one mid-eleventh-century miniature, a double ladder has been figured, its craftsman apparently unable to accept the notion of climbing thirty narrow rungs in a single flight. In the Princeton Codex (1081) one scene depicts the wearied face and an arm of a solitaire protruding from a small cave near the peak of Mount Sinai. He is lowering a basket down the cliff by tattered rope to obtain food from the monastery his superior discipline had bade him to forego.

> The truth is that no searcher can readily forego the ladder.
>
> [Beckett, *The Lost Ones*]

Cartographies of the Other World

E MBEDDED IN THE PLINTH of every Hindu temple is an altar symbolizing the mountain otherworld. Known as the *shikhara*, or tower, this architectural form neatly conveys the meaning of height, an attitude or posture implicit in the Hindu concept of *moksa* or ultimate salvation. The Buddhist equivalent of this form is the *chorten*. Throughout villages in Tibet, *chorten* funeraries line the monasteries, containing the ashes of the deceased lamas. Constructed from adobe, they are segmented sevenfold and conceptually embody the realm of the gods, an Asiatic Olympus.

The most sacred mountain to both Hindu and Buddhist, this Kingdom of Brahma is known as Mount Kailasha, or Kailas. To the Japanese Buddhists it is called Tettchisen; to Indian Buddhists it is known as the mythical Su-Meru; to the Tibetans it is Di Sé. Just over 22,000 feet, the mountain confronts the spiritual aspirant with a tantalizing history. It has never been climbed. Pilgrims from all over Asia have come to this mountain hoping to make *parikrama*. Few of them actually complete the ascetic ordeal which requires a circumambulation of the mountain on the hands and knees, and generally takes two months.

The *Vishnu Purana* delineates a string of other mythological ranges through which the ascetic must pass in his religious trek. The pilgrim's ascent commences in India and continues through ever growing chains leading northward. The first range is known as Himavat, then the Himalaya, the Kimpurusha, the Himakuta, the Harivarsha, and finally the Ilavrita which is centered by the golden mountain Kailasha.

Some four thousand years ago, Indo-European tribes moved across the Kailasha region passing by the sacred Lake Manasarovar. Cattle driving Aryans, these were the people of the Vedas who entered Northwestern India prefiguring the age of the Upaniṣads. Emperor Ashoka built a hermitage in the area and the Tibetan saint, Milarepa, triumphed over a Bön priest by flying to the peak's summit before him, thus ensuring the spread of Buddhism over the previous shamanic faith. In the *Mahābhārata* both Nārada and Arjuna fly to the summit of Meru, Śiva's Mount, in ecstatic trance.

The Hindus believe that Lord Śiva and his consort Parvati, "the most beautiful woman in the world" and daughter of Himalchal, inhabit the summit of this windswept mountain in divine, immortal connubium. Śiva is the patron saint of most Indian ascetics. He is always figured as surrounded by wild animals; he is naked and maintains an erection. The Saivites, or followers of Śiva, are divided into six sects, the last of which are the Yogin. These yogis are wanderers; they worship mountains as the archetypal home of their divine master. In the *Rgveda*, the *muni*—or ascetics—are said to have the wind as their girdle. The seventh-century Chinese explorer Hiuen Tsang, studying ascetic communities of Northern India, described one particular group at Prayāg: these ascetics climbed a high pillar and hung by one foot and one hand "wonderfully" turning slowly with the sun all day until it set.

The Hindus make more pilgrimages than any other people. They are fanatical walkers. Whole families of sadhus, even as far south as Cape Comorin, still uproot their lean-tos once a year to wander barefoot throughout the whole of India toward Kailasha. Since 1962 however, the Chinese have barred access to it. But there are hundreds of other sacred peaks, and thousands of shrines all commemorating Śiva. Miguel Serrano, Chile's ex-embassador to India and an Andean mountaineer and mystic, describes the Hindu relation to these high-altitude altars:

> This extraordinary people had created a mythology as gigantic as the mountaintops which surrounded their country. These very mountains were united to their souls. . . .Like most people who look upon nature as something symbolic, they are forever condemned to the eternal and unmeasurable. In order to survive in ordinary life, and so as not to lose themselves forever on this otherworldly plane, they have had to create an elaborate structure around them, with the result that they live almost entirely according to formulas. Lacking any real way to measure the world around them, they are frequently misunderstood. Their only real measurement is the symbolism of their high mountains, and their gradiose philosophy, which in turn seems modelled on these summits.
>
> *The Serpent of Paradise*

The ranges which lead to the summit of Kailasha are also reflected in the Indian subcontinent as in a still pond. These antipodal strata embrace the flatlands, the rice paddies, the river deltas, and the sweltering village outbacks unchanged since ancient times. Asceticism in this hot and fly-ridden maze of history and poverty is a philosophical rapture of endurance, a masochistic, worldly concentration. The Bodhisattva disciple of Buddha and the Yogi disciple of Siva are volunteers to the divine tension deriving from the excruciating contrast between the Himalyan alpine worlds and those of the plains beneath.

The assimilation of Su-Meru from popular Indian iconography into Buddhist cosmology occurred by way of the Triloka Abhidharma philoso-

Giovanni Di Paolo, *St. John in the Wilderness* (c. 1450-60). Courtesy of the Art Institute of Chicago

phy, an aerial metaphysics of trance heavens and psychological negations. This Buddhist adoption transformed the act of pilgrimage into a mental act, according sheer and rugged stages of contemplative penetration to the *parikrama* circuit. Su-Meru is symbolically 1,680,000 miles high. Milton seems to have envisioned it:

> Against the eastern gate of Paradise,
> levell'd his evening-rays:
> > It was a rock
> Of alabaster, pil'd up to the clouds
> Conspicuous far, winding with one ascent
> Accessible from earth one entrance high;
> The rest was craggy cliff, that overhung
> Still as it rose impossible to climb.

[*Paradise Lost,* Book Four]

Triloka consists of ten levels of psychological implantation and subsequent geographical apportionment. The adept experiences a complicated "summit meditation" which involves his witnessing the infinity of space as the ultimate unrecognition of self. In this transparency of being, there is a silence, cold blue, like lapis, which cuts through the barriers separating subject and object. This abyss constitutes a paradox known as Ākīmcanyāy-atana, which refers to the ultimate limit of perception. Beyond is Nirvāna.

The Buddhist Mahayana schools, particularly during the medieval period in Bhutan, provide us with the essence of Su-Meru's beauty in artwork depicting colorful cosmic spirals and wheels of time. The mandala frescoes in Paro Dzong are "guiding threads" of the movement of consciousness from finite to infinite things; from interior ruminations to the external world of landscape. The threads have become holy formulas which, like Himalayan mantras, are meant to transcend the ambiguities of language, the contradictions, against the backdrop of sublime nature in which self-obsession is plunged.

The essence of sacrality to the Indian mind, the Himalayas were revered in the *Rgveda* (VII, xxxv, 8). "Abode of the Glaciers," to see them even once was enough to remove all sin. To actually drink of their torrential waters was to cast one into paradise. The Sikkimese Lepchas worship Kanchenjunga (28,156 feet) as the great Snow Fortress of the Five Storehouses. They believe it contains minerals, grains, salt, weapons, and, most important, holy scriptures. The mountain's glaciers fall into a small area on the latitude of Florida that is rich in flora and fauna: there, great black bears and snow leopards roam amidst more than six hundred species of orchid. Kanchenjunga is surrounded by other peaks—Kumbakarna, Kang, Simvo, Pandim, Jannu—and together they offer an alluring, heavenly splendor which provides all water, and thus all life. Magnificent, lambent, and hanging over their lives, one can readily understand the Lepcha cultural heritage of mountain worship.

Ruins discovered in this area contain pillars probably erected to simulate the religious aura of height these massifs conjured in the minds of those early inhabitants of the Tibetan plateau (see Wojkowitz). Like the ziggurats, or the pillars of Sinai, these ruins, welling up in an archeology of ladders, suggest a love affair as ancient as man himself. This is not to imply that these people are necessarily fond of their mountains. The mountains mean hardship, constant cold, and danger. And while mountains provide what to some Westerners' minds may be splendid isolation, to the Easterner they are barriers, without amenity. In the Alps, the same dichotomy existed among the Savoyards. Until the British offered money for guide services, there was no widespread interest in wandering unnecessarily through snow. But the Sherpa, like the Swiss mountain farmer, is a member of a hearty breed. In a sense he reflects the character of his mountains as they have permeated his upbringing, his way of seeing the world. Colin Turnbull formulates this symbiosis with regard to the Ik who inhabit the top of Mount Morungole in Northern Uganda:

> Just as the Mbuti Pygmies in their lush tropical rain forest regard the forest as a benevolent deity, so do the Ik in their rocky mountain stronghold think of the mountains as being peculiarly and specially theirs. People and mountains belong to each other and are inseparable. . . .The Ik, without their mountains, would no longer be the Ik and similarly they say, the mountains, without the Ik would no longer be the same mountains, if indeed they continued to exist at all.

Classical Attitudes

WE HAVE NUMEROUS examples of Greek and Roman admiration of mountain landscape, but there is no indication of a tradition of mountain worship per se. A fondness for rugged terrain is couched in literary phrase and pictorial representation, lending a subliminal quality to an expressèd Mediterranean naturalism. From Homer to Saint Augustine there is a sense of the mountain sublime: Homer's "beetling cliffs"; the pastoral epigrams of the poetess Anyte of Tegea; the first, seventh, and tenth *Idylls* of Theokritos associating the cave Nymphs of Nyssa with Pan and the infant Dionysos; and the ascent of Mount Dindymon where the "Makrian heights and all the Thracian coast came out before their eyes as if they could touch it. . . " in Apollonios of Rhodes' fourth-century B.C. epic, the *Argonautica.*

When one observes the sacred shrines constructed on such sites as the Plistus Gorge, Sounion, Mount Athos, on Ida, Rhodes, Atabyrium, Oeta, Parnes, Olympus, and Taletum, it is difficult to isolate the sense of awe, love, and admiration of mountains, as expressed in the mute commemorative stones, from the mountains themselves, their setting and commanding view. The expression is as poised as Greek sculpture.

Dicaearchus, the topographer, Strabo, and Polybius all detail the Greek assimilation of mountain names. And Arcadia, the mountainous region in Greek prehistory, speaks to English literature of a mountain-pastoral paradise imbedded in the humanist psyche.

During the early Hellenistic period, the basic ingredients of landscape painting and pastoral verse—a rocky groundscape and a high pillar within the scene—began to emerge. Vitruvius (first century B.C.) describes the "wanderings of Odysseus" as "good old decoration," referring to a fashion of pictorial art seen today in a sequence of wall paintings discovered in a house on the Esquiline. Its landscapes are mythological depictions of Odysseus among the Laistrygones. In one fresco a mountain god relaxes atop a high crag; he has skinny legs and is apparently sunbathing.

The Romans had a zeal for venerating wild places, although they understated their passion. Livius Andronicus and Naevius cited mountains as "high and rugged." Pacuvius depicted the wild rocky regions of the Bacchae in the *Periboea,* and for Lucretius hills were the homes of primitive people offering welcome contrast to the Roman cities. Catullus called Mount Aetna the "fire of love." In the *Attis* he describes a youth in consecration to Cybele, castrating himself and withdrawing to the loneliness of Mount Ida. The most substantial evidence of Roman wilderness adoration (or cunning) may be found in the inscriptions stamped onto numerous mountain-worshiping seals located along old Roman alpine roads which run through Taurini and the Rhaetien Alps—Roman talismans.

Renaissance Perspectives

SAINT AUGUSTINE'S CREDO, echoing the patrician, manic-bucolia of Virgil's *Georgics,* challenged man toward psychoanalysis by placing Mind in direct opposition to Wilderness. "Men go out to wonder at the mountain heights. . . but they ignore themselves," he mused in his *Confessions* (399 A.D.). This emphatic construance of the indoors with a kind of intellectual and moral presumption triggered a new European perspective. The naturalism of early allegories and picaresque was to be specifically fashioned, its wilds cultivated. Virgins, Madonnas, Dianas, and Fête Champêtres figured amidst tampered environments; crags and meadows adjusted in size and import to accommodate the persuasions of medieval imagination. Upon reading Augustine during an ascent of Mount Ventoux, Petrarch was prompted to descend. However, Gottfried Von Strassburg (early thirteenth century) apparently remained free of this Augustine thraldom. While his evocations of wilderness reveal a legendary naïveté—indicative of the era's allegiance to artistic miniature: the monastic cloisture, the walled gardens of an aristocrat's villa—his work also presents a strain of sentiment that is both lean and tenacious, a realism of stark outlines and suggestive depth that traces back to the penumbra of similarly unusual landscape depictions in *Beowulf.* Strassburg writes:

> Mountains lie all about, with many difficult turns leading here and there. The trails run up and down; we are martyred with obstructing rocks. No matter how well we keep the path if we miss one single step, we shall never know safe return. But whoever has the good fortune to penetrate that wilderness, for his labors will gain a beautiful reward, for he shall find there his heart's delight. The wilderness abounds in whatsoever the ear desires to

hear, whatsoever would please the eye: so that no one could possibly wish to be anywhere else. And this I well know; for I have been there.

[*Tristan und Isolde,*
lines trans. by Joseph Campbell]

In 1492 Antoine de Ville made the spectacular first ascent of Mont Aiguille, a rock peak in the Dauphiné (6,880 feet) which Rabelais termed "the inaccessible." Others were beginning to take an interest in wilderness if only for purposes of economic gain. Between 1500 and 1650 the Americas' Eastern seaboards were to produce some 181 tons of mountain gold for European monarchies. The images conjured by tales of fabulous riches in India and Cathay enabled the European imagination to place its "other worlds" there. "Not only has this navigation confounded many affirmations of former writers about terrestrial things," wrote Francesco Guicciardini (1483-1540), "but it has also given some anxiety to interpretors of the Holy Scriptures." In his *History of the World* Sir Walter Raleigh weighed the "evidence" of Desert Fathers and explorers in an effort to "place" paradise, the Christian New Testament Wilderness. This equation of quasi-Biblical topography with the geographical exploration endemic in Raleigh's time stemmed in part from the literary tradition of the goddesses Fortuna and Natura—Fates and Muses possessed of virtue and cathartic power who were lodged atop inaccessible mountain gardens to which a hundred dozen picaresque heroes would attempt ascent.

Convinced of the possibility of discovering the land of milk and honey, Columbus brought along Hebrew-speaking Louis de Torres, thinking he might be useful in paradise. In his Third Letter, Columbus indicated he knew exactly where it was: on a mythic mountaintop south of the equator. Bacon's *New Atlantis*, Campanella's *City of the Sun*, die-hard Jesuits in Central Asia, the Prester John tales, the letters of Sir John Maundeville, and the flood of expeditionary data generated by the "voyage extraordinaire" genre created an impulsive atmosphere conducive not only to a Don Quixote or a King Lear, but to an eventual Candide, Crusoe, and Humboldt. In his *Treatise of the Sphere* (1537), Pedro Nunes wrote, "New islands, new lands, new seas, new peoples: and what is more, a new sky and new stars."

This exploratory curiosity, commencing with an unprecedented vigor in the Renaissance and continuing through the romantic era into the first century of tourism, debated the whereabouts of paradise. While Christianity maintained its aerial Heaven, there was no way to check the apocryphal melee of other suggested sites, nearly all of them situated on mountains in the "East." John Salkeld's celebrated *Treatise of Paradise and the Contents thereof* (London, 1617) provided the first comprehensive anthology of quotations from saints and obscure journeyers which offered "indisputable proof" that paradise existed in the "Oriental mountains." The romantics were reared on the lyrical overtures of such a zenith. Wordsworth's disappointment on crossing the Simplon Pass stemmed perhaps from the fact that the Alps were so well trammeled—

Joachim Patinier (c. 1480-1524), *St. Jerome in a Rocky Landscape*. Courtesy of the Prado, Madrid

Behold, my son, for ninety-five years I have been in this cave. . . . I even ate dust . . . from hunger, I drank water from the sea. . . . Frequently they (demons) dragged me from here to the base of the mountain until there was no skin or flesh on my limbs . . . finally . . . I saw the realms of the Kingdom.

— *The History of Abba Marcus of Mount Tharmaka*

so accessible—that they failed to meet up to his eager historical expectations.

The late fifteenth century witnessed an extraordinary change in pictorial art—a new visual concept—namely, mountains.

Between 1485, when Giovanni Bellini painted his *Saint Francis in Ecstacy* and Leonardo completed *The Virgin of the Rocks*, and 1717, the date affixed to Watteau's serene *Embarkation for Cythera,* the alpine scene acquired a preeminence, a simultaneous diversity of invigorated perspectives previously unequaled in the West. If one compares the coeval Persian landscapes of a Sultan Muhammad (early Safavid period), where illuminations of satinlike luster display colorful unreal inscapes of paradise and blurred outcrop, or the "Individualists" of early Ch'ing painting in China, where nonobjectivism has taken irreality and stark linearism into threads and ink blots of the other world, one appreciates the cultural daring of the dozen or so Renaissance masters who achieved, for the first time in Europe, an intensely believable feeling for mountains. One can discern in such landscapes a birth of real curiosity. The vague and stunted attributions which had previously branded the alpine world suddenly burgeoned forth with overt admiration, nuance, and flair. An era of discovery—entrenched in long-standing allegory—suddenly, and dauntlessly, careened into the rocks and chasms with disciplined inquiry.

Granted, the Chinese had attained and abstracted such perspicuity eight hundred years earlier. Wilderness fascinated the Asian mind since primitive times. Not so in the West—all the more intriguing Europe's relatively late, but nonetheless fantastic, plunge into the sublime.

Lucas Cranach the Elder's magical *Rest on the Flight to Egypt* (1504) portrays a luscious hilly pine forest in the tones of an alpine setting. Albrecht Dürer's *Alpine Scene* (c. 1495) and *Lamentation of Christ* (c. 1500), and Pieter Bruegel's *Alpine Landscape* (1553-55) portray rock studies which Altdorfer's *Alexander the Great Defeating Darius* (1529) would perfect with splendor and precision in lighting and proportion, as if he had flown over the mountains with a camera. Joachim Patinier's *Saint Jerome in a Rocky Landscape* and Giovanni Di Paolo's *Saint John the Baptist* (c. 1450) lent a symbolic febrility to the Gothic spires and eerie crags distinct from the thematic religiosity upon which the landscapes were otherwise riveted. Bellini and Breughel were largely unrivaled in their treatment of mountain landscape. Both painters were concerned with revealing scenes accurately and in completion. Bellini's *Baptism of Christ* (1500-2), *Allegory of the Progress of the Soul* (1490-1500), *Transfiguration* (1455), and *St. Jerome* (1480-85, and 1505) all portray the literal ideal Renaissance landscape. The rocks are bathed in light, veinlike crooks fanning the geometrical abutments, extravagant color filling the valleys, permeating slopes, and lending life to an era which capitalized on fantasy. In Breughel's *Winter, the Dark Day* the sentience of Bellini has converged with the scope and pageantry of panorama conveyed by Altdorfer. A village scene is set against the ethereal, snowy sentinels of a dramatic mountain range. The entire history of Europe is figured in those crags, and in their monarchial dominance of the foreground. In the works of Mathias Grünewald and Jan de Cock, such steeps came to be identifiable by the governing realism of their awesome verticality. In Grünewald's troubling *Isenheim Altarpiece* (1512-1515) we unmistakeably espy three successive walls, sheer and lime-stonelike, which strike definite resemblance to the spires surrounding the Zugspitz.

In works of El Greco (1548-1614), such as the *Landscape of Toledo* and *Mount Sinai*, religion has merged into the deep-laden meaning of vertical walls. The seventeenth-century Flemish tradition of "paysage montagneux" would alter this symbolic similitude, freeing scenery to exist independent of human subject matter. Hercules Seghers's *Mountain Landscape* (c. 1630) and the works of Jan Loten (c.1618-81) placed all accent and significance in the mountains themselves, illuminating ridges and hanging hillocks with a richness of lighting and texture never before realized in Western art, save for Bellini, Breughel, and Altdorfer. Watteau's peaks behind his *Embarkation* scene, golden and glaciated, reveal a passion whose origins, with an inexorable logic of their own, go back to those famed, half-concealed spires behind the Mona Lisa (1505), as enigmatic as her smile.

Leonardo visited glaciers for both scientific and artistic purposes. During a mountain trip in 1499, he experienced a storm breaking over an alpine valley which he later captured in an extraordinary red-chalk drawing. More landscape drawings from Leonardo survive than from any other fifteenth-century painter. His first signed work, composed at age twenty-one in 1473 and now in the Uffizi, details a cliff-entrenched village. In his *Trattato della Pittura*, the first landscape treatise ever written by an artist in Europe, Leonardo wrote that, "in such walls the same thing happens as in the sound of bells, in whose strokes you may find every word which you can imagine." Compare this to a sentiment of Kuo Hsi, the foremost landscape theoretician in the Sung dynasty: "there are four kinds of landscape paintings: those which can be contemplated; those in which one can travel; those through which one may ramble; and those within which one may dwell" (see Esther J.-Leong).

The Renaissance landscape painters provided a sorely needed impetus for exploration into Europe's interior. In the mid-sixteenth century, the Swiss scientist Conrad Gessner walked each summer through the Alps, and the traveled Englishman, Fynes Moryson, publicized his own delight in mountains early in the next century. And while Saint François de Sales visited Chamonix in 1606 and wrote favorably about its peaks, the average individual probably agreed with the Jesuit Kirchner who spoke out against the demonic nature of the Alps or with William Richards who, in his amusing *Wallography* (1682), noted that the mountains of Wales had a "variety of Precipice to break one's neck." Yet scarcely a decade later, William Nicholas was to write that even under the most "desperate" of conditions, mountains must "strike us with awful Reverence." This combination of linguistic excitability, stemming from a tension ingrained for centuries in the European attitude to wilderness, was to foster the rash of mountain adoration exhibited over the coming centuries.

THE EIGHTEENTH CENTURY witnessed a pronounced shift in mountain perspective. So curious was the scientific and exploratory imagination of the day that within a single generation the pangs of romanticism and ecology were suffered simultaneously. By 1800 thousands of reveling families were rolling across Western Europe in their carriages, visiting Gibbon's house, quoting Rousseau on the rocks of Meillerie, and extending Britain's legacy of the Grand Tour to the glaciers. Voltaire, Chateaubriand, Rosseau, and Bernadine de St. Pierre had paved the way with enamoring pledges to the noble savage upon whom they based their revolutionary ideologies of nature. This syndrome of rustification has been well documented (see Marjorie Nicolson).

What most characterized the mountain reveries of romanticism was the initial excitement of tourism—public exploration. Enlightenment poets such as Gray and Addison had latched onto the delightful oxymorons which expressed their wavering aesthetic convictions—"agreeable kinds of horror"—the reverberations of which would be felt 150 years hence in Henry Adams's *Education.* But to those swooning followers of Byron on the Wengern Alp, the mountains had crystallized certain fundamental longings. Seventy-five years later, the great literary critic and mountaineer Sir Leslie Stephen would lament the destruction of the Alps resulting from excessive British tourism. Ironically, his own Victorian enthusiasms encouraged the onslaught.

John Martin remained in London essentially his entire adult life. When he took up painting in 1812 at the age of twenty-three, his first canvas required only a single month to complete. He titled his work *Sadak In Search of the Waters of Oblivion.* Although he had never seen a mountain, it tells the story of the nobleman Sadak who climbs his own Mount Analogue in search of the immortal waters. A pastiche titan with a body like Michelangelo's Adam, Sadak is portrayed mantling atop a dark abyss onto the rocky ledge of a pool formed by waterfalls from higher glaciers. The peaks are captured in their essence, an otherwordly splendor shattering the intoxicating storm which bursts concentrically over them. The rocks are incandescent, straining to burst into light. There is no coherent detail in the upper spheres. Lightning breaks beneath rock; rock becomes cloud which in turn merges into ice. The human fledgling grapples on the edge of the world, his musculature golden and dwarfed. The awe is ravaging; it surpasses in hallucinatory realism, in sublimity, anything ever produced by De Loutherbourg, Turner, or Friedrich.

Yet no reading of the period could have provided Martin with the precise details and proportions his sedentary life precluded. His biogra-

Sadak in Search of the Waters of Oblivion

Leonardo da Vinci, *Virgin of the Rocks* detail (1485). Courtesy des Musées Nationaux, The Louvre, Paris

Chosen are those artists who penetrate to the region of that secret place where primeval power nurtures all evolution. . . . Who is the artist that would not dwell there? In the womb of nature at the source of creation, where the secret key to all lies guarded.

— *Paul Klee on Modern Art*

pher, Mary Pendered, asks with bewilderment how Martin acquired such a magnitude of vision, having never experienced the mountains. Martin was so precise that in a pamphlet written for one of his exhibits, he stated that "the highest mountain in the picture will be found to be 15,000 feet."

Martin's great rival was Francis Danby, who between 1825 and 1841 traveled extensively in Wales, Norway and Switzerland. Though his mountain paintings lack Martin's mythological breathlessness, they possess greater believability. Danby never attempts to encapsule infinity; his focus is real. J. Romney's engraving, *The Climber of Helvellyn* (1825) based on Danby's lost *Death of An Alpine Hunter* (1825) reflects the Danby style at its Romantic best. The death posture might as well be the scene of lovemaking. The flesh is sterling, unmarred, in graceful repose amidst rocks which seem almost sympathetic. There is a listless ease.

Percy Shelley, A Wilderness Exile

SHELLEY MOVED RELENTLESSLY from one outpost to the next, relating the details of his wanderings in ruminative missives while refashioning those confessional exultations throughout the body of his work. The "mountain" provided an effective vehicle for generating metaphors relevant to his state of mind: a desert, a repressor of energy, the material embodiment of transcendence, of poignant inaccessibility—it was a sensual vortex for him, eternal, alien, and most of all, beautiful. It overpowered him, lending an autobiographical allegory, a reliable shape for his lyrical transports. More than any other romantic poet, Shelley responded to the wilderness with a vision, a personal equation that set him apart from his era. Unlike their effect on many of his contemporaries who worshiped objects of Nature in trendy cults of adulation, the wilds worked more soberly to stimulate the dramatist, philosopher, and political theorist that was Shelley. Cathartically refining his doubts, the mountains provided one setting after another for his poetic schemes, and shaped the ironic, devastating fabric of his unfulfilled ideals.

A study of the *Shelley Concordance* reveals over four hundred usages of the words *mountain, hill,* and *rock*; several hundred references to *wilderness, river,* and *wild*. It is in "The Assassins," "Alastor, or The Spirit of Solitude," "Mont Blanc," and *Prometheus Unbound,* as well as in his letters, that the relationship between Shelley's journeys and his intellectual leanings is made apparent.

Traveling with Mary Godwin and Jane Clairmont in July of 1814, Shelley visited the Alps for the first time, following three years of Welsh and Lakeland roaming. Having been thrown out of Oxford for asserting his atheism, he had been disowned by his father. At twenty-one, Shelley was fiercely alone, save for his two female devotees. In the onrush of the spectacular scenery around Lake Lucerne, he found a landscape which almost mirrored—in its isolation—his own resolute exile. He composed several chapters of a political story entitled "The Assassins" detailing a group of Christians who sought refuge in the wilds of a mythologic Lebanon. The allegorical isolation served to nourish his experience of Switzerland. In a reverie of earth, and with a purpose that would later project his Übermensch Prometheus, Shelley drew upon a vivid legacy of utopian paradise after Samuel Johnson's "Rasselas":

> Piles of monumental marble and fragments of columns . . . flowering orange-tree, the balsam, and innumerable odoriferous shrubs, grew wild in the desolate portals. . . . The immensity of these precipitous mountains, with their starry pyramids of snow, excluded the sun, which overtopped not, even in its meridian, their overhanging rocks. . . . No spectator could have refused to believe that some spirit of great intelligence and power had hallowed these wild and beautiful solitudes to a deep and solemn mystery. . . . To live, to breathe, to move, was itself a sensation of immeasurable transport.

Shelley continually used the word *desolate*, infusing it with an etymologically incorrect lavishness. The contradiction offers an example of the romantic inclination to emphasize extremity. Eighteenth-century prescriptive aesthetics provided linguistic precedents for such usage. Rousseau's Saint Preux, Beattie's Minstrel, and Montesquieu's troglodyte all shared an ethos of rapture which proclaimed the barren beauty of the wilds. The visual arts of Shelley's age further accented the convenient duality of oxymoron. Multiple interpretation, freeing the viewer's imagination, was crystallized on sprawling canvases that revealed the entire spectrum of alpine evocations at a whimsical glance. Philip de Loutherbourg's *An Avalanche in the Alps* (1803) provided the cue symptomatic of both Manfred's and Childe Harold's outbursts:

> Lo! Where it comes like an eternity,
> As if to sweep down all things in its track,
> Charming the eye with dread, a matchless cataract,
> Horribly beautiful!   ["Childe Harold," IV, 69-72]

Friedrich extended this tendency with *Chalk Cliffs of Rügen* (c. 1818), *Watzmann* (1824-25), *Landscape in the Harz Mountains* (1820), *Rocky Ravine* (1812), and his Riesengebirge paintings. Such portraitures were characteristic of the romantic passion for remote mountains which could lend their forbidding if alluring prospects to the tablature of human destiny. In the charged admixture of landscape and mind was something akin to creative insomnia, a wilderness calling that brought an entire generation of artists out into the open.

Though we cannot be precisely certain what Shelley read between his 1814 summer in the Alps and his journey to Chamonix exactly two years later, we can assume, based on the details of Mary's journal, that he was generally familiar with the current scientific and literary reviews. Three lengthy articles published in the *Edinburgh Review* presented Humboldt's findings in South America as well as newly acquired data from the leading

Himalayan explorers of the day. In the November 1814 *Review* there are descriptions of Cotopaxi's eruption, of the caldera, of the lava flows and snow fields. Humboldt is quoted: "In scaling the volcano . . . it would be impossible to reach the brink of the crater." It is likely that Shelley saw this prior to the fall of 1815 when he wrote "Alastor."

Meaning "evil genius," "Alastor, or The Spirit of Solitude" is cast in a setting as remote and impossibly wild as Shelley could configure. The Poet in the work is Shelley's doppelgänger visionary. This second-self probes a solipsism which is self-destructive and epical. He tracks a cliff-girded dream-torrent to its source in a pathological quest for pure experience. The pursuit undermines itself in a revelation without value, that of death. Verse in synonymity with stones underfoot, the poetic abandonment of "Alastor" lays its claims to credibility in the light of Shelley's own mountain and river experiences. Through "many a wide waste and tangled wilderness," the Poet travels from Athens to "Cachmire" via Africa. "Nature's most secret steps/He, like her shadow, has pursued, where'er/The red volcano overcanopies/Its fields of snow, and pinnacles of ice." The Poet wanders among "eternal pyramids" and "desert hills" suggesting with his whole being a reason behind the awesome shapes, a sphinxian gravity which is transcendental.

The Poet ponders his fate, staring down into water which reflects the endless labyrinth of the cliff face above. We feel the epic burden, the predicament of Shelley's own driven restlessness. Both Humboldt and Milton invoke the "impossible" climb. Shelley is spurred on and jettisons his Poet farther afield. Wan and confused, he arrives at the river's source surrounded by the "ethereal cliffs/Of Caucasus, whose icy summits shone/Among the stars like sunlight." Traversing the outback of transfiguration, crossing "polished stones," he quests frantically after a vision with incandescent resolve. Acres of air and the roar of cataracts embracing him, he reaches a small alcove on a mountain's edge where he surrenders his life "on the smooth brink/Of that obscurest chasm."

The wilderness setting in "Alastor" is fashioned to evoke the ideal landscape for exile. Shelley wants to acknowledge the dangerous destiny— which is isolation—but he cannot do so entirely, because his despair contains the seed of its own perpetuation, a mechanism characteristic of the romantic Weltschmerz. "Alastor" could never have been philosophically confined to urban topography. Few of Shelley's works were. Ironically, while the poem moves with ardent ferocity over an immense cartography, Shelley had in fact settled in Bishopsgate, England, leasing a house, facing defeated permanence.

As exemplified in the details of his life, the fate of the wanderer is one of Shelley's most graphic motifs. The disarray of peaks and ponds reflecting abject nothingness in rhythm offered Shelley the spatial coordinates he required. The undefiled, illimitable wilderness, a tradition of inaccessible paradise, evoked a topophilia, a private touchstone which was his profound sense of place. It is no coincidence that the story behind

"Alastor" resembles Martin's *Sadak* painting. It is likely that Shelley saw the work exhibited at the British Institution in London since he later wrote an eighty-line poem entitled "Sadak the Wanderer—A Fragment" which was published posthumously in 1828.

Shelley was lodged between the aesthetic formulas of an Edmund Burke, and the first intimations of a Whymper. He lived lyrically on the edge of an age, in the shadows of a new influx, still able to generate contexts of lore which served his mysticism with a vitality no other poet so simultaneously sensitive to personal, social, and natural details would have sustained. Shelley's situation was fraught with longings which extended like brilliant tentacles in two opposing directions.

By 1783 there had developed among foreign visitors "the fashion of viewing mountains and glaciers," wrote Gibbon in his *Autobiography*, and by 1812, the Benedictine monk from Disentis, Placidus Spescha, informs us that "Englishmen, Frenchmen, Germans, Italians, [came] every year." By July 1816, when Shelley visited Chamonix, Mont Blanc had been climbed eleven times and had seen many other attempts. He was familiar with this climbing activity, as were most other visitors to the Vale who hired guides and heard the infamous stories. In the preface to *History of A Six Weeks Tour* (1817), an apologetic note admits to incomplete accounts of "scenes which are now so familiar to our countrymen." In his *Travellers in Switzerland*, Gavin De Beer provides an invaluable chronological bibliography of all Swiss travel literature, citing 195 individuals who visited Chamonix prior to 1816 and published books or articles incorporating landscape descriptions of the area. One Lady De Clifford writes, "On the day when we visited these icy wilds [the Mer de Glace—1816] there were not less than thirty persons who came to indulge a similar curiosity. Almost all these were English."

Gottlieb Gruner had published his three-volume *Die Eisegebirge Des Schweizerlandes* in 1760, the same year the young Saussure had visited the Vale and offered a prize to the first ascent party up Mont Blanc, a challenge untried for fifteen years, and not successfully met until 1786 by Paccard and Balmat. An account of Saussure's own third ascent was included in his celebrated, and syndicated, *Voyages dans les Alpes* (1796), published three years after Wordsworth's *Descriptive Sketches* of *his* own first alpine journey. An entire genre of ascent narrative had come into vogue: W. Coxe's *Sketches* (1779) and *Travels in Switzerland* (1789), T. Martyn's *Sketch of a Tour through Swisserland* (1788), Plinkerton's *Voyages and Travels, etc.* (1814), and G. W. Bridge's *Alpine Sketches* (1814). Shelley's adamant departure from these fashionable excursuses, his insistence upon upholding a pure symbol in conjunction with his *own* experience, creates an ambiguity of special historical interest. Mary's *Frankenstein, or, The Modern Prometheus*, her journal, and Claire's journal, along with Shelley's extensive letter to Thomas Peacock offer a portrait of Shelley during his three-day sojourn in Chamonix in late July of 1816, when he wrote "Mont Blanc."

Joseph Severn, *Shelley Contemplating Amidst the Baths of Caracalla* (1845). Courtesy of the Keats-Shelley Memorial House, Rome

But how shall I describe to you the scenes by which I am now surrounded.
—To exhaust epithets which express the astonishment & admiration—the
very excess of satisfied expectation, where expectation scarcely acknowledged any boundary— ...I too had read before now the raptures of
travellers. I will be warned by their example. I will simply detail to you,
all that I can relate...I never knew I never imagined what mountains
were before. The immensity of these aerial summits excited, when they
suddenly burst upon the sight a sentiment of extatic wonder not unallied
to madness ...

The seven-and-a-half-page letter to Peacock covers his entire journey with
the exception of one day, July 23, the date affixed to the composition of
"Mont Blanc."

The sculptor Henry Moore has said that "every idea has a physical
shape" lending it reality. Shelley's system of seeing Mont Blanc is trans-
fixed in that envelopment of catalysts. In her note to the poem published
in the 1839 American edition of his collected poems, Mary quotes
Shelley:

It was composed under the immediate impression of the deep and powerful feelings excited by the objects which it attempts to describe; and as an
undisciplined overflowing of the soul, rests its claim to approbation on
an attempt to imitate the untameable wildness and inaccessible solemnity
from which those feelings sprang.

To combat the incomprehensibility of Mont Blanc, Shelley merely
abandoned himself to it, as best he might, hoping to merge with the awesome visage that had overwhelmed him. The whole alpine teleology—from
sunsets on the leaning seracs to the boulder fields and downrushing
cascades—eluded his craftsman's usual ability to convert such immensity
and mystery into song. In its pursuit, Shelley found himself in a world of
alien beauty he had never thought possible. The poem reads like the
invention it is. Indeed, Mont Blanc was for Shelley a revelation.

Forging acrostics ("a mysterious tongue") from atmospherics,
Shelley addresses his wilderness ideology in a passage that arrests the
otherwise interminable reverie. It is a relief, a nonphilosophical salve. The
surroundings, rather than the poet's vicarious iconography, impose their
own ceaseless, inspirational antiphon—Mont Blanc itself. There, midway
into the third strophe, we are riveted to the image of the twenty-three-
year-old Shelley standing on a bridge over the fast-moving glacial runoff,
pondering the dazzling massif:

I look on high;
Has some unknown omnipotence unfurled
The veil of life and death? or do I lie
In dream, and does the mightier world of sleep
Speed far around and inaccessibly
Its circles? For the very spirit fails,
Driven like a homeless cloud from steep to steep

That vanishes among the viewless gales!
Far, far above, piercing the infinite sky,
Mont Blanc appears, —still, snowy, and serene—   [52-61]

The similitude of idea and sense becomes a haunting at the end. Embellishing sentiment with metaphysics, Shelley cultivates the incomprehensible which he has identified with inaccessibility. At the poem's finale he can confidently question an enigma he has no desire to denude:

The secret strength of things,
Which governs thought, and to the infinite dome
Of heaven is as a law, inhabits thee!
And what were thou, and earth, and stars, and sea,
If to the human mind's imaginings
Silence and solitude were vacancy?   [139-144]

The meaning was Shelley's own. Mary provided an apt commentary on Shelley's intellectual autism in the character of Frankenstein who visits the Mer de Glace glacier only to encounter his own creation—the monster. Wrote Shelley to Peacock, "All was as much our own as if we had been the creators of such impressions." Shelley's only experience with a glacier occurred when he briefly stepped onto the periphery of the Mer de Glace. But the following year, in the preface to his "Revolt of Islam," Shelley was to write:

I have been familiar from boyhood with mountains and lakes, and the solitude of forests; Danger, which sports upon the brink of precipices, has been my playmate. I have trodden the glaciers of the Alps, and lived under the eye of Mont Blanc. I have been a wanderer among distant fields. . .

Shelley had come to Chamonix for much the same reasons as Frankenstein —to forget his troubles in the "eternity of such scenes." Over the next four years the poet was to move constantly in a geometry of turmoil. First to Bath, then Marlow, London, Milan, Bagni di Lucca, Venice, Rome, Naples, Livorno, Florence, and finally to Pisa. He continually intimated his desire to visit the vast geography outlined in "Alastor." In discussing this self-imposed rootlessness, Richard Holmes argues that "the deep cause of this need to move is certainly one of the profoundest questions which can be asked about his life."

The year 1818 saw his permanent exile to Italy. The path over Mount Cenis which Charles the Bold and Montaigne tobogganed, the Shelleys crossed by Napoleon's carriage route. In late October they took up residence in Naples, and from their hotel window Shelley could see the dull red smoke slowly rising from Vesuvius. In mid-December he climbed the volcano, and his letter to Peacock describing the adventure has been called one of the finest examples of descriptive prose in the English language. Shelley would later utilize the volcano metaphor politically: Asia would liken Prometheus' insurrection to a "sun-awakened avalanche."

Shelley completed Acts II and III of *Prometheus Unbound* during the Spring of 1819 while living in Rome. Each morning he would routinely hide himself in the Baths of Caracalla, which he described to Peacock as "mountainous ruins. . . which are extended in ever winding labyrinths upon its immense platforms and dizzy archs suspended in the air." Nature had reclaimed civilization, verdure toppling over history, and this sweet evidence that nature was in fact more powerful than man, as Mont Blanc had intimated for him, swept over Shelley. He was no longer the English tourist, but a thriving Greek visionary. Mary would write in her note to the play that his "dearest pleasure" was "the free enjoyment of the scenes of nature."

Prometheus Unbound opens in a "Ravine of icy Rocks in the Indian Caucasus," the same Himalayan setting as in "Alastor." Asia (Prometheus' lover) describes the scene in Act II:

> Some Indian vale. . .
> Under the curdling winds, and islanding
> The peak whereon we stand, midway, around,
> Encinctured by the dark and blooming forests,
> Dim twilight lawns and stream-illumined caves,
> And wind enchanted shapes of wandering mist;
> And far on high the keen sky-cleaving mountains,
> From icy spires of sunlike radiance fling. . .
> The vale is girdled with their walls, a howl
> Of Cataracts. . .
> As thought by thought is piled, till some great truth
> Is loosened, and the nations echo round,
> Shaken to their roots, as do the mountains now.
>
> [II, iii, 12-19; 23-24; 30-32]

Prometheus and Asia are reunited in a cave within this vale. The martyr is seen to be stubborn but no fool. Love enshrines him in Nature, and, like the wise man, he settles down on the fringe of civilization. The cave is the closest form of matter providing wildness a human habitation. Shelley dwelt there. The elicitations for this final setting in *Prometheus Unbound* accrued over an eight-year period during which Shelley explored the allusiveness offered by rugged terrain and the spectacular particulars of nature. The "lonely Vale in the Indian Caucasus" was to remain for him the purest expression of his own ambivalent alienation from a public which, unlike his wife Mary or his best friend Byron, he never succeeded in reaching.

Shelley's unfulfilled dream of ideal love, the comprehensive insulation which marked his sudden turnabouts, and his tragic early death in a sailing accident aboard the *Don Juan* all seem to stem from his relentless identification with desolate and inaccessible places. His own intense inwardness plagued him with an obvious irony, for the idyll he courted constituted a legacy of wide expanse, immense exposure, and untouchable summits, entrenched in the lore of paradise which titillated his age and the three centuries preceding it. The mountain environment was Shelley's self-induced isolation. Such exile he ceaselessly converted into a setting of itself.

Some six months after he moved to Pisa, in July of 1820, two years before his sudden death, Shelley wrote to his friend, Thomas Medwin, who was in Geneva at the time:

> How much I envy you, or rather how much I sympathise in the delights of your wandering. I have a passion for such expeditions, although partly the capriciousness of my health, and partly the want of the incitement of a companion, keep me at home. I see the mountains, the sky, and the trees from my windows, and recollect, as an old man does the mistress of his youth, the raptures of a more familiar intercourse, but without his regrets, for their forms are yet living in my mind.

Wilderness Paradox, A Synopsis

I HAVE DISCUSSED SHELLEY at length because he so poignantly evokes the tension which is the necessary compromise between wilderness and civilization. I might equally have chosen John Muir, Lermontov, Hokusai, or Basho as preeminent examples of significant mountain immersion. Shelley is particularly intriguing because his literary aspirations coincided with the beginnings of the golden age of mountaineering.

Today, Shelley's feelings for nature seem dated, whereas Muir's "mountain metaphysics" suggest an informed, if wishful modernity. Shelley was an aristocrat, an obsessed genius, and a cognoscenti of taste, while Muir was a humble rustic, an enlightened philanthropist, a backwoodsman-poet comfortable hiking with Teddy Roosevelt or riding the crest of an avalanche. While Shelley and Muir each loved wildness, they expressed divergent orientations. If Muir was the seminal, driving force behind a sudden cultural infatuation with pristine landscapes and camping—prefigurements of the Jack London era—Shelley was the major *example* of Rousseau and Wordsworth's testament. It is the paradoxical combustion of these two evocations—the romantic and the ecological—which agonizes us today, though the distinction lies half-concealed beneath our contemporary wonderment with Oriental ideas about nature that seem, on the surface, to shadow our own ignorance. The romantic poets and painters anticipated Stendhal, Tennyson, and Camus—authors of revolt, of altruistic despair—as well as later poets who would seek in the natural world the only supposed sanity remaining. The popularization of such vogues has paralleled our fashionable return to nature. Existentialism has moved out-of-doors.

As a child I relished the world atlas and would imagine the deserts and great mountain ranges to my heart's delight. They provided me with an infinite, spiritual privacy. Human beings have always worshiped and delighted in sacred space. When first formalized, conceptions of sacred space were in themselves a wilderness, that is, the ideas were unmarred by a confusion of cultural opposites. But what of the twentieth-century psyche, as overrun and intricate as its cities? We speak of *our* wilderness areas with bewildering conviction. Addicted to certainty and convenience, bolstered by the 747, mass media, overpopulation, and rampant "alternatives," we frantically accelerate the loss of wonder and captivation which other centuries felt in the wake of exploration, and with them the values, the honed religiousness, nourished on adventure's mystique. We usurp an ancient quiet with excess self-awareness whose leisure has merely estranged us further from the original intuitions of our rural forebears, and from the mythology of impulses, the state of mind, even the musculature which once generated our atavistic thrills and philosophical flights.

Modern progress is synonymous with this physical disjunction. Muir wandered most of his life, as did such literary *exaltés* as Nikos Kazantzakis and André Malraux. Thoreau managed two years at Walden, Melville lived with cannibals for four months, Mendelssohn retreated to his cabin in the summer. But the average American experiences all of two weeks a year to himself. Such a reality dictates an environmental experience whose quality is comprehensively stunted.

Each of us relates differently to the outdoors. But what clearly distinguishes contemporary relationships to the environment from earlier ones is the potential destructiveness—the permanent damage—of a paradox whose increasing contagion has ushered in an era of bitter wilderness politics. Our unfortunate penchant is to love the wilderness to death.

The contamination of every cubic inch on the planet stems, with unwavering ardency, from a glut of overwrought technology and from tourism, the caravanserai of mobile-home curiosity seekers who are doing "what they came into the world to do." However, these are not the worst culprits: arrogance is. Too much of it in the wrong places. With our laws, our technicalities, our press, even with our best inspirations we have cordoned off the anterooms of wilderness, zoning primaeval country for recreational, industrial, and political investiture. In a national frenzy to domesticate wildness, we are smothering it. The remaining redwoods are like noble vestiges, resplendent reminders of our species' unwise audacity. And to a disciplined sensibility, even the most remote glacier in Nepal is beginning to have about it the trammeled, doomed aura of a caged animal. There is no matter-of-fact remedy for this paradox, as there is none for famine. What accentuates the fascinating dilemma of twentieth-century curiosity —of imagination—is that this ineluctable trespass is as conceptual as it is environmental.

Throughout history, luminaries in the avant-garde of solitude have provided cues to the resolution of "reality" versus "nature." The one spectacular discovery of this abundant daring—of ascetics, mountain wayfarers, roving diplomats of the spirit, and farmers in the outback of consciousness—is that of a sacred, inviolate space which is the natural world. Anachronism or guide?

While the mind is fraught with turmoil, with conflicting desires which it registers in the intellectual, risk-free cancellation of opposites, while it is plagued by a contradiction which molests it on the condition of living, this space—the mountains—continues to exist as it always has: pure, without meaning, other than that which, if we are hapless, we will probably achieve for ourselves amidst their mute and more serene worlds.

I think back to the words of the "ghost poet of the T'ang," Li Ho (791-817): ". . . then quietly comes the dream of an aged woman on an ancient mountain. . . " In the Middle Ages perhaps, somewhere in the Karakoram, or New Guinea. Her ideas inhabit her mountains. There is a wildness about her thoughts, despite whatever practical concerns embellish them; a universal wildness which philosophers on all continents have idealized for millennia, perhaps nostalgically.

NOTES
AND
BIBLIOGRAPHIES

Editors' note:
The notes and bibliographies follow the order of the book and are set forth under the writer's name, save that when a translator has supplied the material his name precedes the writer's. A uniform citation system has not been imposed, it being decided that each system is appropriate to the matter it is supporting. The annotation of the Eastern material has in most cases been reduced. A few books will be encountered in more than one section; and in one or two cases, where page numbers are cited, the use of different editions has been allowed to stand.

Lyon *NOTES*

1. Robert Ornstein, *The Psychology of Consciousness* (New York: The Viking Press, 1972).

2. Garma C. C. Chang, *The Buddhist Teaching of Totality* (University Park: Pennsylvania State University Press, 1971), see p. 85, for example.

3. Robert Marshall, "The Problem of the Wilderness," *Scientific Monthly* 30 (February 1930): 141-48.

4. Reinhold Messner, *The Seventh Grade* (New York: Oxford University Press, 1974), p. 103.

5. Kenneth E. F. Watt, "Man's Efficient Rush Toward Deadly Dullness," *Natural History* 81 (February 1972): 74-82.

6. C. G. Jung, *Psyche and Symbol* (Garden City, New York: Doubleday, 1958), p. 86.

7. Biographical information on Muir is found in Wolfe, Linnie Marsh, *Son of the Wilderness: The Life of John Muir* (New York: A. A. Knopf, 1945).

8. Linnie Marsh Wolfe, ed., *John of the Mountains: the Unpublished Journals of John Muir* (Boston: Houghton Mifflin, 1938), p. 53.

9. Quoted in Edwin Way Teale, ed., *The Wilderness World of John Muir* (Boston: Houghton Mifflin, 1954), p. 312.

Bielefeldt/Dogen *NOTES & ADDITIONAL READINGS*

1. *Chia-t'ai p'u-teng lu*, II (ZZ.IIB. 10.1.41.b). Ta-yang is better known as Fu-jung Tao-k'ai (1043-1119), seventh patriarch of the Ts'ao-tung school of Ch'an.

2. After the line, "A flower opens and the world arises," in the transmission verse attributed to Bodhidarma's master Prajñātārā. *Ching-te ch'uan-teng lu*, II (T.2076.216b).

3. These four views appear to follow a similar list in the *Hsiang-fa ch'üeh-i ching* (T.2870.1337a).

4. It should be noted that these three practices are all characteristic teachings of the Ch'an tradition.

5. The various types of stones mentioned here can all be found in secular Chinese literature.

6. *Yün-men K'uang-chen ch'an-shih kuang-lu*, I (T.1988.547c). Yün-men is better known as Yün-men Wen-yen (864-949), founder of the Yün-men school of Ch'an.

7. "Nan-ch'üan's 'sickle'" refers to the well-known koan recorded in the *Lien-teng hui-yao*, IV: "Nan-ch'üan was cutting thatch. A monk asked, 'Which way is the Nan-ch'üan road?' The master held up his sickle and said, 'I got this sickle for 30 cash.' The monk said, 'I didn't ask about that. Which way is the Nan-ch'üan road?' The master replied, 'And now that I use it, it's really sharp.'" (ZZ.IIB.9.3.246a).

"Huang-p'o's stick and Lin-chi's roar," below, refers to the famous Ch'an teaching methods of beating and shouting developed by these two masters.

8. Or "they are the children of the heresy of naturalism," a reference to the heretical view that things arise, not from causes and conditions, but spontaneously.

9. From the famous dialogue between the Sixth Patriarch and Nan-yüeh Huai-jang: "The Sixth Patriarch asked, 'Where do you come from?' Nan-yüeh answered, 'I come from Sung-shan.' The Patriarch said, 'What is it that comes thus?' He replied, 'To say it is like anything is not accurate.' The Patriarch said, 'Is it contingent on practice and verification?' He said, 'Practice and verification are not non-existent, but they cannot be defiled.'" *Ching-te ch'uan-teng lu*, V (T.2076-240c).

10. These various views of water are based on the Vijñānavāda teaching known as "the four views of water": *devas* see water as jewels; men see it as water; *pretas*, as blood; and fish, as a dwelling.

11. According to traditional Buddhist cosmology, the earth rests on mandalas of the other elements.

12. The source of this quotation has not been traced. It is generally thought to be based on the *Ratnakuṭa* (*Ta pao chi ching*, LXXXVII [T.310.499a]).

13. After the Tao-yüan chapter of the *T'ung hsüan chen ching*.

14. See, e.g., the *Suvarna-prabhasa* (*Chin-kuang-ming ching*, II [T.663.340b]).

15. From the *Cheng-tao ko* of Yung-chia Hsüan-chüeh (T.2014.396b).

16. In the T'ien-ti chapter of the *Chuang-tsu* the Emperor Yao has an interview with the Hua Guard. In the Tsai-yu chapter Huang-ti visits the Taoist sage Huang Cheng-tzu on Mount K'ung-t'ung, and is instructed in the secret of immortality.

17. At the time of the T'ang persecution of Buddhism (845), Ch'uan-tzu Te-ch'eng (d.u.) left his teacher Yüeh-Shan Wei-yen and became a boatman on the Hua-t'ing River. There he met Chia-shan Shan-hui (805-881). After transmitting the dharma to Shan-hui by throwing him in the river, Te-ch'eng himself leaped into the water and disappeared. *Ching-te ch'uan-teng lu*, XIV (T.2076.315b).

18. The "true dragon" refers to the well-known Chinese story of She Kung, who loved paintings of dragons, but was one day visited by a real dragon and frightened out of his wits.

19. Probably the words of Yün-men Wen-yen: "Monks, do not have deluded notions. Heaven is heaven, earth is earth; mountains are mountains, rivers are rivers, monks are monks, laymen are laymen." *Yün-men K'uang-chen ch'an-shih kuang lu*, I (T.1988.547c).

Abbreviations:

ZZ. *Dai Nihon zoku zōkyō*. Kyoto: Zōkyō Shoin 1905-12. 750 vols.

T. *Taishō shinshū daizōkyō*. Tokyo: Taishō Issaikyō Kankōkai 1923-34. 85 vols.

Additional readings

In recent years several works on Dōgen have appeared in Western languages. Interested readers may wish to consult the following:

Kim, H. J. *Dōgen Kigen: Mystical Realist.* Tucson, Arizona: University of Arizona
    Press, 1975. A study of Dōgen's religious sy
    Press, 1975. A study of Dōgen</p>

Kim, H. J. *Dōgen Kigen: Mystical Realist.* Tucson, Arizona: University of Arizona
    Press, 1975. A study of Dōgen's religious system.
Matsunaga, R., trans. *A primer of Sōtō Zen.* Honolulu: East-West Center Press,
    1971. A translation of Dōgen's *Shōbōgenzō zuimonki.*
Mishiyama, K., and Stevens, J., trans. *Shōbōgenzō*, I. Sendai, Japan: Daihokk-
    aikaku, 1975. The first volume of a complete but rather free translation.
Yokoi, Y., trans. *Zen Master Dōgen.* New York and Tokyo: Weatherhill, 1976.
    Selected translations.

In addition, mention must be made of the reliable translations by N. Waddell and M. Abe which have been appearing regularly since 1971 in *The Eastern Buddhist* (The Eastern Buddhist Society, Otani University, Kyoto).

Grapard/Kūkai *NOTES*

These notes are restricted to matters of general interest or to crucial points. A fully supported text would be annotated at perhaps four times this length, but much of the material would be of value only to students of classical Chinese.

In the title itself I have rendered as "in His Search for Awakening" a group of words originally meaning "polishing the pearl obscure." The pearl has often been used to refer to the Mind of Awakening because of its round perfection. The word *obscure* seems to indicate existence beyond the appearance of phenomena.

The quoted lines introducing the text may be seen as the formal request addressed to Kūkai by Doctor I (about whom we know nothing beyond what Kūkai tells us). See also the conclusion of the text.

1.   The Buddha, seen as an Essence and as an eternal principle, chooses to manifest itself in this world to save it. The form it appears under is that of the historical Buddha, or that of numerous divinities of the pantheon, which in turn manifest themselves as the divinities of religions other than Buddhism. This theory is at the basis of syncretism, and if the residence of the Buddha is seen as the sky, the most natural manifestation point is the mountain.

2. The "obscure" refers to the first chapter of Lao-Tzu's *Tao Te Ching*. "Both being and non-being appear out of the Obscure—to make this obscure even more obscure is what I call the gate to all marvels."

3. From the *Analects* of Confucius.

4. The age of fifteen or sixteen was taken as that at which one starts to show compassion for all forms of life.

5. The ideogram used in the original is that meaning "following one's lord into death," thus showing the seriousness of the determination.

6. In the Buddhist view of the universe, this sevenfold range of mountains surrounds the base of Mount Sumeru (Japanese: Tettchisen).

7. One li was, in the T'ang dynasty, equivalent to 560 meters.

8. "The True Aspect of the Phenomena," that is to say, the Ultimate Reality hidden beyond the appearances, is for Kūkai hidden *in* the appearances, which he sees as direct manifestations of the Essence of the Buddha. To see this Reality, one has to scale a high mountain from which the view is perfect and without obstacles; here, this mountain is identified with Mount Sumeru.

9. From the *Analects* of Confucius, where he says that he is very happy when just eating herbs, drinking water, and sleeping on his elbow.

10. This sentence also has the following meaning: "the fame of the low monk reached the ears of the high Emperor." The double meaning allows Kūkai to make an elegant transition.

11. Kyoto, where Kūkai was living at the time.

12. The text to this point serves only to introduce the poem, which was to be engraved on a stone. This type of composition, in which the central poem is seen as standing like a jewel on a ring, became very fashionable in Japan. Kūkai proved to be one of the very few Japanese who mastered Chinese prosody. The text, however, is at times obscure and my rendering conjectural. Nor does the translation allow any insight into the original rhythm, sound harmonies, and visual appearance of the ideograms, inherent aspects of the poem's beauty.

13. These four lines express Chinese mythology: after the breaking of the original egg, the moon (where a toad resides) and the sun (where a crow resides) appear. The three-legged crow is the emblem for the Kumano area in which are located the sacred Ise Shrines where the Sun is worshiped. It was the Kumano region which came to replace Nikkō as the "Pure Land" of the Bodhisattva Avalokitesvara. Japan's most famous mountain is there, Mount Koyasan, which Kūkai made the center of the Shingon School.

14. In Buddhism, the phenomena have been compared to the impermanent, ever-changing waves on the surface of the Constant Essence, water.

15. A Buddhist statement: there is as much "water-essence" in one single drop, as in all the oceans; as much "earth-essence" in one single particle of dust as in all the mountains; as much potential for awakening in one single man as in all Buddhas.

16. That is to say, Mount Fudaraku.

17. See note 2 above. Words may have "whitened" the obscure. In the West we would say: "they have not been clear enough . . ."

18. Kūkai often signed with this title, meaning All-Illuminating Diamond. The Western Mount indicates Takao in the northwestern part of Kyoto.

Drasdo *SOURCES CITED*

Daumal, René. *Mount Analogue.* San Francisco: City Lights Books 1972. The words quoted appear on the inside cover of the book but not, I think, in the text itself.

Edwards, John Menlove. "Scenery for a Murder," in G. Sutton and W. Noyce, *Samson: the Life and Writings of Menlove Edwards.* Stockport, England: privately published, 1959.

Gardner, W.H. *Gerard Manley Hopkins (1844-1889): A Study of Poetic Idiosyncrasy in Relation to Poetic Technique.* London: Secker and Warburg, 1944.

Hawkins, Ellie. Quoted from a letter in *Mountain* 32, London 1974

Keats, John. *The Letters of John Keats.* Edited by M.B. Foreman. Letter 15, to Haydon, 10th-11th May 1817. London: Oxford University Press, 1947.

Long, Jeffery. "The Soloist's Diary." *Ascent,* 1974, Sierra Club, San Francisco.

Malory, Sir Thomas. *Morte D'Arthur* (1469-70).

Tejada-Flores, Lito. "Games Climbers Play." *Ascent,* 1967, Sierra Club, San Francisco.

Smuts, Jan. Quoted in G.W. Young, *The Influence of Mountains on the Development of Human Intelligence.* Glasgow: Jackson, Son & Co., 1957.

Snyder, Gary. Quoted from his essay in R. Disch, ed., *The Ecological Conscience: Values for Survival.* Englewood Cliffs, N.J.: Prentice-Hall, 1970.

Amy *WORKS CONSULTED*

Alyn, Marc. *La Nouvelle Poesie Francaise.* Ed. Robert Morel, 1968.

Delas, D., and Filliolet, J. *Linguistique et Poetique.* Coll. Langue et Langage, Librairie Larousse, 1973.

Drasdo, Harold. "Climbing as Art." *Ascent,* 1974. Sierra Club, San Francisco.

Kerouac, Jack. *Les Clochards Celestes.* Coll. Folio, Gallimard, 1963.

Revue *Poetique,* no. 7, 1971.

Rousselot, Jean. *Les Nouveaux Poetes Francais.* Ed. Seghers, 1959, p. 243.

Sonnier, Georges. *La Montagne et l'Homme.* Albin Michel, 1970.

Suzuki, D.T. *Essais sur le Bouddhisme Zen.* Albin Michel, 1970.

Watts, Alan. *Le Bouddhisme Zen.* Petite Bibliotheque Payot, 1972.

The final quotation is from Proust.

Earhart NOTES

1. Marjorie Hope Nicolson, *Mountain Gloom and Mountain Glory: The Development of the Aesthetics of the Infinite* (New York: W.W.Norton and Company, 1963), p.3.

2. Ibid., pp. 34-35.

3. Ibid., p. 34, quoting Andrew Marvell, "Upon the Hill and Grove at Billborrow," *Poems and Letters,* ed. by H.M.Margoliouth (Oxford: The Clarendon Press, 1927), I, 56.

4. Ibid., p. 50.

5. Ibid., p. 2, quoting Wordsworth, "To_____on Her First Ascent to the Summit of Helvellyn."

6. Mircea Eliade, *The Sacred and the Profane. The Nature of Religion,* trans. Willard R. Trask (New York: Harcourt, Brace, 1959), p. 50.

7. J.D.Frodsham, "Landscape Poetry in China and Europe," *Comparative Literature* XIX (Summer 1967): 193-215; see p. 194. Frodsham compares the third-century change in Chinese aesthetic values from fear of mountains to adulation of mountains, with a similar transformation in Western aesthetic values in the eighteenth century. Sōkichi Tsuda draws an interesting *contrast* between the Chinese view of nature (as emphasizing the larger, sublime aspect) and the Japanese view (as emphasizing the smaller, delicate aspect). ". . . Generally speaking, as a natural result of the geographical conditions peculiar to their home land, the Chinese not only have a predilection for the grandiose in natural scenery but are also apt to find pleasure in letting loose in it their unbounded desire for absolutely unfettered freedom. And so they are scarcely capable of appreciating the delicacy of beauty in nature." See Sōkichi Tsuda, *An Inquiry into the Japanese Mind as Mirrored in Literature—The Flowering Period of Common People Literature,* translated by Fukumatsu Matsuda (Tokyo: Japan Society for the Promotion of Science, 1970), p. 282. This gives food for thought in any consideration of mountain aesthetics.

8. *The Manyōshū. The Nippon Gakujutsu Shinkokai Translation of One Thousand Poems* (New York and London: Columbia University Press, 1965), pp. 187-88. For general comments on mountains in the *Manyōshū* and citation of poems, see p. 1x-1xi.

9. Quoted in Ryūsaku Tsunoda, et al., *Sources of Japanese Tradition* (New York and London: Columbia University Press, 1964), Vol. I, p. 112.

10. Quoted in ibid., p. 10.

11. Quoted in Yoshito S. Kakeda, *Kūkai: Major Works* (New York and London: Columbia University Press, 1972), p. 47.

12. Ibid. For a more detailed treatment of the Buddhist transformation of nature in Japan, see William R. LaFleur, "Saigyō and the Buddhist Value of Nature," *History of Religions* XIII, no. 2 (November 1973); 93-129; XIII, no. 3 (February 1974); 227-48. LaFleur makes interesting comparisons and contrasts with Chinese materials; he also claims that the Buddhist poet Saigyō (1118-90), in valuing nature itself as responsible for salvation, went far beyond figures such as Kūkai, who valued nature more as "an excellent locale for the performance of austerities" (p. 236).

13. For a general article see Ichirō Hori, "Mountains and Their Importance for the Idea of the Other World," in his *Folk Religion in Japan: Continuity and Change* (Chicago and London: The University of Chicago Press), pp. 141-79. Fascinating materials can also be found in Carmen Blacker, *The Catalpa Bow: A Study of Shamanistic Practices in Japan* (London: George Allen and Unwin, 1975), especially "Mountain Oracles," pp. 279-97.

14. H. Byron Earhart, "Shugendō, the Traditions of En no Gyōja, and Mikkyō Influence," in *Studies of Esoteric Buddhism and Tantrism* (Kōyasan, Japan: Kōyasan University, 1965), pp. 297-317; see p. 306.

15. Ibid. pp. 306-7. See also Kyōko Motomochi Nakamura, trans., *Miraculous Stories from the Japanese Buddhist Tradition: The Nihon ryōiki of the monk Kyōkai* (Cambridge, Mass: Harvard University Press, 1973), pp. 140-42.

16. The three major Western works on Shugendō are: H. Byron Earhart, *A Religious Study of the Mount Haguro Sect of Shugendō: An Example of Japanese Mountain Religion* (Tokyo: Sophia University, 1970); Gaston Renondeau, *Le Shugendō. Histoire, doctrine et rites des anachorètes dits Yamabushi* (Paris: Imprimerie Nationale, 1965; Cahiers de la Société Asiatique, 18); Hartmut O. Rotermund, *Die Yamabushi. Aspekte ihres Glaubens, Lebens und ihrer sozialen Funktion im japanischen Mittelalter* (Hamburg: Kommissionsverlag Cram, de Gruyter and Co., 1968; Monographien zur Völkerkunde, 5).

17. For a general account see H. Byron Earhart, "Four Ritual Periods of Haguro Shugendō in Northeastern Japan," *History of Religions* V, no. 1 (Summer 1965); 93-113.

18. The fall peak is described briefly in my "Four Ritual Periods of Haguro Shugendō in Northeastern Japan," and more extensively in my *A Religious Study of the Mount Haguro Sect of Shugendō*, pp. 110-46.

19. See Robert S. Ellwood, Jr., *Religious and Spiritual Groups in Modern America* (Englewood Cliffs, N. J.: Prentice-Hall, 1973), pp. 262-67.

20. More practical considerations are assessed in my "The Ideal of Nature in Japanese Religion and its Possible Significance for Environmental Concerns," *Contemporary Religions in Japan* XI, nos. 1-2 (1970): 1-26.

Echevarría *NOTES*

1. Arnold Lunn, *A Century of Mountaineering* (London: Allen & Unwin, 1957), p. 28.

2. Francisco J. de San Román, *Desiertos i Cordilleras de Atacama* (Santiago: Imprenta Nacional, 1896), vol. I, p. 145.

3. Sir William M. Conway, *Climbing and Explorations in the Bolivian Andes* (London: Harper & Brothers, 1901), pp: 56-57.

4. Centro de Investigaciones Argueológicas de Alta Montana, *Volumen Uno* (San Juan, Argentina: 1973), pp. 36-37.

5. Witold Paryski, "Indianie na szczytach Ameryki," *Taternik* 3-4 (Zakopane, Poland: 1956), pp. 165-195.

6. Greta Mostny, *La Momia de Cerro Plomo* (Santiago: Museo Nacional de Historia Natural, 1957).

7. Mario Fantin, *A settemila metri: gli Inca precursori d'alpinismo* (Bologna: Tamari Editori, 1969), pp. 22-23.

8. Centro de Investigaciones, op cit., pp. 11-16.

9. William Rudolph, "Licancabur: Mountain of the Atacamenans." *Geographical Review,* vol. XLV·2 (New York, 1956): 156.

10. Bión González, "Llullaillaco," *Revista Andina* 79 (Santiago, 1952): 15.

11. Centro de Investigaciones, op cit., pp. 38-39.

12. Centro de Investigaciones, op cit.; Evelio Echevarría, "The South American Indian as a Pioneer Alpinist," *Alpine Journal* 73 (London, 1968): 81-88; Mario Fantin, op cit.; Witold Paryski, op cit.; Universidad Nacional de Cuyo, *Anales de Arqueología y Etnología* (Mendoza, Argentina, 1966), vol. XXX.

13. Lothar Herold and Thomas Kopp, "Primera ascensión a la cumbre sur del Cerro Aconcagua," *Revista Andina* 56 (Santiago, 1947): 11-15.
    The peaks known to have been ascended by the Indians are as follows:
    Peru: Chachani, 6,087 m.; Sarasara, 5,949 m.; Misti, 5,877 m.; Pichu Pichu, 5,640 m.
    Bolivia: Bonete, 5,656 m.; Salla, 5,036 m.
    Chile: Llullaillaco, 6,723 m.; Cerro del Toro, 6,386 m.; Cerro de las Tórtolas, 6,323 m.; Cerro Pular, 6,225 m.; Cerro Copiapó, 6,072 m.; Serro Salín, 6,060 m.; Cerro Pili or Acaramachi, 6,045 m.; Cerro Socompa, 6,031 m.; Licancabur, 5,930 m.; Miñiques, 5,910 m.; Cerro del Potro, 5,830 m.; Nevada Tambillos, 5,800 m.; Juriques, 5,710 m.; Cerro Doña Ana, 5,690 m.; Cerro Plomo, 5,430 m.; Cerro Chuculai, 5,421 m.
    Argentina: Mercedario, 6,670 m.; Antofalla, 6,440 m.; Cerro de los Patos, 6,250 m.; Cerro Quéhuar, 6,160 m.; Cerro Negro Overo, 6,150 m.; Cerro Arácar, 6,080 m.; Nevado de Chañi, 6,060 m.; Tebenquincho, 5,790 m.; El Peinado, 5,740 m.; Cerro Galán, 5,650 m.; Cerro Macón, 5,490 m.; Cerro Mogotes, 5,380 m.; Cerro El Imán, 5,070 m.

14. Marcel Kurz, editor, *Berge der Welt* (Zürich: Buchverlag Vergandsdruckerei A.G., 1948), vol. III, p. 356.

15. Maximino Fernández, *Hombres indígenas en las montañas chilenas* Santiago: privately printed, 1972), 16.

16. Marcos Yauri, *Ganchiscocha* (Lima: Ediciones Piedra y Nieve, 1961), pp. 78-78.

17. José Frederic Finó, "¿Por qué ascendemos las montañas?" *Revista Andina* 63 (Santiago, 1948): 17.

18. Arthur Chapman, *The Story of Colorado* (New York: Rand McNally, 1924), p. 63.

Doub NOTES

1. For various discussions of Chinese views on the place of humanity in the natural world, none purely on Taoism, see Tuan Yi-fu, *China, The World's Landscapes,* ed. J.M.Houston (Chicago: Aldine, 1969); Li Chi, "The Love of Nature," ch. 1 of Li Chi, *The Love of Nature: Hsu Hsia-k'o and his Early Travels,* Program in East Asian Studies, Occasional Paper no. 3, ed. Henry G. Schwartz (Bellingham, Washington: Western Washington State College, 1971); Michael Sullivan, *The Birth of Landscape Painting in China* (Berkeley; University of California Press, 1962); Joseph Needham, *Science and Civilisation in China* (Cambridge: Cambridge University Press, 1956), II.

2. For an excellent discussion of Taoism, including so-called philosophical and religious Taoism (with references to other discussions of this question) see Norman J. Giradot, "Part of the Way; Four Studies on Taoism," *History of Religions* 11 (1972); 319-37.

3. For probably the best treatment in Western languages of mountains in China, though only partly on Taoism, see Paul Demiéville, "La Montagne dans L'Art Litteraire Chinois," *France-Asie/Àsia* 20 (Autumn, 1965): 7-32.

4. William H. Neinhauser, Jr., et al., *Liu Tsung-yüan,* Twayne World Author Series no. 225 (New York: Twayne Publishers, 1973), p. 67.

5. See Demiéville, "La Montagne," op cit., pp. 10-12, for discussion of mountains in the *Chuang Tzu.* Mountains are mentioned some forty-four times in the *Chuang Tzu.* For a discussion of mountains in a largely Taoist text compiled some two hundred years later, see the unpublished Ph.D. dissertation by John H. Major, "Topography and Cosmology in Early Han Thought: Chapter Four of the *Huai-nan-tzu,"* Harvard, 1973.

6. On the Chinese recluse, see Li Chi, "The Changing Concept of the Recluse in Chinese Literature," *Harvard Journal of Asiatic Studies* 24 (1962-63): 234-47; Frederick W. Mote, "Confucian Eremitism in the Yüan Period," in *The Confucian Persuasion,* ed. Arthur F. Wright, Stanford Studies in the Civilizations of East Asia, no. 4 (Stanford: Stanford University Press, 1960), pp. 202-40, 348-53.

7. Kristofer M. Schipper, "Gogaku Shingyō zu no Shinkō" (Beliefs in the chart of the True Form of the Five Peaks) in *Dōkyō Kenkyū* II, eds. Yoshioka Yoshitoyo and Michael Soymié (Tokyo: Shōshinsha, 1967), p. 121. In Japanese. Note that all Chinese and Japanese personal names are given in their original order with the family name before the given name.

8. Ko Hung, *Pao p'u tzu,* (Tapei: Shih-chieh shu chu, 1958) p. 78, and James R. Ware, trans., *Alchemy, Medicine, Religion in the China of A.D. 320: The Nei P'ien of Ko Hung (Pao p'u tzu),* (Cambridge: M.I.T. Press, 1966), p. 279. Note the severe criticism of these views in the largely Confucian sections of the *Pao p'u tzu* where it is said that the Tao is not to be found in the mountains and forests and that those who said in ancient times that it was necessary to go into the mountains to cultivate the Tao were far from the mark (pp. 202-3).

9. Ibid., p. 76, and Ware, trans., p. 279.

10. T'ao Hung-ching, *Chen kao* (Revelations of the perfected), *Tao Tsang* (1447; rpt. Shanghai: Commercial Press, 1924-26), *ts'e* 640, *chuan* (of *Chen kao*) 18, p. 7a. For the Hut of Silence, see R.A.Stein, "Remarques sur les mouvements du Taoisme politico-religieux au IIe siecle ap. J.-C.," *T'oung-pao* 50

(1963), pp. 69-73; Needham, *Science,* op. cit., V:2 (1974), p. 152, and William C. Doub, "A Taoist Adept's Quest for Immortality," Dissertations, University of Washington, 1971, pp. 53-56.

11.   *Pao p'u tzu,* op. cit., p. 76, 1.13, and Ware, trans. p. 279.

12.   Kristofer M. Schipper, *L'Empereur Wou des Han dans la legende taoiste. Han Wou-ti Nei-chuan,* Publications, Ecole Franciase d'Extrême-Orient, Vol. 58 (Paris, 1965), French trans., p. 78, and Chinese text, pp. 3, 1.15-4, 1.1.

13.   *Chin shu* (635; rpt. of Po-na or Palace edn., Shanghai: Commercial Press,) *chüan* 80, p. 8a. Biography of Hsü Man.

14.   T'ao Hung-ching, *Chou-shih ming-t'ung chi* (Records of communications with the occult of Mr. Chou), *Tao tsang, ts's* 152, *chuan* 2, p. 14b, and *chuan* 4, p. 16b. See also Doub, "A Taoist Adept's Quest," op. cit., pp. 47-48.

15.   Tao, *Chen kao,* op. cit., *chuan* 1, p. 5a-b.

16.   "The Changing Concept," op. cit., p. 239. For a translation of the poem, see David Hawkes, trans., *Ch'u Tz'u The Songs of the South* (Oxford University Press, 1959), pp. 119-20.

17.   *Pao p'u tzu,* op. cit., and Ware, trans., ch. 17, passim.

18.   Ibid., p. 77, 1.21, and Ware, trans., p. 283.

19.   Ibid., pp. 76-78, and Ware, trans., pp. 280-81, 283-85. Ko gives extensive lists with specific days, hours, etc.

20.   Quoted in ibid., p. 76, 1.17-18, and Ware, trans., p. 280.

21.   For studies, all in Japanese, of mountain talismans with references to the original Chinese sources, see Schipper, "Gogaku shingyō," op. cit.; Kogawa Takuji, *Shina Reikishi Chiri Kenkyū* I (Kyoto: Kōbundo Shobō, 1928), pp. 32-40, et passim; and Inoue Ichii, "Gogaku shingyō zu ni tsuite" (On the chart of the True Form of the five Peaks) in *Naito Hakase Kanreki Shukuga Shinagaku Ronsō,* ed. Haneda Tōru (Kyoto: Kōbundo Shobō, 1926), pp. 43-91.

22.   *Pao p'u tzu,* op. cit., pp. 89, 97, and Ware, trans., pp. 298, 315. See also Schipper, *L'Empereur Wou,* op. cit., French trans., p. 103, and Chinese text, p. 10, 1.10-11. For an extensive list of mountain talismans see *Pao p'u tzu,* pp. 82, 97 (trans. pp. 295-96, 313, 384-85).

23.   Ibid., p. 77, and Ware, trans., p. 282.

24.   Ibid., p. 89, 1.12-13, and Ware, trans., p. 298. For additional details about how to make and use the talismans, see ibid., pp. 82-88, and Ware, trans., pp. 296-97.

25.   To see how this works, see the explanation (in English) by Ch'en Hsiang-ch'un of a talisman called "Talisman to be Hung on the Belt to Exorcise Miasmas of the Mountains and Valleys," in his article, "Examples of Charms Against Epidemics with Short Explanations," *Folklore Studies* I (1942): 47-48. For illustrated discussions of mainly more recent talismans of various kinds, see Henri Doré, *Researches into Chinese Superstitions* (Shanghai: T'usewei Printing pr., 1914-16), Vols. I-III. See also J.J.M.de Groot, *The Religious System of the Chinese* (1892; rpt. Tai-pei: Ch'eng Wen Publ. Co., 1969), VI, 1024-61.

26.   Schipper, "Gogaku Shingyō, op cit., p. 119.

27.   Ibid., pp. 139-40.

28.   For detailed discussions with many references to primary sources of the Talismans of the Five Peaks, see Schipper, "Gogaku shingyō," op cit., and the articles by Ogawa and Inoue referred to above. There is an extensive literature in Chinese and in Western Languages on the Five Sacred Mountains of China.

See Edouard Chavannes, *Le T'ai Chan Essai de Monographie d'un Culte Chinois* (Paris: Leroux, 1910; rpt. England: Gregg, 1969); William E. Geil, *The Sacred 5 of China* (Boston: Houghton Mifflin, and London: John Murray, 1926); Dwight C. Baker, *T'ai Shan An Account of the Sacred Peak of China* (1925; rpt. Tai-pei: Ch'eng Wen, 1971); Mary A. Millikan and Anna A. Hotchkis, *The Nine Sacred Mountains of China* (Hong Kong: Vetch and Lee, 1973); Hedda Morrison, *Hua Shan, The Taoist Sacred Mountain of China* (Hong Kong: Vetch and Lee, probably 1974); and Michel Soymié, "Le Lo-feou Chan; Étude de Géographie Religieuse," *Bulletin de l'Ecole Francaise de l'Extrême Orient* 48 (1956): 1-139. In Chinese, a vast collection of writings on mountains is *Ku-chin T'u-shu chi-ch'eng* (1726; rpt. Taipei: Wen hsing Book Co.,), *ts'e* 183-199 (bound as Vols. 23 and 24 in Wen hsing rpt.).

29. Schipper, "Gogaku shingyō," op. cit., p. 121.

30. Ibid., pp. 133-34, 142, and Schipper, *L'Empereur Wou*, op. cit., French trans., p. 103, and Chinese text, p. 10, 1.1-6.

31. This translation from *hsiang* to "image" is doubtful. The meaning of *hsiang* is uncertain in this passage.

32. *Chi* here translated to "traces" has a second meaning suggesting the traces or marks of one's activity which one would prefer if possible not to leave in the world. If it means that here, it would appear to be repeating the meaning of the previous phrase.

33. The Three Realms (*san chieh*) is usually a Buddhist term but might not be here. One non-Buddhist meaning is heaven, earth, and humanity. In Buddhism its most common use is to refer to the realms of sensuous desire, form and pure spirit.

34. *Yun-ch'i ch'i ch'ien, Tao tsang, ts'e* 677-702, *chüan* 80 (*of YCCC*), pp. 19b-20b. For discussion of the passage see Schipper, "Gogaku shingyō," op. cit., pp. 42-43. Although it is little more than a guess, it seems likely that this text dates from the sixth to eighth centuries A.D.

35. *Pao p'u tzu*, op. cit., p. 77, 1.11, and Ware, trans., p. 282.

36. Ibid., p. 98, 1.1-2, and Ware, trans., pp. 315-16. See also Schipper, "Gogaku shingyō," op. cit., pp. 119-20.

37. Schipper, *L'Empereur Wou*, op. cit., French trans., pp. 102-3, and Chinese text, p. 10, lines 3-4.

38. Schipper, "Gogaku shingyō," op. cit., p. 128.

39. Eleventh year of Duke Hsiang, Section 5. See James Legge, trans., *The Chinese Classics* (1872; rpt. Hong Kong: Hong Kong University Press 1970), Vol. V, pp. 450, 453. The *Tso chuan* was probably written during the fourth or third centuries B.C., but the year of the events referred to in this passage is approximately 561 B.C.

40. Schipper, "Gogaku shingyō," op. cit., pp. 127-28. See also Stein, "Remarques," op. cit., pp. 14, 60, 69, et passim; and Doub, "A Taoist Adept's Quest," op. cit., pp. 120-25.

41. For the beginnings of these essays and a great deal of additional discussion of the place of humanity in the natural world, see Obi Kōichi, *Chūgoku Bungaku ni Arawareta Shizen to Shizenkan—Chūsei Bungaku o Chūshin to shite* (Nature and the concept of nature as they appear in Chinese literature—with the emphasis on medieval literature), (Tokyo: Iwanami Shoten, 1963).

Blakeney NOTES

1. Adam's Peak is the subject of a chapter in John Still, *The Jungle Tide* (London: W. Blackwood & Sons, 1930).

2. This hill is discussed by Paul Brunton in *A Search for Secret India* (London: Rider and Co., 1934) ch. 9.

3. Sherring, Charles A., *Western Tibet and the British Borderland* (London: Ed Arnold, 1906).

4. *Alpine Journal* 69, p. 171 (London: 1958).

5. *Alpine Journal* 40, p. 23 (London: 1929).

6. *Alpine Journal* 66, p. 118 (London: 1955).

7. Heim, A., and Gansser, A., *The Throne of the Gods* (London: MacMillan, 1939).

8. Hamsa, Bhagwan Shri, *The Holy Mountain* (London: Faber and Faber, 1934).

9. Harrer, Heinrich, *Seven Years in Tibet* (London: Rupert Hart-Davis, 1953).

10. Pravavananda, Swami, *Geographical Journal* 93 (1939).
    ————*Explorations in Tibet* (Calcutta: University of Calcutta Press, 1934).
    ————*Kailās-Mānasarovar* (Calcutta: S. P. League, 1949).

11. I understand that Major R. K. Saker visited the peak in 1941, and Dr. Herbert Tichy presumably saw the mountain during his 1936 attempt on Gurla Mandhata.

12. *Nine Lives: The Autobiography of an Old Soldier* (London: Hollis and Carter, 1955).

13. Mr. Mackworth Young visited Tuling in 1912 and found relics of the old kingdom. Mr. Hubert Calvert in 1906 made his way to Rudok, as did E. B. Wakefield in 1929. Captain Robert Hammond records a visit to Western Tibet in 1938 (*Geographical Journal* 99).

14. *Alpine Journal* 60, p. 268 (London: 1949).

15. The draw of Tibet to travelers has always been very evident. Remote from the rest of the world, it aroused a curious awe, not only because it was an obvious "blank on the map," but also because of the reputed Wise Men of the East believed to inhabit it. Shambala, the mysterious region in the north, may perhaps have been the source of James Hilton's Shangri-la (in his *Lost Horizon*); at an earlier date Guy Boothby's fabulous Dr. Nikola owed no small part of his learning to his gleanings from Tibet. Travelers of our own day, such as Ella Maillart, Andre Migot, and Rowena Farre have experienced the attraction of the Himalayas and the great tableland that lies beyond.

16. I remember talking during the war to some of the African troops (East and West) in India and learning of their impressions: a frequent comment was "a sad people."

17. Murphy, Dervla, *Tibetan Foothold* (London: John Murray, 1966).

Bueler   *SELECTED BIBLIOGRAPHY*

In English:

> Li Chi, *The Love of Nature: Hsu Hsia-k'o and His Early Travels* (Bellingham, Wash.: Western Washington State College, 1971).
>
> Li Chi, *The Travel Diaries of Hsu Hsia-k'o* (Hong Kong: The Chinese University of Hong Kong, 1974).

In Chinese:

> Ting Wen-chiang, *Hsu Hsia-k'o Yu-chi* (Hsu Hsia-k'o Travel Diaries), (Shanghai, China: The Commercial Press, Ltd., 1928).

Watson/HanShan   *NOTES*

A Note on Han-Shan

Han-Shan probably lived around the end of the eighth century. His poems suggest that he was a scholar-farmer who left his family and retired to a place called Han-shan or Cold Mountain in the T'ien-t'ai mountain range of Chekiang, where he became a layman follower of Ch'an or Zen Buddhism. The poems attributed to him, some three hundred, are untitled, generally quite short, and cast in simple, often colloquial language. Some are satires on the follies of the world or sermons on Buddhist practice and belief, others descriptions of the rugged mountain scenery of the poet's retreat and the austere but unfettered life he lived there.

At some unknown date a preface was attached to his poems depicting him as a carefree, laughing eccentric dressed in rags who went about with a fellow Zen follower called Shih-te or the Foundling. On the basis of this description, Chinese and Japanese painters in later times have produced spirited and humorous renderings of the pair, sometimes in company with a Zen priest named Feng-kan and a sleepy tiger.

Han-Shan's poetry was probably widely read in China, particularly in Buddhist circles, in the centuries following his death. The eminent statesman and poet, Wang An-shih (1021-1086), for example, wrote imitations of his poems. But as Buddhism declined in China, Han-Shan's work fell into relative obscurity. This was not the case in Japan, however, where Zen continued to flourish. All the extant commentaries on his poems are the work of Japanese monks and scholars, and his poems continue to play an important part in Zen study today.

Translations and Notes

Arthur Waley was probably the first to produce English translations from Han-Shan's poetry, publishing versions of twenty-seven poems in *Encounter*, vol. II, no. 3, September, 1954. A scholarly article by Wu Chi-yu, entitled "A study of Han Shan," *T'oung Pao* 45, 4-5, 1957, included translations of a number of poems. Twenty-four poems translated by Gary Snyder appeared in *Evergreen Review,* vol. II, no. 6, Autumn, 1958, and have since been reprinted in various places. *Cold Mountain: 100 Poems by the T'ang Poet Han-shan*, translated by Burton Watson, was published by Grove Press in 1962 and reissued by Columbia University Press in 1970.

In the six poems tanslated here, the Cinnabar Hills and Four Bright in II are place names in the T'ien-t'ai range; the Seven Treasures in III are precious minerals used in Buddhist literature to symbolize things of great worth. Poems V and VI use an unusually brief three-character line.

Siegel   *NOTES AND BIBLIOGRAPHY*

Notes

1. Frederick Copleston, *A History of Philosophy* 7 vols. (New York: Doubleday, 1963), VII, Part I, p. 152.
2. Robert M. Wernaer, *Romanticism and the Romantic School in Germany* (London: D. Appleton, 1901), p. 48.
3. Günther Grundmann, *Das Riesengebirge in der Malerei der Romantik* (Munich: Bergstadt Verlag-Wilhelm Gottlieb Korn, 1965), p. 70.
4. Wilhelm Heinrich Wackenroder, *Herzensergiessungen eines kunstliebenden Klosterbruders* (Stuttgart: Reclam, 1955), p. 50.
5. Ibid., p. 79.
6. Theodor Körner, *Sämmtliche Werke* 2 vols. (Berlin: G. Grote'sche, 1885), I, p. 84.

Bibliography

Grundmann, op. cit.

Hoffmann, Werner; Grohn, Hans; Reichert, Eleanore; and Schaar, Eckhard, *Caspar David Friedrich*, Munich: Prestel Verlag, 1974.

Korner, op. cit.

Schlegel, Friedrich, *Aesthetic and Miscellaneous Works*, trans. E. J. Millington. London: George Bell, 1900.

Sumowski, Werner, *Caspar David Friedrich—Studien*. Wiesbaden: Franz Steiner Verlag, 1970.

Wackenroder, op. cit.

———,*Phantasien über die Kunst*. Hamburg, 1797.

Vaughan, William; Supan, Helmut Börsch; and Neidhardt, Hans Joachim, *Caspar David Friedrich*. Catalogue of the Tate Gallery Exhibit, September 6—October 16, 1972.

Tobias *SELECTED BIBLIOGRAPHY*

Abbey, Edward. *Desert Solitaire: A Season in the Wilderness.* New York: Ballantine, 1977.

Adams, Eric. *Francis Danby: Varieties of Poetic Landscape.* New Haven: Yale University Press, 1975

Amy, Bernard. "The Greatest Climber in the World." *Mountain* 24 (November 1972): 18-21.

Bates, Robert. "A Study of the Literature of the Mountains and of Mountain Climbing Written in English." Ph.D. dissertation, University of Pennsylvania, 1947.

Beckett, Samuel. *The Lost Ones.* New York: Grove Press, 1972.

Bielefeldt, Carl. "The Mountains and Rivers Sutra." Oriental Language and Literature master's thesis, University of California, Berkeley, 1972.

Cahill, James. *Chinese Painting*, 2d ed. New York: Rizzoli International Publications, 1977.

Campbell, Joseph. *The Mythic Image.* Bollingen Series C. Princeton: Princeton University Press, 1974.

Chakraborti, Haripada. *Asceticism In Ancient India.* Calcutta: Punthi Pustak, 1973.

Chi, Li. *The Love of Nature: Hsu Hsia-k'o and his Early Travels.* Occasional Paper No. 3. Bellingham: Western Washington State College Program in East Asian Studies, 1971.

Clark, Kenneth. *Landscape Into Art*, rev. ed. New York: Harper and Row, 1976.

Cohn, Robert L. "The Mountains and Mount Zion." *Judaism* (Spring 1977): 97-115.

Collingwood, Robin George. *The Idea of Nature.* Oxford: Clarendon Press, 1962.

Coomaraswamy, Ananda Kentish. *The Transformation of Nature in Art.* New York: Dover Publications, 1934.

Daumal, René. *Mount Analogue*, 4th ed., trans. with introduction by Roger Shattuck. Baltimore: Penguin Books, 1968.

Drasdo, Harold. *Education and the Mountain Centres*, 2d ed. Llanrwst: Tyddyn Gabriel, 1973.

Earhart, H. Byron. *A Religious Study of the Mount Haguro Sect of Shugendō: An Example of Japanese Mountain Religion.* Tokyo: Sophia University, 1970.

Eliade, Mircea. *Shamanism: Archaic Techniques of Ecstasy*, trans. Willard R. Trask. Bollingen Series LXXVI. Princeton: Princeton University Press, 1972.

_____ *Patterns in Comparative Religion*, trans. Rosemary Sheed. Cleveland: World Publishing Company, 1958.

Encyclopedia of Religion and Ethics, 1915 ed. S.v. "Mountains, Mountain God," by J. A. MacCullough, pp. 863-869.

_____ S.v. "Asceticism," several authors, pp. 63-111.

Frankfort, Henri. *The Birth of Civilization in the Near East.* Bloomington: Indiana University Press, 1959.

Frodsham, J.D. *The Murmuring Stream*, 2 vols. Kuala Lumpur: University of Malaysia Press, 1967.

Gayet-Tancrède, Paul. *Hommes, Cimes et Dieux: Les grandes mythologies de l'altitude et la légende dorée des montagnes a travers le monde, par Samivel.* Paris: Arthaud, 1973.

Giamatti, A. Bartlett. *The Earthly Paradise and the Renaissance Epic.* Princeton: Princeton University Press, 1966.

Greitbauer, Karl. *Das Ganze der alpinen Idee, eine geistige Analyse des Bergsteigens.* Wien: W. Braumüler, 1973.

Guénon, Réné. "The Heart and the Cave." *Studies in Comparative Religion* (Winter 1971).

Hamsa, Shri Bhagwān. *The Holy Mountain-Being the Story of a Pilgrimage to Lake Manas and of Initiation on Mount Kailas in Tibet.* London: Faber and Faber, 1934.

Holmes, Richard. *Shelley—The Pursuit.* New York: E. P. Dutton and C., 1975.

Hornbein, Thomas F. *Everest The West Ridge.* San Francisco and New York: Sierra Club and Ballantine Books, 1968.

Jones, Frederick L. *The Letters of Percy Bysshe Shelley*, 2 vols. Oxford: Clarendon Press, 1964.

Kazantzakis, Nikos. *The Odyssey—A Modern Sequel*, trans. with introduction by Kimon Friar. New York: Simon and Schuster, 1958.

———. *Report to Greco*, trans. Peter Bien. New York: Simon and Schuster, 1965.

Krawczyk, Chess. *Mountaineering: A Bibliography of Books in English to 1974.* Metuchen: Scarecrow Press, 1977.

Lacarriere, Jacques. *Men Possessed by God; the Story of the Desert Monks of Ancient Christiandom*, trans. Roy Monkcom. Garden City: Doubleday, 1963.

Leong, Esther Jacobson. "Place and Passage in the Chinese Arts: Visual Images and Poetic Analogues." *Critical Inquiry* 3, no. 2 (Winter 1976): 345-68.

Lermontov, M. Yu. *A Hero of Our Time*, trans. with introduction by Paul Foote. Middlesex: Penguin Books, 1974.

Long, Jeffery. "The Soloist's Diary," edited by Michael Tobias. *Ascent Journal* (July 1974): 16-27.

Mallory, George. "The Mountaineer as Artist." *Climbers' Club Journal* (1914).

Martin, John. *The Illustration of the Heavenly Ladder of John Climacus.* Princeton: Princeton University Press, 1954.

Mather, Richard. "The Landscape Buddhism of the Fifth-century poet Hsieh Ling-yün." *Journal of Asian Studies* 18, no. 1 (1958): 67-79.

———. "The Mystical Ascent of the T'ient'ai Mountains: Sun ch'o's Yu-T'ien-T'ai' Shan Fu." *Journal of Oriental Studies* 20 (1955-56): 226-45.

Matsunaga, Alicia. *The Buddhist Philosophy of Assimilation: The Historical Development of the Honji-Suijaku Theory.* Tokyo: Sophia University, 1969.

McShine, Kynaston, ed. *The Natural Paradise Painting in America 1800-1950.* New York: The Museum Of Modern Art, 1976.

Nash, Roderick. *Wilderness and the American Mind*, 5th ed. New Haven and London: Yale University Press, 1975.

Nicolson, Marjorie Hope. *Mountain Gloom and Mountain Glory: The Aesthetics of the Infinite.* Ithaca: Cornell University Press, 1959.

Noyce, Wilfrid. *Scholar Mountaineers; Pioneers of Parnassus.* London: Dobson, 1950.

Olschak, Blanche C. *Mystic Art in Ancient Tibet.* New York: McGraw-Hill, 1973.

Panish, Paul. "Hsieh Ling-yün's 'Poetical Essay on my Mountain Dwelling,' an Annotated Translation." Oriental Language and Literature master's thesis, University of California, Berkeley, 1973.

Patch, Howard. *The Otherworld According to Descriptions in Medieval Literature.* Cambridge: Harvard University Press, 1950.

Pearson, Mike. "Pondering the Imponderable." *Mountain* 31 (January 1974): 15-17.

Salkeld, John. *A Treatise of Paradise.* London: N. Butter, 1617.

Serrano, Miguel. *The Serpent of Paradise: The Story of an Indian Pilgrimage*, 2d ed., trans. Frank MacShane. New York: Harper and Row, 1972.

Shelley, Percy Bysshe. *The Poetical Works of Percy Bysshe Shelley*, 1st ed., ed. Mary Shelley. Philadelphia: Porter and Coates, 1839.

Singh, Madanjeet. *Himalayan Art*. New York: Macmillan C., 1971.

Skrobucha, Heinz. *Sinai*, trans. Geoffrey Hunt. London: Oxford University Press, 1966.

Strassburg, Gottfried Von. *Tristan und Isolde*, trans. with introduction by A. T. Hatto. Baltimore: Penguin Books, 1960.

Sullivan, Michael. *Birth of Landscape Painting in China*. Berkeley: University of California Press, 1962.

Tayler, E. W. *Nature and Art in Renaissance Literature*. New York: Columbia University Press, 1964.

Thompson, Stith, ed. *Motif Index to Folk Literature*. Bloomington: Indiana University Press, 1955.

Tobias, Michael Charles. "The Mountain Obscure—A Selected Bibliography." *Climbing Magazine* (May-June 1978): 35-41.

_____ "A Biography of Self-Consciousness," 2 vols., Ann Arbor Microfilms, no. 77-17, 277, Diss. Ab. Int., Vol. 38, no. 2, 1977.

_____ "The Anthropology of Ascent." *Mountain* 44 (Summer 1976): 31-36.

_____ *Tsa*. San Francisco: IMAJ Publishers, 1974.

_____ *Dhaulagirideon*. Yellow Springs: Agni Review, 1973.

Tuan, Yi-Fu. *Topophilia: A Study of Environmental Perception, Attitudes, and Values*. Englewood Cliffs: Prentice-Hall, 1974.

Turnbull, Colin. *The Mountain People*. New York: Simon and Schuster, 1972.

Watson, Burton, trans. *Cold Mountain: 100 Poems by the T'ang Poet Han-shan*, 2nd ed. New York: Columbia University Press, 1970.

Wentz, Walter Evans. *Tibet's Great Yogi Milarepa: A Biography from the Tibetan*. London: Oxford University Press, 1928.

Zimmer, Heinrich. *Philosophies Of India*, ed. Joseph Campbell. Bollingen Series XXVI. Princeton: Princeton University Press, 1969.

Zink, Daniel David, III. "The Beauty of the Alps: A Study of the Victorian Mountain Aesthetic." Ph.D. dissertation, University of Colorado, 1962.

Zweig, Paul. *The Adventurer*. New York: Basic Books, 1974.

Contributors

BERNARD AMY is engaged in mathematical research in information theory at Grenoble. He has served on the editorial board of *La Montagne et Al-Pinisme* and on the management committee of the Federation Francaise de la Montagne. He has climbed on five continents and is the author of *La Montagne des Autres*.

SAMUEL BECKETT holds a Nobel Prize for Literature. Within his diverse, often baffling works, he has evoked a variety of desolate landscapes and settings among which none is more strange than that of the searchers and climbers of *The Lost Ones.*

CARL BIELEFELDT is an assistant professor of Japanese Religion at the University of Virginia, and a special research fellow at the Research Institute for Humanistic Studies, Kyoto University. He has published previously in the field of Ch'an and Zen.

T.S.BLAKENEY died in 1976 at the age of seventy-three, not long after writing this account of his journey to Kailas. Formerly a tea planter in Ceylon and South India, he served with the Indian Army during the Second World War. He was secretary of the Mount Everest Foundation for twenty-five years, and his encyclopedic knowledge of the history of alpinism and of mountain travel generally lent an added distinction to the pages of the *Alpine Journal,* of which he was for many years an assistant editor.

WILLIAM M. BUELER was formerly a translator of Chinese for the U.S. Government and now works in journalism. He has written several books, including *Chinese Sayings*, a guide to literary expressions used in colloquial Chinese, *Roof of the Rockies*, and *Mountains of the World*.

JOHN CLEARE is a British climber and photographer whose work may be viewed in two publications he has co-authored, *Rock Climbers in Action in Snowdonia* and *Sea Cliff Climbing in Britain*, and in his own record of his climbs and journeys, *Mountains*, which has been published in the United States and Britain.

ED COOPER played a leading part in the first ascent of Dihedral Wall on El Capitan, initiating a new phase in big-wall climbing in Yosemite Valley. However, he is chiefly known as a photographer and his work covers an extraordinarily wide span, ranging from studies of rock detail to views of the grandest mountain panoramas in North America.

WILLIAM C. DOUB is a professor of Chinese religion and language at the University of Colorado, Boulder, and has also taught at the University of

Kyoto. During the 1950s he climbed with a number of America's leading rock climbers, and he is still active as a skier and climber in the Rockies today.

H. BYRON EARHART, of the Department of Religion at the University of Western Michigan, Kalamazoo, is the author of the principal work on Shugendō in the English language.

EVELIO ECHEVARRÍA has been involved in South American mountaineering for many years and is often called upon to provide the annual summaries of developments in that hemisphere for the *Alpine Journal* (Britain) and the *American Alpine Journal.* He is a language professor at Colorado State University.

JOHN GILL is the protagonist in the promotion of the boulder problem as a kinaesthetic art form, and he has also played a part in setting standards to define the concept of good style in American "climbing ethics." Dr. Gill teaches mathematics at Southern Colorado State College, Pueblo.

RAWDON GOODIER is a biologist with a special interest in mountain ecology. He has served as the regional officer of the Nature Conservancy both in North Wales and Eastern Scotland. He is now an advisory officer to the Nature Conservancy Council for Scotland. He has climbed in the Alps and in East Africa and was the originator of some of the classic rock climbs on the Cornish sea cliffs.

ALLAN GRAPARD is a Frenchman who studied in schools and monasteries in Japan for seven years. He is an assistant professor at Cornell University, Ithaca, New York.

AL CHUNG-LIANG HUANG is the author of *Embrace Tiger—Return To Mountain, Living Tao: Still Visions and Dancing Brushes,* and the collaborator with Alan Watts of *Tao: The Watercourse Way.* A native of China, trained in the theater and movement arts, he has performed and conducted seminars throughout North America and the Far East. A lecturer at the Lan T'ing Institute in Sausalito, and at the Esalen Institute in Big Sur, he is the founder-director of the Living Tao Foundation.

SI CHI KO was born in Taiwan and trained at the College of Photography in Tokyo. He now lives in New York City.

JEFFERY LONG is an accomplished American mountaineer whose imaginative writings have appeared in *Ascent* (San Francisco) and *Mountain* (London).

TOM LYON teaches at Utah State University and edits the journal, *Western American Literature.*

ARNE NAESS is an eminent Norwegian philosopher. He has been an active mountaineer since the 1930s and has climbed extensively in the Alps, the Himalayas, and America, as well as in his own country. In later life he has taken a prominent part in conservation struggles in Norway. He is Professor of Philosophy at Oslo and has published several works in the English language.

DAVID ROBERTS has been a regular visitor to Alaska throughout the past fifteen years and has described two of his expeditions in his books, *Mountain of My Fear* and *Deborah: a Wilderness Narrative.* He is also the author of some notable essays on contemporary mountaineering literature in *Ascent.*

GALEN ROWELL, author of *The Vertical World of Yosemite,* and *In The Throne Room of the Mountain Gods,* was a member of the American K2 Expedition in 1976. He has recently led successful ascents of Nun Kun and the central Trango Tower in the Karakorum. An early protagonist of Big Wall climbing in Yosemite, he is currently a contributing editor to the magazine *Outside.*

LINDA SIEGEL, Associate Professor of Music and Art at the College of Notre Dame in Belmont, California is a leading authority on German romanticism. She has written extensively on Friedrich and her forthcoming book, *Caspar David Friedrich and the Age of German Romanticism* will be published in 1978.

GEORGE STEINER is eminent in the world of letters, and his major works —*The Death of Tragedy, Language and Silence, In Bluebeard's Castle,* and *After Babel: Aspects of Language and Translation*—have won international acclaim. A regular contributor to *The New Yorker,* he makes his home in Geneva.

REUBEN TAM is of Chinese extraction and was born in Hawaii. His paintings—many of which use mountains as vantage points—are to be found in the collections of more than thirty American galleries and museums. He lives in New York City. His poetry has been published in *A Sense of Place* (Friends of the Earth, 1971) and will appear in a forthcoming anthology of Hawaiian poetry.

PHILIP TEMPLE was born in Britain but settled at an early age in New Zealand where he has established himself as one of the foremost writer-mountaineers. His books include *Nawok!, The Sea and the Snow, The World At Their Feet, Castles in the Air,* and *Ways to the Wilderness.*

AMOS TUTUOLA is one of the most widely admired of those African writers to have gained recognition in the West. His novels include *The Palm-Wine Drinkard, Brave African Huntress,* and *My Life in the Bush of Ghosts.* He works for the Nigerian Broadcasting Corporation.

BRADFORD WASHBURN was one of the most enterprising American mountaineers of the first half of this century and has since achieved world-wide recognition for his remarkable aerial photographs of high mountains. He is a tireless worker whose most recent projects include a new book on Mount McKinley and a new map of the Grand Canyon. He is the director of Boston's Museum of Science.

BURTON WATSON has taught at Columbia and Stanford Universities and at Kyoto University in Japan, where he has lived for many years. He is the author of numerous works on Chinese history, philosophy, and poetry, and his translations include the two-volume *Records of the Grand Historian* and *The Complete Works of Chuang-Tzu.*

The Editors

MICHAEL TOBIAS received his Ph.D. in the History of Consciousness Department of the University of California, Santa Cruz. His fields of interest include comparative literature, philosophy, and art history.

Author of two limited edition books, *Dhaulagirideon* (Agni Review, 1973) and *Tsā* (IMAJ Publishers, 1974), as well as numerous articles, Tobias first conceived of *The Mountain Spirit* while climbing and doing research at Saint Catherine's Monastery in the Sinai Peninsula in 1972. Since then, he has studied artwork and monasteries, mountains and mountain people in the Himalaya, mainland China, the Soviet Union, Europe, and North America. A frequent lecturer at college and universities, he has taken study groups to Bhutan, Sikkim, Indian Tibet, and other remote mountain ranges.

He is presently assistant professor of Environmental Studies at Dartmouth College.

HAROLD DRASDO was born in Bradford, Yorkshire, England in 1930. Responsible for numerous first ascents and one of the first climbers to establish routes still graded in the Extreme category, he has been a leading figure in British rock climbing for many years. He has traveled widely and is familiar with the mountain ranges of Europe and some North American regions.

As the author of *The Eastern Crags* and *Lliwedd*, he is the only British climber to have produced authorized guidebooks for the mountain areas of both the English Lake District and North Wales. His writings on mountains and on the outdoor education movement in Britain are used as texts for a number of university and college courses. He has also written on politics and literature. A polemical work, *Education and the Mountain Experience*, will be published in Britain in 1979.

Formerly a teacher of English, he has been in charge of a government maintained Outdoor Education Center in Snowdonia for the past twelve years.

Acknowledgments

We gratefully acknowledge a large number of persons who, in one way or another, have been involved in this project. First, we must mention those writers and artists whose work would have appeared here but for a variety of circumstances: Al Alvarez, Michel Ballerini, Christian Bonington, Robin Campbell, Stephanie Evanitsky, J.D. Frodsham, Tom Frost, Toni Hiebeler, Philip Holmes, June Layson, Gordon Mansell, Stephen Mullen, Sasuke Nakao, W.W. Sayre, Doug Scott, John Svenson, Giuseppe Tucci.

We thank Gary Snyder for his initial encouragement and advice. For a while we hoped to include a section from his work-in-progress, *Mountains and Rivers without End*, but poetry cannot be completed to a deadline. It was Snyder, however, who first drew our attention to Carl Bielefeldt's translation of Dōgen.

Thanks are extended to Kimon Friar, Helen Kazantzakis, Blanche Olschak, and Miguel Serrano for their friendship and advice.

The cooperation of the following museums and individuals in the obtaining of photographs must be acknowledged: Art Institute of Chicago; Baghdad Museum; M. Bazan; Birmingham Museums and Art Gallery; Museum Boymans-van Beuningen, Rotterdam; Cleveland Museum of Art, Purchase Fund, John L. Severance; Leo Dickinson; Peter Eichner; Photographie Giraudon; Hamburger Kunsthalle; Keats-Shelley Memorial Association and Sir Joseph Cheyne; Si Chi Ko; Kunstmuseum Basel Kupferstichkabinett; Des musées nationaux-Louvre; Matija Maležič—1977 American Makalu Expedition; Michigan-Princeton-Alexandria Expedition to Mount Sinai; Oslo-Nasjonalgalleriet; New Orleans Museum of Art and Kurt Gitter, M.D.; Prado, Madrid; Smithsonian Institution, Freer Gallery of Art; Southampton Art Gallery; Tate Gallery; Tetryakov Gallery, Moscow; Tokyo National Museum, Mariko Togashi, Zauho Press; Walter Steinkopf; The Museum of Science, Boston; Whitworth Art Gallery, University of Manchester; and the William Rockhill Nelson Gallery of Art, Atkins Museum of Fine Arts, Kansas City.

To Grove Press, Calder & Boyars Ltd., and Samuel Beckett we are grateful for permission to reproduce extracts from *The Lost Ones*.

Ken Wilson, former editor of *Mountain* magazine (London), recognized the value of our project at an early stage and gave valuable assistance.

Gratitude is due to Maureen Drasdo and to Elizabeth Johnston (Gretel) for their commitment to this work and their painstaking labors to help see it through to completion. To Eric Hoffman, Carol McGee, Sandra Slone, Alain Balladeur, Michael and Susan Wagner, and Tenzing Norgey, thanks are extended for reasons each will know.

We must put on record the crucial, last-moment support of two persons. After a series of plans had miscarried, and at a point where it seemed we might have to wrestle with its technicalities ourselves, Elizabeth Cartwright translated Bernard Amy's essay for us. And in a couple of hours' work each evening, Valerie Siviter, who saw the first pages of our difficult and severely disorganized manuscript on August 10, 1977, typed an immaculate text by the last day of that month.

And finally, much appreciation is extended to the University of California, Santa Cruz, Humanities Patent Fund, for two consecutive research fellowships for one of the editors, which helped defray the costs arising over a period of three years from a collaboration plagued by the vastness of an intervening ocean.